TAKING SIDES

by the same author

THE PENDULUM YEARS

TAKING SIDES

BERNARD LEVIN

JONATHAN CAPE
THIRTY BEDFORD SQUARE LONDON

First published 1979
© 1979 Bernard Levin

Jonathan Cape Ltd, 30 Bedford Square, London WC1

British Library Cataloguing in Publication Data
Levin, Bernard
Taking Sides.
I. Title
082   PR6062.E91/

ISBN 0–224–01730–6

Printed in Great Britain by
The Anchor Press Ltd and bound by
Wm Brendon & Son Ltd, both of Tiptree, Essex

Acknowledgments

Most of these articles originally appeared in *The Times*; five appeared in the *Observer*; two in the *New Statesman*; one in the *International Herald Tribune*. I am grateful to the Editors concerned for enabling me to reproduce them here; if it comes to that, I am grateful to them for employing me to write them in the first place. I had two secretaries during the period covered by the volume, who typed the articles for their original appearance and checked a great deal of the material in them, besides providing countless other varieties of assistance and support; to Claudia Fraser-Orr (now Mrs Jon Swain) and Sally Chichester I therefore offer my warmest thanks. I am additionally indebted beyond all repayment to my colleagues at *The Times* and elsewhere who not only put up with my tantrums but in discussion and argument provided me with many new ideas and a most valuable corrective to those I had already. The inexhaustible patience and unfailing encouragement of my publisher, Tom Maschler, and my literary agent, Graham Watson are, to put it mildly, a great deal more than I deserve. Brian Inglis kindly read the proofs; this action was the fruit of a pact he and I made many years ago, by the terms of which we pledged ourselves always to proof-read each other's books. Since then, however, he has published nine, and this is only my second; *sunt lacrimae rerum*. Finally, I have to thank that unseen and many-headed friend, my readers, whose letters in response to what they read under my name has always astonished me by its quantity and astounded me by its generosity.

Contents

Introduction

IT HAS OFTEN occurred to me that journalism is a very odd profession. The rest of mankind spends its time jostling, raising its voice, interrupting and even engaging men in red coats to pray silence, in order that it may express its views. 'What I say is ... if you want my opinion ... let me tell you what *I* think ... it seems to me ... ' – the air is full of such pleas for attention, battling, usually in vain, against a host of identical claims, and at any given moment there must be fully ten talkers to every listener. Nor is that particularly surprising; it is of the essence of thoughts that they should demand to be expressed, and very few of those who form them ever stop to wonder whether anybody else is interested in attending to their expression.

The journalist, however, is *paid* to indulge in this universal practice, and so far as I am aware, no newspaper proprietor has ever, even by way of experiment, insisted on exacting a fee from the journalists for affording them the hospitality of his columns in order that they may therein express views which have rarely been solicited, and are even more rarely felt to be indispensable, by those to whom they are addressed. Yet it must be clear that many journalists, and certainly most of the successful ones, are not in the profession for the material rewards, pleasant though these are and amazing though it is that they exist at all; whether journalism is an art, a science, a craft, a confidence trick or a disease,* its leading practitioners are in it mostly and mainly because

---

* The last possibility should not be too hastily ruled out. Juvenal, indeed, even found a name for the malady: *scribendi acoethes.*

they have something to say. I am afraid that I have a very great deal to say.

I have been in the business of expressing my views in writing for a little over a quarter of a century; for most of that time I have also been engaged, on and off, in expressing them on radio and television. I do not know how many words I have thus committed to print or the airwaves, and I certainly do not wish to be told; but it must be a good many millions by now, and with the exception of *The Pendulum Years,* a book I wrote a decade ago (it is an account of the 1960s), all the words I have ever put one after the other have been born to live for only a few hours and to disappear as swiftly as they came.

That has never worried me in the least. On the contrary, I have always felt decidedly uneasy at the prospect of preserving any of my journalism, and have until now resisted the blandishments of my publisher, rationalizing my reluctance by saying that I did not want to compile an anthology of my ephemera until I had written another custom-made book. But the truth is much more curious. I have had, for as long as I can remember, an obsession, doubtless neurotic, with rolling up the past behind me like a carpet. I keep no files of correspondence, or of anything else for that matter; indeed, I keep no pieces of paper at all any longer than is necessary for dealing with the business or pleasure they concern. Letters are destroyed when they are answered; bank statements and cheque books as soon as the income tax return has been agreed; diaries on the morrow of the New Year. No one, not actually deranged, is ever likely to wish to write my biography; even if it were otherwise, no one would be able to. (Perhaps I had better pause here to assure the reader that my past conceals no startling secrets that must at all costs go to the grave with me. I am not an illegitimate scion of the Royal Family, nor am I on the run from the Foreign Legion; my name is what I say it is, and I am the thing I seem, whatever that may be.)

It follows, therefore, that in clapping a selection of articles between boards I am breaking a self-imposed canon, and I shall no doubt pay for this act of subjective impiety with some sleepless nights. What may be less obvious is that the work of selecting, marshalling and annotating my choice has itself constituted a deeply disturbing experience. But this has been only partly for the weird reason I have given; even stronger was the appalling sensation of meeting not one *Doppelgänger* but hundreds, so that at times I have felt like a man trapped between two mirrors, with reflections on both sides reproducing themselves to infinity.

For of course, I have not remained the same man over the years of my career, and in the yellowing pages that I have scanned for this compilation I have met every one of the men I have been. I found this so distressing that eventually I had to make it easier for myself by limiting the catchment area; with only three exceptions, from the mid-sixties, all the articles in this volume come from the period during which I have been writing a regular column (at first twice weekly, then thrice) for *The Times* – that is, since the beginning of 1971. For the first six years of this period I also contributed regular book reviews to the *Observer,* and a small selection of these is included. But before that, nothing. For some years, for instance, I was the Parliamentary and political correspondent of the *Spectator,* under the pseudonym of Taper; before that I had been television critic for the *Guardian;* I had also been theatre critic for both the *Daily Express* and the *Daily Mail,* and for the latter I had in addition written, for five years, a column five days a week. And I began my career in journalism on *Truth.* I have chosen not to include any of this work in the present book, and I shall not use any of it in a second volume which will, I hope, appear about a year after this one; in that I propose to include a further selection of my work for *The Times* and *Observer,* together with a choice of my articles in the *Sunday Times,* of which I became the theatre critic in 1976. The two volumes will thus comprise all the journalism that I wish to preserve.

I rejected the earlier work because a cursory inspection (which was all I could bear) suggested that it was not sufficiently substantial to be worth putting into a book; I suppose this, too, is a rationalization, designed to protect me from the parade of ghosts that re-reading my journalism has summoned. And presumably those ghosts represent intimations of mortality.

On the other hand (and at this point I shake myself like a dog coming out of the water, banishing these gloomy thoughts) it may be that the discomfort I have had to endure in the preparation of my anthology reflects no more than a reliving of the public horrors I was chronicling, together with a reminder of the misjudgments, disproved prophecies, untenable conclusions and hitherto unnoticed inconsistencies for which I had been responsible.* (In one respect, however, I can claim perfect judgment, unfailing consistency and accurately prophetic insight; I believe I was the very first journalist to write regularly, frequently and unequivocally about Harold Wilson, in terms which from the very beginning made clear my conviction that he was, and would even more fully become, what everybody else has only belatedly recognized. Cassandra's gift of prophecy did no good, as nobody believed her; nor, alas, did more than a handful share my assessment, made well over twenty years ago, of Harold Wilson's character, nor did anyone believe my exact prediction of the inevitable catastrophe of his national leadership. Any reader who recalls any of my early writing on this subject may be surprised to find none of it here, and even more so at the absence of any of my more recent comments on him. There is a reason for that, too, which I shall discuss in a moment.)

* A note on the text seems appropriate here. In reproducing the articles in more enduring form, I have taken the opportunity to correct a few errors of fact, punctuation and style, as well as of typography; I have also made three or four small cuts where I felt on reflection that extraneous matter had obscured the meaning. These alterations do not amount to more than a score or so, and none is of any substance; I have altered nothing whatever in the *views* originally expressed. A name or reference has occasionally been rendered puzzling with the passage of time, and some mildly elucidatory footnotes have therefore been added; in two cases the elucidation seemed hardly worth the trouble and I have simply omitted the item concerned. Finally, I have extended one originally abbreviated quotation.

Most of these articles, as I have said, appeared in *The Times*,* and thereby hangs a tale that has some relevance to their nature. When, in 1970, I left my employment with the *Daily Mail*, I received a flatteringly substantial number of invitations from editors to write for their journals. These included the then Editor of the *Guardian*, Alastair Hetherington, as well as William Rees-Mogg, who at that time had been Editor of *The Times* for some three years. I was much tempted by these conflicting proposals (both editors wanted me to write a general column), and at one point even had a wild notion of suggesting that I should write for both simultaneously. (Does anyone still read C. E. Montague's *A Hind Let Loose*? It is worth the reading; it tells of a journalist who writes for two rival papers of opposite political persuasion, though it is true that in his case neither editor knows of his work for the other.) I chose *The Times*, but my reason now seems very strange to me; I told the Editor of the *Guardian*, in declining his offer with very genuine regret, that I felt (as indeed I did) that I wrote more comfortably against the grain of the paper I worked for rather than with it. And I felt so closely identified with the stance of the *Guardian*, and so— well, not opposed to, but detached from, that of *The Times*, that the latter seemed to provide a more fruitful partnership both for me and for my hosts.

Eheu fugaces, nos et mutamur in illis. The *Guardian* has moved a long way since those days, and I have moved as far, and perhaps further, mostly in the opposite direction. But this is not simply a matter of right and left, let alone of political parties. The greatest issue of the years during which I have written for *The Times* has been the sharpening conflict between collective solutions to national problems on the one hand and the primacy of individual liberty on the other. Readers of the following pages will find a good deal about liberty in them, both at home and abroad, and regular readers of the column from which they are culled will

* This seems the right point at which to say that the work of preparing the selection for book publication was done during the period when *The Times* and *Sunday Times* were suspended. (I am reminded that Danny Kaye, the comedian, once defined a bassoon as 'an ill wind that nobody blows good'.)

have seen a very great deal more. But to be in favour of freedom is comparatively simple (though a surprising number of people are not – even as I was settling down to write this introduction my eye fell upon a report of a statement by Haringey Council, setting out its view of the responsibilities of the public libraries in its bailiwick, which ended with an enchanting instruction to the librarians to 'reaffirm that racist and sexist writing have [*sic*] no place in libraries and that censorship must be opposed'); it is less easy to find and pursue consistently a line through the inevitably conflicting claims to a wide variety of freedoms, some of which are genuinely incompatible with others.* Through the years of my contributions to *The Times* it has been more and more pressingly borne in upon me that the greatest illusion from which societies like ours suffer is the belief that proposals which diminish the liberty of individuals can increase that of the people in general; the most important lesson I have learned during those years is that that is a ruinous fallacy. The reason for its fallaciousness is obvious, or should be; liberty only exists for and in individuals, not for or in abstractions called society, let alone the state. Moreover, the attempt to make the abstractions more free by making the individuals who constitute their only reality less so can only lead to a continuing decline in liberty; to reach the collectively inhabited sunlit upland seems to those desiring it to require only one more small step, and then, when it is still not reached, a consequent further step, and ...

In my increasing emphasis on this definition of freedom (I find that I summed it up in March 1977 in the words 'There is no such thing, in the long run, as a state which is both collectivist and democratic') I have marched in step with a similar movement on the part of *The Times*, as expressed in its editorial columns, and of its Editor, as expressed in the countless conversations we have had on the subject. (Of course, you may say that I am nothing but a boss's man, but on the whole I think you had probably better not.) And until very recently indeed, when the tide began at last to

---

* If only in the traditional sense that 'your fist's freedom ends where my nose begins'.

turn, the road has been hard, dusty and uphill all the way. (Mind you, that has been the fun of it. I once wrote that 'there is a fellowship on the sinking vessel that the torpedo can never know', and I take little pleasure in pushing on an open door; my need for a position in which I can be *Athanasius contra mundum*, long un-supplied by *The Times*, has been amply assuaged by the general drift of Britain.)

Of course, it has not all been an argument about liberty. My own complete liberty to choose my subject has enabled me to indulge to the full (some would say to the brimming over) my devotion to the pursuit of hares of the most extraordinary diver-sity. It is just as well that there is no alleyway too narrow, ill-lit or obviously without issue for me to feel impelled to wander up it; I could not possibly write a general column three times a week if I were not inquisitive, to the point of impertinence, about almost everything, and off-hand I can only think of two subjects on which I almost never write at all, one being education, in which I find myself simply uninterested, and the other Northern Ireland and its troubles, on which I have never been able to think of anything to say that has seemed to me worth saying.

But that has left plenty of room. Not long ago, inspired by nothing more than idle curiosity, I tried to count the number of distinct subjects I had written about in my *Times* column, restrict-ing the list to those I had discussed several times, and I discovered that they numbered something like seventy. I shall not impose the list on the readers of this book, as I am entitled to hope that they are about to browse among its constituent elements, but I am obliged to say something about the omissions, before making some general observations about the inclusions.

A very large proportion, of course, fell because they dealt with something so tied to a particular and limited event or moment that they have lost all interest now; in one instance, indeed, I had the unnerving experience of reading a column and finding myself without the slightest idea of what it was about, even in the most general terms. (I thought of including it in this volume and offer-ing a small prize to the reader who could explain it to its author, but in the end decided to let it die peacefully in its newsprint bed.)

I had, for instance, found myself acting as fugleman for the moderate forces in a number of trades unions, including those of the engineering workers, the civil servants, the journalists and the actors.* In seeking ways of publicizing their struggles against the extremist minorities within their ranks, I found that the most efficacious help I could give was the provision of crucial information about their internal elections and other ballots, and my readers were sometimes outraged to find my day's inches entirely devoted to lists of moderate union candidates on whose behalf I was vicariously soliciting the votes of those who had them. Obviously, these columns would be of no interest now; and there were many others which served an equally limited purpose which a reader today would find it difficult to recognize and impossible to respond to.

Similarly, there were subjects on which I have written repeatedly, but for which a single, representative example of my views was clearly enough for the book; many of my regular readers have their particular likes or, more frequently, dislikes, among my regular subjects (Wagner, to whose music I am incurably addicted, was the one that aroused most hostility, but he was used to that himself), and whereas in a column appearing three times a week I could ride hobby-horses as often as I pleased, it seemed to me a mistake to ride too many in a collection of this kind. And again, there were subjects to which I returned again and again but which were inevitably subject to a law of diminishing returns as far as my readers' interest was concerned. The area in which this has been most bitterly true is that of persecution in totalitarian coun-

---

* These last were – and still are, for that matter – engaged in a struggle with a group led by Miss Vanessa Redgrave; I dubbed the group 'Vanessa's Loonies', and the name appears to have stuck. I mention this because it enables me to answer a question often put to me, and almost as often wrongly answered by those who have not made inquiry of me before offering confident ascriptions of their own; I did *not* (though I wish I had) think of calling Sir Hartley Shawcross Sir Shortly Floorcross, but I *did* call Sir Reginald Manningham-Buller Sir Reginald Bullying-Manner.

tries; I have given many scores of such accounts in my column, and have found it increasingly difficult to meet the necessity of devising every time a new way of saying the same thing, the same thing being that terrible rubric of our times: Country X is committing an injustice against Citizen Y. (In this connection I must here disclose that I am barred by the governments concerned from entering the Soviet Union and the lands of her Empire on the one hand and South Africa on the other. These decrees constitute a pair of campaign medals that I wear with considerable pleasure, and I have a profound suspicion of those who rebuke me for partisanship while wearing only one.)

Some columns I rejected because they no longer interested me, from which I concluded that they were unlikely to interest others; some seemed to me to require a familiarity with my writings that I had no right to expect from purchasers of this book; some expressed a view I have since abandoned. But none of this explains the omission of a subject on which I have certainly written more columns than on any other two put together; the reader will seek almost entirely in vain for direct evidence of my chronicling of the British party-political scene, and will find almost as sparse the discussion of Britain's economic condition.

When I was planning this anthology, but before I started to read through the material from which I was to select it, I had desultorily planned to make my political and economic columns something like the spine of the book; they would, I thought, run throughout it, with the rest being fitted in as the ribs and other ancillary bones of the skeleton. But that was in theory; when I turned to practice, I got such a shock as I had never had before in my life.

The only suitable image is the most familiar one; it *was* like looking through the wrong end of a telescope. This is not just a matter of the inadequacy of the men, though certainly a close spectator of politics in the Heath–Wilson years is likely to have been immunized against hero-worship for the rest of his life, and indeed to have got the antibody so firmly entrenched in his veins as to ensure its passing on, Lamarckianly, to countless generations beyond him. *Did* people like Harold Wilson and Denis Healey, Edward Heath and Anthony Barber, govern us, and oblige us, by virtue of that fact alone, to take them seriously? I suppose so; in the files I worked through there they were, those and a score more, grinning and shouting at us, pushing and shoving and gibbering, laying waste the country in the name of schemes for its improvement and mulcting us of uncountable millions to feed their own pride. People like me are always being accused by politicians and their hangers-on of 'denigrating democracy' by drawing attention to the flaws in the character and capacity of those who hold office under it. But it is precisely out of a love for democracy, and an increasing concern at its condition, that people like me find themselves increasingly often under the necessity of warning any who will listen that we are ill-governed by *this* lot and unlikely to see the situation markedly improved merely by exchanging them for *that*.

But it is not for that reason that the reader will find very little discussion of politics and economics in these pages, despite the very large proportion of my weekly space I have devoted to these subjects. It is the subjects themselves that now loom so small, not just *sub specie aeternitatis*, but in the context of a day that is only the morrow of theirs but which already seems aeons later. The turning tide is carrying out to sea not just this or that claim to the cure of all our national ills, but the very idea of political cures; what diminishes politics so rapidly is the growing realization that we have been looking in the wrong direction, literally for centuries, in our search for a solution to problems considerably more profound, enduring and important than the balance of payments or industrial relations, and that only when we change the direction of our gaze and look inwards shall we begin to understand anything worth understanding. It is because the political and economic remedies offered in the years covered in this book no longer seemed to me worth understanding that I have omitted almost all of what I said about them.

So much for what I have left out; now for what I have put in. A journalist who writes about everything that interests him inevitably produces, over time, a complete picture of his mind; in my case, my friends are wont to describe my form of personal map-making by saying that from reading my column regularly they can find out everything about me except the most important things. Thus, a reader of this book, let alone of the articles not included in it, will discover, among a good many other things, that music means a great deal to me and has played a large part in my life, that I am a cat lover, that the vast impersonal institutions of our society, like the Post Office and the Gas Board, are not close to my heart, that lawyers and judges are even further from my affections, that Alexander Solzhenitsyn is one of my heroes, that I do not admire busybodies, censors and suppressors but that I am often as unimpressed by the case made against them as that made on their behalf, that my political instincts go quite a long way towards anarchism, that *humani nil a me alienum puto*, and that I am more willing to proclaim my own ignorance than to undertake the work of remedying it.

The picture that emerges is, I suppose, of a liberal increasingly aware of the inadequacies of liberalism and a rationalist who finds himself less and less able to rely on rationalism; a man at ease with the art of the eighteenth century but distrustful of the basis of the Enlightenment's optimism; above all one who, day by day, finds himself more and more convinced of the importance of the inexplicable.

It is in this last area that I can recognize most clearly what my friends mean when they complain about the ground I fence off even from them while perfect strangers are given conducted tours over my passion for Mozart, *haute cuisine* and the English language.* I plead guilty, but beg leave to make a statement before sentence is passed. First, a man who describes in print as much of his activities as I do must inevitably become all the more fiercely determined to guard the areas of privacy that he retains for the sole use of himself and his intimates. Second, I promise to reform,

---

* There is nothing here on the subject of friendship itself. But to discuss in public what has hitherto been the most important thing in my life is, I have found, quite impossible. I beg my friends' pardon, if not my readers'.

and can bring evidence that I have already to some extent done so. In one respect, for instance, this book is already out of date; I have begun to write (because I have begun to think) very much more about what I have called, above, the importance of the inexplicable. This in itself has involved revealing more of myself than I have previously felt comfortable about doing, and I have no doubt that the second volume of my selected writings will amply reflect this development.

Meanwhile, here is the first selection; if anyone who has followed me as far as this feels by now that I have concentrated to excess on the first person singular, I can only say that the newspapers I have written for have invariably hired me to express my own opinions; those who find that matter for surprise are invited to re-read the first sentence of this introduction.

In the end I return to liberty, on which all depends, including, of course, my ability to express my opinions. During the past decade Britain has never been free of the totalitarian threat from within as well as from without, though it has been as depressing as it is ironic to observe that the internal threat has grown as the external has diminished; I have said that I confidently expect Britain to be proclaimed a Soviet Republic at about the time the people of Moscow put their rulers on trial. But in truth lovers of liberty have less to fear from those who deliberately seek to bring about liberty's destruction than from those who fail to see that there is nothing of value – *nothing* – in any society other than the individuals who compose it, and, so failing, pursue ends which, designed to enlarge the lives of many, succeed only in narrowing the lives of all; he who most loudly proclaims himself his brother's keeper all too often turns out to be literally and grimly just that.

Yet it is necessary to ask *why* the individual is all-important; if asked, I can offer only a tentative and interim answer. It is surely because if the universe makes any sense at all it only does so in terms which imply that the individual soul – an unfashionable word, but one for which no fully adequate substitute has yet been devised – has a duty to develop itself towards the highest of which it is capable. Some say that this task can only be accomplished over many lifetimes; it is not necessary to believe as much to insist that the argument is not to be understood in terms of material betterment; many who have nothing in this world are far richer in spirit, because they have understood the truth of which they are part, than those who are poor beyond the dreams of misery, though they lie on mattresses of soft down, and on their backs, too, because their stomachs are uncomfortably full. That is why many a political prisoner is more free behind the barbed wire than the guard who patrols it, as half the world's prison literature makes clear.

This is not an argument (though it has often been used as one) for telling the poor not to mind their poverty. It is an argument for believing that only as individuals can we hope to realize our full potentiality, and that anything which denies or restricts that realization denies salvation itself. 'If you wanted to put the world to rights', asks Solzhenitsyn's Nezin in *The First Circle*, 'who should you begin with: yourself or others?' And Evelyn Waugh put it even more neatly in a radio interview, part of which Ronald Harwood incorporated in his stage adaptation of Waugh's autobiographical novel *The Ordeal of Gilbert Pinfold*. Asked 'You have not much sympathy with the man in the street, have you?', Pinfold replies:

> You must understand that the man in the street does not exist. There are men and women, each one of whom has an individual and immortal soul, and such beings need to use streets from time to time.

But only from time to time. Some suggestions as to what happens to them for the rest of the time will, I think, be found in this volume, and more, I hope, in its successor. At any rate, that is my own view of what I have tried to do; whether others share it I shall no doubt now discover.

March 1979   B.L.

London pride doesn't mean a thing to us

I CANNOT BE the first to have noticed, but I believe I am the first to point out in print, that when nowadays one sees, above a shop window, the word 'Books', unaccompanied either by the name of the bookseller or by an indication of the nature of the books sold, it is probable that what the shop is selling is pornography, mostly in the form of magazines.

In saying that this phenomenon marks yet another sign that the world is coming to an end, I am not basing the claim on the fact that pornography is being sold; I have no need of the stuff myself, but do not (unlike some) believe that what I don't want nobody else should be allowed to have. No; what saddens me is that the word 'books', which is surely, in whatever language, the noblest sound the human race has yet uttered, should now come to mean something so far removed from its original concept.

Habent sua fata libelli. But it is not only books. The word 'sauna' for instance, when written up on a building in a public street, now has two entirely distinct meanings; it can indicate either that inside you can have the curious heat-and-water treatment that has become so popular in recent years, or that inside you can find women willing to engage in prostitution on the usual terms.

Again, my objection is not to the service, but to the melancholy implications; purveyors of pornography feel inhibited from telling the passers-by what they are selling, so they use (they prostitute, you might say) a word designed for a very different purpose; purveyors of flesh, similarly constrained (no doubt by similar feelings of delicacy), write up above their premises not 'Women for hire', but 'Sauna'. And if it comes to that, establishments which sell various venereal accessories are as likely to be labelled 'Lovecraft' or 'Ann Summers' as 'Sex shop'.

I cannot maintain, though I would like to, that it is only a matter of language. Nor is it even a matter of corrupted thought issuing, as sooner or later it always does, in corrupted words. (Read Orwell on 'Politics and the English Language' for the definitive statement on the subject.) But the most striking and disagreeable aspect is the whole sleazy, furtive atmosphere of this inability to call a spade a spade, together with the apparently un-caring acceptance of it by almost everybody.

Of course, this particular phenomenon has a long history. I remember the cards which used to appear on newsagents' win-dow-boards (that exchange and mart for unwanted sewing-machines, urgently sought bed-sitting rooms and lost kittens): there were always ladies with 'Large chest for sale', others who were engaged in the scaffolding business and therefore naturally expressed willingness to dismantle erections, and still others who would simply assert that they offered 'Tuition', though without specifying in what, presumably feeling (not without cause) that merely giving the name 'Miss Wipply-Rodley' would be suffi-cient indication, often adding – just in case it wasn't – 'Stern disciplinarian'.

But such devices existed to enable the users to get round the laws on prostitution. Those laws have changed since then, and the laws on pornography have changed even more. The shops selling 'books', for instance, may well include among their stock items that could lead to a prosecution under the Obscene Publications Act or at least to a forfeiture order; but it is not in itself a crime to sell magazines showing pictures of couples coupling, let alone of naked women in suggestive poses, and certainly it is not an offence to sell pornography under that name (the word itself is unknown to the law). If the shops announced plainly that that was the business they were in, nothing would be lost, and much, I cannot help feeling, gained.

The 'saunas' present rather more of a problem, for if they were labelled 'brothels' they would invite prosecution (keeping a brothel is still an offence), apart from which many of them are not, strictly speaking, brothels anyway, since the employees are not resident upon the premises. But there are real saunas, too, and although a man (let alone a woman) would have to be naïve beyond the bounds of sympathy to enter a fake one under a misapprehension that it was genuine, I do feel rather strongly that an institution associated with fitness, cleanliness, cold water, steam and deep breathing should not suffer the indignity of having to go under the same name as one in which the object is a commercial exercise in sexual stimulation carried out by grim harridans on unhappy men in the shabby back rooms of garishly lit premises in the less pleasant areas of our larger cities.

But of course, the less pleasant areas of our larger cities are less pleasant in more ways than these. Take—it is part of the same phenomenon after all—the proliferation of cinemas showing pornographic films. Now as a matter of fact most of what looks like cinematic pornography, and is criticized as such by the terrible army of banners, consists of harmless frolics of which the most titillating aspect is the title. All the same, though the widespread display of the advertisements for these films, together with the array of 'stills' outside the cinemas themselves, does not, in my view, do anybody any harm, it does give a somewhat narrow view of life, suggesting that it consists entirely of people tearing off other people's underwear. (Besides, since the manufacturers can rarely recruit real actresses for the films, and no serious model would appear in them either, the women waving their bosoms at passers-by from the photographs outside the cinemas in question are generally so wretched-looking, if not downright ugly, that they cause a shudder to pass through even the hardiest frame.)

Add those filthy hot-dog stands, from which the stench of rancid fat spreads for an appalling distance around; add the yobbos propping up the walls; add the crooks relieving gullible foreigners of their money by pretending to take photographs of them; add the litter; add the picturesque drunks being sick on the pavement and the addicts shooting-up in the telephone-boxes; add all that and stir, and we have powerful evidence that the Devil is abroad in the land, that old England's winding-sheet has already been woven, or at the very least that Gresham's Law is of considerably wider application than Gresham supposed.

Manichaeism is one of the few heresies that has never tempted me. All the same:

> God's plan had a hopeful beginning,
> Till man spoilt his chances by sinning;
> They tell me the story
> Will end in God's glory,
> But at present the other side's winning.

And the victories may be seen, literally, all around us. It is unpleasant to walk after dark through entire central areas of London and other British cities; it can even be truly dangerous. But that is not my main complaint, for the danger is still fortunately rare and the unpleasantness bearable. What occasions my gloom is what it implies for the decline of *civilitas*, of self-respect, of an interest in and care for our surroundings, of London pride and London character, and the pride and character of our other cities too. Whatsoever things are true, said St Paul, whatsoever things are honest, whatsoever things are just, whatsoever things are pure, whatsoever things are lovely, whatsoever things are of good report; if there be any virtue, and if there be any praise, think on these things. He said it, of course, to the Philippians; what would he have said if he had been writing to the Londoners? More to the point, what would they have written back?

The Times July 11th, 1978

A just price for a teacher's passion

I N THE MATTER of Mr Clement Vogler, the schoolteacher dismissed (justly, in the view of the Industrial Tribunal to which he appealed) for having sexual relations with a sixteen-year-old girl at his school, I do not propose to offer any comment of a moral nature, though I can hardly be expected to refrain from pointing out that 'Vogler' is the German for 'bird-catcher'.* What interests me is the nature of one important part of Mr Vogler's defence. It was argued on his behalf that he should not have been dismissed because the Hertfordshire Education Committee, the authority responsible, had never made any formal statement to the effect that teachers within their jurisdiction were forbidden to go to bed with their pupils, and that there was nothing to that effect in his contract, either. Assuming (as I do) that Mr Vogler has the facts on his side in both of these contentions, the question I wish to ask is: whatever next?

To start with, it is agreed on all sides that any offence Mr Vogler had committed was against such canons as good order and discipline, not the criminal law. Now, surprising though it may seem, I can find nothing in Archbold's *Criminal Pleading* (the only volume from my law library that I have to hand as I write, assuming that Copinger's *Copyright* is not germane to such matters) to suggest that the practice of cannibalism is, in itself, against the law. To murder someone for the purpose of eating the corpse would certainly be a criminal offence, and to eat the whole of a corpse, even without bringing about its demise first, might be

* It is also the German for something much ruder, and even more appropriate in this instance.

held to constitute either the prevention of the burial of a dead body or the disposing of a corpse with intent to prevent a coroner's inquest, both of which are unlawful; but it is, I contend, lawful to eat parts of a dead body.

The point is, however, that there is nothing in the regulations, by-laws or contracts of employment of the Hertfordshire Education Committee (I can say this with some confidence, as they have been my nightly study for many years) which forbids a teacher under its auspices, should one of his pupils unfortunately expire from natural causes on the school premises, to eat, say, an arm or leg before getting in touch with the parents, or for that matter after. Would Mr Vogler, therefore, maintain that, if cannibalism is not a criminal offence on the one hand, and not forbidden by his contract on the other, he would be unfairly dismissed if he were to be sacked for practising it?

Let us be so presumptuous as to assume that Mr Vogler would not so maintain (though even if he would not, we would be unwise, particularly these days, to rule out altogether the possibility that others might take a contrary view, and even that at, say, the North London Polytechnic there is an active and popular movement for Cannibals' Lib). But there are other acts, also not prohibited in what I believe Mr Vogler calls black and white, which raise more directly pedagogical questions.

For instance, I cannot believe that the Hertfordshire Education Committee has ever specifically forbidden teachers to bring the larger beasts, *ferae naturae*, into class; were Mr Vogler to appear one day leading an orang-utan or a tarantula on a string, however, I think he would be asked to go away, and quite possibly to refrain from coming back. Would he complain at such a response, and if he did, would his complaint be upheld?

Or suppose Mr Vogler should take to singing his lessons in a monotonous plainsong chant, or giving them while standing on his head, or convincingly disguised as a Zulu warrior, a circus clown or a woman? None of these, I think, is against the law or the Hertfordshire regulations; yet any of them might be held — and some would say reasonably — to warrant his dismissal.

It all comes back, I think, to the case of Dorothy Parker and the maid. Miss Parker, so the story runs, was given an alligator's egg, brought it home and put it, for want of anywhere better, in the bath. She then went out, and when she returned she found that the egg had hatched in her absence, and that her maid had quit her employ abruptly, leaving her a note saying that she was unable to work in a house where there were alligators, and adding the memorable words: 'I would have mentioned this before, only I never thought the subject would come up.'

So let it be with Vogler. If we tell him that there are certain things that ought not to be done, we have, by introducing that word 'ought', set off a debate on Mr Vogler's morals, which I at least am determined to avoid. What we have to get into his head, though I fear it may need a pickaxe to do it, is the fact that there are certain things which grown-up people are supposed to know, and that the inevitable consequences of his action come, most decidedly, under this heading.

He cannot, unless he is in a state of mental confusion so extreme that it would in itself justify his dismissal, seriously believe that a teacher who has an affair with one of his sixteen-year-old pupils would or could be permitted to continue in his employment if it were discovered. The girl might, perhaps, be presumed not to know this, but if so, that is precisely the point, for the adult would be expected to make up any deficiency in her understanding with the surplus of his own presumed responsibility. Mr Vogler may reply that he was not, in the grip of his passion, fully responsible for his actions, and we should beware of rejecting this explanation too quickly (assuming, that is, that we believe it), unless we can say, hand on heart, that we come into Hamlet's admired category of men,

> Whose blood and judgement are so well commingled
> That they are not a pipe for Fortune's finger
> To sound what stop she please.

But Hamlet did not claim the protection of the *lex Voglerensis*; he understood the consequences of his actions, even if he could not control their cause, and died without pretending otherwise. He did not, it is true, die at the hands of the Hertfordshire Education Committee, but neither, it seems worth pointing out, did Mr Vogler. It is, no doubt, a hard world that puts a price on things, and demands that the purchaser pay the price. But it is the world in which Mr Vogler lives, and he cannot say, when the bill is presented, that it comes as a surprise to him. There is a man in a poem by Kipling who loses his life because of his fastidiousness, as Mr Vogler has lost his job because of his lack of it. 'How is this matter for mirth?' he asks; 'I have paid my price to live with myself on the terms which I willed.' So has Mr Vogler, and he would be wise to accept the fact.

The Times November 11th, 1975

How an old geyser fell on hard times

AN ELDERLY WIDOWED lady of whom I am rather fond was notified some time ago that she was about to undergo the full horrors of conversion to Natural Gas. Resigning herself to a future of uncontrollably fluctuating gas-pressures, burnt saucepans and higher bills, she awaited the coming of the converters. The day dawned. Two men came; they converted her stove, her kitchen water-heater, her refrigerator and her gas fires. She also has, however, in her bathroom, a geyser of ancient design and dilapidated condition (I suppose we had better pause here for the one that goes 'Mornin' lady; 'ave you got an old geyser 'ere what won't work?' – 'Yes, 'e's just gone down to the Labour Exchange to draw the dole'), but which – mark these words, and mark them well – has operated adequately and served her well.

Obstinate in its faith, the geyser resisted conversion. The two gas men explained that it needed a device that they did not have with them, but which they would bring; meanwhile, the geyser was out of action. The lady bore her bathless state with as much fortitude as she could muster, and awaited their return.

They did not return, of course. Nor, of course, did she hear from anybody at all on the subject. So she telephoned the office from which the men had come; they had left a form with its address and telephone number. (It was the Conversion Report Centre, Oakington Road, London W9, telephone 349 3171, and I put these details in so that whoever is in what is laughably known as charge shall know exactly where the finger is pointing.) She explained that she had now been without a bath for a week, that a promise had been made and broken, and what was going to be done about it? The reply was that action would be taken. About a week later (nobody, of course, had told her anything at all in the interim) two more men turned up. They too, tinkered with the geyser; they too, said that it needed an extra device that they had not got with them; they, too, said that they would return with it; they, too, of course, did no such thing. Nor, of course, did anybody at all get in touch with her.

The lady in question, I will have you know, likes to bath regularly and often; moreover, she is not accustomed, or for that matter able, to take a bath in a kettle. So when another week had gone by, she telephoned the Gas Board. The office for the district in which she lives is North Thames Gas Board Area 5, telephone number 328 1717, address not given in the telephone book (I suppose they are afraid of violence from their customers, and well they might be). An official of the Gas Board came round (she cannot remember how long after her call, though she doubts if it was immediately, and so, by God, do I); he explained that the Gas Board and the conversion programme are independently run (if 'run' is the right word, and my own opinion is that it is most emphatically not the right word), but that he would inspect the geyser. He did so, told her that he knew exactly what was needed, and left with the memorable words, 'Leave it to me, Mrs Levin.' The reason he addressed her thus was that Levin is her name, and this seems as good a moment as any to reveal that the fact that it is the same name as mine is not a coincidence; she is my mother.

She did indeed leave it to him; she is a patient and trusting soul, and – rather more to the point – she had no option. He did not return, of course; nor, of course, did anybody get in touch with her. So she rang the Gas Board again. She was assured that action would be taken. It was: another man arrived (this made six she had actually seen, plus several more she had spoken to on the telephone). Had he, she asked, brought the necessary device? 'I have brought nothing,' he replied with candour; nor had he. (He also explained that he knew nothing of any extra and needed part.) He would, however, go back to the office and report the situation. He went; that was on Monday. Not long after he left

an official (female) telephoned from the Gas Board to ask if he
had been. Yes, said my mother, grinding her teeth, he had; but
he had not brought the magic device, and had therefore gone
away. In that case, said the official, I will see what the situation is,
and ring you back and let you know. She didn't, of course, and
at the time of writing this (Wednesday afternoon), my mother
had heard nothing more from anybody.

I now want three things to happen. First, I want my mother's
bathroom water-heater fixed, and at once. Second, I want a
written apology to my mother to be sent from both the Natural
Gas Conversion office and from the Gas Board.

That will satisfy my mother. But I also want a third thing on
my own behalf; or rather, on behalf of the public in general,
who have to put up with the kind of behaviour I have just described. I want a public answer to this question: what is wrong
with a national organization which gives its customers not the
service they pay for but, instead, incompetence and a string of
broken promises?

Later:
The nation, I gather, is agog to know whether my mother is
clean. This is not, I take it, a matter into which a well-bred nation
would normally seek to inquire. But since I sang the saga of my
mother's bathroom water-heater and the North Thames Gas
Board, recounting how she was without hot water from her geyser for over three weeks, its normally copious supply being replaced only by a flow of broken promises from officials of the
North Thames Gas Board, I have had virtually uncountable numbers of letters wishing to know whether my words have had the
desired results.

All in good time. But first, about those letters in general. To begin
with, their number exceeded, by a very considerable margin,
those I have received on any single topic arising out of this column
since I began writing it two and a half years ago. Next, in the
ovewhelming majority, the writer recounted experiences, at the
hands of the North Thames Gas Board, that were undoubtedly at

B

least as bad as, and in a substantial number of cases very much worse than, those undergone by my mother. Finally, the pattern of behaviour on the part of North Thames Gas Board was the same in almost all the accounts: promises of action unfulfilled, and no coordination whatever between any two people in that organization, so that the men who supposedly come to fit a part which a previous visitor has declared necessary and promised will be sent, come without either the part or any knowledge of a previous visit or the conclusions formed by the previous visitor. (My mother had four sets of such visitors: one correspondent had nineteen.) Several sufferers, incidentally, seeing the advantage of being my mother, offered to adopt me; one asked if I would adopt *her*.

I am also informed by *The Times* Business News that the subject on which they regularly receive the largest number of letters is the North Thames Gas Board and its incompetence, though incompetence, to judge by my postbag on the subject, is too mild a word; the organization seems to be putrescent from top to bottom, its officials leaving letters unanswered, phone calls ignored, and customers offered nothing but false assurances of action.

Which brings me to the question of my mother and her bath. The first conclusion to be drawn from the affair is that top officials of the North Thames Gas Board read *The Times*. Not long after breakfast on the morning the article appeared, my mother's flat was filled from wall to wall with North Thames officials — eventually, at least seven. There were engineers, and fitters, and executives, and one man who, from my mother's account, appears to have been the apologizer. Anyway, just as the place was about to collapse from the weight of Gas Board men (some of them even arrived from outside, by ladder) they finished the job and left. My mother, exhausted by the weeks of battle, and no doubt in addition emotionally drained by the abrupt discovery that she was the owner of the most famous bathroom geyser in the world, immediately went away on holiday, pausing only to take a bath.

When she returned (she got her written apology, incidentally) she found that North Thames had, while doing the work, apparently installed a fascinating and novel system. Whenever she takes a bath, and much of the time now even when she does not, water pours out of the ceiling in the room next door. This, of course, enables her to offer a visitor, in addition to tea and cakes, an informal shower in the kitchen, but she cannot help feeling that the degree of informality in the arrangement is excessive, and the bucket she puts underneath does tend to fill rather quickly, besides adding little if anything to the kitchen's appearance. ('It seems', she says – she is a woman long accustomed to seeing into the heart of a problem – 'that they must have knocked a hole in something.') Unless the Gas Board, feeling that it has done its final duty by the tribe of Levin, has now given up *The Times*, perhaps any senior official reading this might care to indicate to his colleagues that something in the nature of a return to square one is urgently needed.

The Times August 16th and 28th, 1973

Two fingers and the long arm of the law

THEY DO HAVE fun in Middlesbrough that we don't in the Strand, I must say. A Mr Bangs, who is herewith invited to blow the froth off a pint of mine any time he finds it convenient to call, has been arrested and hauled into court in that part of the world on a charge of contempt, the particular judge to whom he was alleged to have shown it being Mr Justice Lawson. (I read the name first as Lawton, and the room spun around me, for Mr Justice Lawton is a very wise old bird indeed, whereas the one with an 's', at any rate in this case, seems to be perhaps not quite the most — well, well, perhaps we had better leave the sentence there.)

Mr Bangs has recently had his rates increased, and is, understandably enough, displeased in consequence. When, therefore, a large and official-looking car passed him, in which he saw a gentleman in colourful, not to say ridiculous, clothes, he suited his actions to his feelings and extended the first and second fingers of his right hand, knuckles outwards, in its direction, believing that the gorgeously-caparisoned traveller was the Mayor. In this, it speedily appeared, he was mistaken, for the man at whom he had made his rude gesture was not only blameless in the matter of the rates; he was Mr Justice Lawson, on his way to clock in for the morning shift at Teesside Crown Court, and what is more he was accompanied by his oppo, Mr Justice Mais by name and rank.

This, as it turned out, was a dangerous mistake for Mr Bangs to have made, for he shortly afterwards found himself in a dungeon, and after cooling his heels there for some hours was brought before Mr Justice Lawson (careful with that 's', Mr Compositor,

I beg you), who said to him, 'It is a very serious matter indeed to do what you did to two of Her Majesty's Justices on their way to court. I have jurisdiction, you know, to send you to prison.'

And the question for discussion this morning is, of course: *is* it 'a very serious matter indeed' to give the high-sign to two or even twenty-two of Her Majesty's Justices on their way to court, or for that matter their way from court to the nearest fish-and-chip shop? I mean, is it *really*?

Of course, it is wrong, and naughty, and worthy of reproof. As soon as I read the report of what Mr Bangs had done, my face became stern and solemn, though it is true that this was mainly because I had taken the precaution of injecting a quart of novocaine into it, lest I should burst into unseemly giggles. But 'a very serious matter indeed'? How, I wonder, if he uses such language about a mere gesture, would Mr Justice Lawson describe an attempt by a disgruntled litigant to defenestrate him? Or the action of a gang of scoundrels who were to debag him and paint his bottom bright green? Would he not, in such genuinely outrageous circumstances, be hard put to it to frame a suitable rebuke if he had used up 'a very serious matter indeed' on what Mr Bangs did?

It is true, of course, that Mr Justice Lawson is not simply Mr Justice Lawson. Lineal descendant of Sir Edward Coke and Lord Mansfield, heir to Blackstone and Pufendorf, he represents, not just mortal man with a wig on, but the majesty of the Law itself. Even so, is the Law so damaged in the eyes of all right-thinking persons that its incarnation on the Teesside bench must needs talk of prison to a bus-driver who did to him what Mr Harvey Smith did to Mr Bunn?* And even if the answer is yes, would not the good justicer have done well to remember whether it was Mr Smith or Mr Bunn who came out of that episode with the greater quantity of egg on his face? I realize, of course, that the Law is

* Mr Smith was a show-jumper; Mr Bunn a judge of such contests who had somehow displeased Mr Smith, and who promptly displeased him even more by depriving him, for his rude gesture, of the prize he had just been awarded.

the true embodiment of everything that is excellent, but it may
not necessarily follow, even in the case of Mr Justice Lawson,
that,

> It has no kind of fault or flaw
> And I, my Lords, embody the law.

Proportion, surely, is what Mr Justice Lawson may be thought,
however unjustly, to have displayed on this occasion a very
slightly defective sense of. And I cannot help feeling that the law
and those who dispense it would have been better served if, when
Mr Bangs had done his dreadful deed, Mr Justice Lawson had
turned to Mr Justice Mais, sitting beside him in the car, and dismissed the incident by murmuring some appropriate tag, such as
'*Nunquam in vita mihi fuit melius*', which is from Plautus, and
means 'I never felt better in my life', or '*Re ipsa repperi, facilitate
nihil esse homini melius neque clementia*', which is from Terence,
and means 'I have found by experience that there is nothing
better for a man than an easy temper and complacency', or
even, 'The object of the discipline enforced by the Court in case
of contempt of court is not to vindicate the dignity of the Court
or the person of the Judge, but to prevent undue interference with
the administration of justice', which is from Lord Justice Bowen,
and means what it says.

I have written before about that great heroine of mine, that
Grace Darling of jurisprudence, the lady who, finding her suit
dismissed by the Court of Appeal, rose from her seat (she had
been pleading in person) and flung an entire row of lawbooks,
one by one, at the judges. They took no action, and indeed no
notice, but left the court gravely and unhurriedly, as had been
their intention. Mr Justice Lawson would have done well to
follow the example of his seniors, rather than the less dignified
one of Dogberry:

Dost thou not suspect my place? Dost thou not suspect my
years? O that he were here to write me down an ass! but,
masters, remember that I am an ass; though it be not written

down, yet forget not that I am an ass. No, thou villain, thou art full of piety, as shall be proved upon thee by good witness. I am a wise fellow; and, which is more, an officer; and, which is more, a householder; and, which is more, as pretty a piece of flesh as any in Messina; and one that knows the law, go to; and a rich fellow enough, go to; and a fellow that hath had losses; and one that hath two gowns, and everything handsome about him. Bring him away. O that I had been writ down an ass!

The Times May 24th, 1973

The mercy of the cruel sea

THERE WAS A little-regarded news item the other day, about a woman and her fifteen-year-old son being found floating in a collapsible dinghy in the Baltic; her husband and their two daughters, aged twelve and fourteen respectively, had been in a similarly frail vessel, but had drowned.

The cruel sea, you may think, up to its usual tricks. The family's boat had been swamped; they had taken to the dinghies which, as prudent sailors, they had been careful to have aboard, dividing the family as they had no doubt long planned against the possibility of just such a disaster; probably they had had regular lifeboat drill, joking as they did so. And now the grey, impersonal waves had shown themselves stronger than all the precautions, and the world contained one more widow and one more fatherless child. And that is really all there is for any outsider to say about it.

Or rather: almost all. For there is an extra dimension to the story, which it now behoves me to disclose. The family had not taken to their rubber dinghies from a sinking yacht; they had embarked in those very craft. And they were not indulging a taste for hazardous sport, or putting their children through some kind of Outward Bound toughening process. They were not seeking fitness, relaxation or sunken treasure; what they were after was freedom. For they were a family of East Germans, from the western marches of the Soviet Empire, and they were trying to get away from it. The mother and the son did; the father and the two daughters did not. We record a 40 per cent success rate (or, if we are of a pessimistic tendency, a 60 per cent failure rate), and pass on.

We pass on to a fairly obvious reflection. How peculiarly vile must a system of government be if citizens compelled to live under it are willing to trust their lives, and the lives of their children, in a challenge to the might of a northern sea, to a couple of toy boats? (If your first thought is that they were foolhardy not to wait until the weather was better, have a second; when the weather around the shores of Soviet Germany is such as to make the waters navigable without risk, the State watchers are on permanent alert for any kind of boat putting out to sea, be it never so innocent in appearance. Only when it is very dangerous indeed to sail such seas is there any chance of the vigilance being sufficiently slack to offer any chance of escape.)

I ask how vile a regime must be if its citizens are compelled to take such chances to get away from it. For consider: the Soviet imperialists have been in occupation of Eastern Germany for a third of a century; an entire generation has been born, and grown up, and created another, under Soviet rule.

They have never read any permitted printed word, never heard or seen anything on their country's radio or television program-mes, never learnt anything in school or university, never had any public instruction or exhortation, never come across any public information at their place of work or of social relations, that had not been carefully searched and screened by people highly skilled in the appropriate techniques, to ensure that not a single word of truth about the world, or communism, or their Soviet masters, or their own puppet government, would get through. Whatever it was that this family felt, and that drove all of them to danger and most of them to death, came from their lifetime's experience of the delights of communism.

That these delights are insufficient to keep seventeen million people indefinitely delighted is made plain by the episode I have recounted. But it is made plainer by the fact that the regime lines its western borders, land and sea, with guards and guns, electrified fences and lethal mines, watchtowers and dogs and pursuit ves-sels, all intended not to keep invaders out but to keep the regime's citizens in.

When the Berlin Wall was built I thought, and I have never seen reason to revise my view, that the standard excuse for it among Soviet apologists in the West—that it was justified because of the 'brain drain' of East Germany—was the most squalid item the fellow-travellers' repertoire had ever encompassed. Students of such matters will have noticed that in recent years the line has changed; now we are expected to believe that East Germany is an immensely wealthy state, its citizens revelling in a standard of living that puts Stockholm and California to shame. Some might say that if the new line is true, the Wall has become something of an anomaly, but I have not detected many suggestions that it should now be demolished, and I have even less expectation that it actually will be.

In the end, we have to turn to that much (and ill) used word, empathy. It should be possible, by an effort of the moral imagination, to put ourselves in the position of that family, so that we can see the beach from which they set out, feel their hearts beating with fear and resolution, look upon the sea that faced them, entrust our minds, as they their bodies, to a bubble of air and a film of rubber, and set off with them into the darkness. Beyond that it would be indecent to follow them, to death and deprivation; and beyond that, it is unnecessary to follow them; two, at any rate, reached the freedom that is so familiar to us that most of us have no idea why it is so precious, and that some work day and night to stamp out. But if we can get far enough towards merging our feelings with the feelings of a family to whom death was an acceptable alternative to communism, we shall understand two things it is important to understand—more important, it may be, than we know.

First, we shall be virtually immune to all the lies, all the excuses, all the apologies, all the breathlessly enthusiastic travelogues, that the servants and fellow-travellers of totalitarianism pour out incessantly. Next time one of them is telling us that the system is of course different from ours, but in its way valid, and that anyway the people who live under it seem to like it, all we have to do is to close our eyes; then we can hear the waves lapping, feel the cold, see the darkness, and remember that the waves, the cold, the darkness and the death were considered preferable to continued existence under Soviet communism. And in a single moment the whole edifice of deceit will vanish like a nightmare at dawn.

That is one half of what we may gain from the exercise in empathy that I have proposed. The other half is even more important. By trying to feel what the family felt, we can remind ourselves of what is in some ways the most wonderful and extraordinary of all the attributes of man, the inextinguishable spark of freedom in his soul. For what did that family know of freedom? East Germany went directly from Nazism to communism; today, a citizen of that repulsive helotry would have to be sixty-five* to have lived as an adult in a free society; a Soviet citizen would, of course, have to be much older. And yet in both there are men and women who divine what freedom is, though all their lives they have been denied it, and seek it though they perish in the search.

So the story of the family that fled together and died apart can teach us something of enduring value; that the most valuable thing of all is also the most enduring. Just as science teaches us that matter, however many times it may change its form, is ultimately indestructible, so we can see that at the core of Man's being is a rock that, though it can be cracked, scored, crushed, ground to rubble, cannot be made to disappear; and it was upon that living rock that five human beings set sail into the Baltic. And eloquent testimony to its eternal strength is given by a woman and her son who live now in Federal Germany; and by a man and his two daughters who sleep now beneath the Baltic waves.

The Times March 16th, 1977

---

* Now sixty-seven. 'Hang out our banners on the outward walls; the cry is still "They come".'

Who was that lady?

Shakespeare the Man by A. L. Rowse*

WHAT ANT HAS got into Dr Rowse's trousers and bites him so that he leaps and capers and yells and makes such an egregious ass of himself with his ridiculous boasting, his absurd claims that his speculations are proofs, that he has settled all outstanding questions for ever?

> ... puts out of court all the existing editions of the Sonnets ... all the biographies of Shakespeare ... impossible to impugn the historian's account of the matter ... definitive answers ... nonsense written about William Shakespeare ... comes from ignorance of the Elizabethan age ... my new finds ... impossible to impugn because borne out by historical fact ... we now know, after centuries ... complete and absolute corroboration ... imperceptive generations have missed ... complete vindication of fact and argument ... there can be no mistake about it... vague conjectures, for generations, have told us nothing ... now all quite clear ... commentators with no historical sense have totally lost themselves ... disregard mountains of otiose commentary ... see my *The Elizabethan Renaissance* ... see my *The Elizabethan Renaissance* ... see my *The Elizabethan Renaissance* ... see my *The Elizabethan Renaissance* ...

Cucullus non facit monachum; Dr Rowse is entitled to reply that his buffoonish behaviour does not itself invalidate his claims. True: so let us now ignore the conduct of the accused and proceed to the evidence. It is no secret (at least if it is a secret it is a

* Macmillan, 1973.

bloody miracle, in view of the author's pre-publication trumpet-tings) that Dr Rowse, in this book, claims to have established be-yond any further doubt the identity of the Dark Lady of the Sonnets, and to have done so by the use of 'strict attention to chronology, the correlation of what Shakespeare tells us, the topical references with historical circumstances at every point, the minute and precise corroboration of internal with external information'.

Let us take a few examples of his rigorous method. His candi-date for the role of Dark Lady is one Emilia Lanier, née Bassano, and she appears in the manuscripts of a shady Elizabethan astrolo-ger named Simon Forman, whom she consulted, and with whom she (according to Forman's account) had an affair. Now Shakes-peare's love was, as he repeatedly insists, dark; brows, eyes, hair were all black. We cannot be so sure about her skin, for Sonnet 130 (ignored here by Rowse) says 'If snow be white, why then her breasts are dun' – only, it seems, by comparison with snow; still, if she existed at all (Rowse does not even consider here the 'anti-personalist' view of the Sonnets as flights of pure poetic imagination), she was dark. So Rowse takes us to Forman for confirmation of the fact that Emilia was dark. And *all* Forman says on the subject is 'She was very brown in youth'. This, for Rowse, is enough; 'evidently,' he says, 'she was exceptionally dark.' Why he imagines Forman added 'in youth' if Emilia was still dark, and how Forman's 'brown' becomes the repeated 'black' of the Sonnets – on all this the man of 'minute and precise corro-boration' is silent.

That's nothing. Shakespeare's Dark Lady was musical; indeed, played a musical instrument (Sonnet 128), which seems to be the virginals. It is therefore necessary for Rowse to find that Emilia played the virginals, too. Watch now how the Doctor does it. Forman says that her husband was 'a minstrel'; on page 100 Rowse embellishes this, saying that *she* was 'musical ... married off to another musician'; on page 111, discussing Emilia's pros-pects on the death of her mother, he says that she 'no doubt had been taught to play on the virginals'; and finally on page 156 we read of Shakespeare that 'we know that Emilia's playing on the virginals was one of the arts by which he had been ensnared'. Such is Dr Rowse's method; from a total lack of any evidence whatever that Emilia played any musical instrument to 'we know that Emilia's playing on the virginals' helped to ensnare Shakespeare. This is not scholarship; it is pyramid selling.

But there is even worse to come. For after all, even if Emilia was dark, there are many brunettes; even if she was musical, other women have been so; even if she led Forman a dance, other women may have led Shakespeare one. We turn the page faster, eager to find the moment at which Forman complains that the playwright is his rival. *No such moment comes*; from first to last, Dr Rowse has been unable to find the slightest suggestion that Shakespeare ever met, or even knew of the existence of, Emilia Bassano-Lanier. But stay: there is a character called Emilia in *Othello*, and when Rowse gets there he exclaims 'with that name!' and rests his case.

I have dwelt on the Dark Lady because Rowse claims that, having solved all other problems in his previous book, this was the only one outstanding. But it is not the only example of his slipshod methods. For instance, on page 137 Rowse is discussing the actor Will Kemp, who played many comic roles. 'Would he not then have played the part of Falstaff?' he asks. By page 161 he feels able to dispense with the question mark: 'The part of Falstaff', he says firmly, 'would have been taken by Will Kemp.' Furthermore, at one point, 'It would seem' that Shakespeare played the part of Chorus in *Henry V*; at another ('Seems, Madam! Nay, it is; I know not seems'), 'He himself spoke as Chorus what he had penned at the end of *Henry V*.'

Rowse also suffers from the same complaint as Dr Leslie Hotson; the conviction that Shakespeare was determined to fill his plays with topical and autobiographical references of every kind – at times, from both these great speculators, one could almost believe that he wrote them only as a cover for his allusions, as the madder Baconians believe that the plays were nothing but elaborate cyphers concealing the identity of their true author. But Rowse goes too far for patience when he quotes Sonnet 110's:

> Alas, 'tis true I have gone here and there
> And made myself a motley to the view ...

and then adds 'i.e., he has been touring about the country as a player' – which is on a par with the theory that there is a dog in *Hamlet* called Amazement, giving rise to the line 'But see, Amazement on thy mother sits'.

Dr Rowse is also repetitive (I lost count of the number of times he says 'We shall see', and repeats that some of Jonson's plays were not as popular as Shakespeare's, and regrets that he cannot go into a particular play in any detail), dogmatic (Hamlet was 'psychotic', *sans phrases*), silly ('it is rarely that one of the world's writers takes us into the innermost crevices of his own heart and experience'), wrong ('Gielgud's production' of *The Winter's Tale* was in fact produced by Peter Brook), vulgar (Shakespeare was 'possibly the sexiest writer in the language') and in need of a better dictionary ('conditions that irradiate around genius').

So why am I going on at this length? Why not just recommend the prompt dispatch of the book into the wastepaper basket and leave it at that? Because *Shakespeare the Man* is *not* worthless, and could have been very useful. We do need literary popularizers like Rowse, whose enthusiasm for, and love of, Shakespeare (these qualities leap from the page again and again) communicate themselves to the reader, firing his imagination and making him see the plays, the lines, the characters, vividly and in the round. Rowse's extensive knowledge of the Elizabethan background *is* valuable, *does* enable us to place Shakespeare and his work in the context of their time. And then again, Emilia Lanier *might* be the Dark Lady, the 'only begetter' of the Sonnets *could* be the man who procured them for the printer rather than the subject of them, Marlowe *is* quite possibly the Rival Poet.

With all his understanding of the era and all his love of Shakespeare, Dr Rowse could have written – could still write, if he would only scrap both this book and its predecessor – a work of real value that could replace shelvesful of those lifeless academic studies he despises so much; such a book, if he would only write it, could be the perfect introduction, particularly for young people, to Shakespeare's life. As it is, the book Dr Rowse has written is only the perfect introduction to his own foolishness, which is not at all the same thing.

Observer April 29th, 1973

Baby into guerrilla

THE MOST EXTRAORDINARY thing about the remark that Dr Bridget Rose Dugdale is reported to have made at the first sight of her new-born son – 'He's going to be a guerrilla' – is that she probably did make it. Indeed, it is quite possible that it was not even said with conscious thought of its effect; 'He's going to be a guerrilla' may actually have been the first thing she thought when she saw her child. For

> Cruelty has a human heart
> And Jealousy a human face;
> Terror the human form divine,
> And Secrecy the human dress.

And it is therefore not at all impossible that Dr Dugdale is so far removed from consciousness of her own inadequacy, so unable to see the nasty futility of her own life, so achingly devoid of any trace of a sense of humour, that all she could see in the infant was something as mad, bad and dangerous to know as herself. One would not expect Dr Dugdale to declare that her son was a little bundle of joy sent from the angels, nor that his tiny fingers and toes were as beautiful as fairies, footprints; nor would one expect her to announce his birth in the appropriate column of *The Times*. All the same, even for a woman whose most notable achievements to date have been to rob her own parents and then to terrify two gentle people and steal their pictures, probably for no better reason than that in her poor broken mind the people represented her parents and the pictures something as eternal and immutable as her beliefs are insubstantial and ramshackle, you might suppose that her first thought at the sight of her first-born would be something less fatuous.

'He's going to be a guerrilla.' No doubt Dr Dugdale would dismiss with contempt anyone who found anything odd in such a response to the sight of her new-born child. The 'revverlution' is all that matters, and for her I suppose a baby is not, as it might be to other women who had just given birth, a creature who might take any one of a million paths through life, who might achieve fame or happiness or suffer pain or failure, but an empty vessel into which she will pour all her ignorance, all her desperate need to turn her self-hatred outwards, all her intolerance and dark desire to inflict pain, until the vessel is full of it and it spills over into the same waste and folly as she has made of her own life. She thinks of herself as a guerrilla, though in truth she is nothing but a fool: so she thinks of her son as a guerrilla, though in truth he is nothing but a baby.

One might think that even a woman as confused as Dr Dugdale would stop for a moment and think of her own birth and of her own parents. It is not recorded what her mother's first words after giving birth were, though I think it is unlikely that they were 'She's going to be a fascist-capitalist-imperialist-bandit', still, it is even more unlikely that they contained even a passing guess at what she did in the end become. No doubt, human nature being what it is, Dr Dugdale's mother hoped that her daughter would grow up to be a credit to her parents; no doubt it did not cross her mind that the child would grow up to be a violent termagant in a rotten cause. Is it not possible, then, that Dr Dugdale's son may grow up to be something less than a credit to his parents, that he might, while loving his mother no less than her parents still clearly love her, confound her hopes by becoming say, a stockbroker, an army officer or a poet? She will, of course, do her best to inculcate him with the bent and grubby values by which she lives; but then, her parents did their best to imbue her with the spirit of the straight and honourable values by which they lived, and although of course she would reverse those pairs of adjectives, doing so might not, in itself, be quite enough to ensure that her proud boast – 'He's going to be a guerrilla' – is fulfilled.

Feeling sorry for Dr Dugdale, which I do and which I hope any person of sensibility would, is presumably something that would make her much angrier than hatred and denunciation. However just a prison sentence may be, and however impossible it may be to have people like that walking about free to be a menace to everybody else, the sheer horribleness of locking human beings up in a cage, whatever they have done, still comes into any contemplation of crime and punishment. How much more, then, must one feel sorry for Dr Dugdale. In the first place, she committed her crimes because her poor, soft, impressionable head had been so crammed with crazy rubbish by her lover and her own psychological problems that everything else was pushed out of it. And in the second place, of course, she has given birth to a child in prison, and since it is inconceivable that the Irish authorities will allow the child to grow up in prison, there will come a parting which for her will be doubly bitter in that it will not only be the parting of a mother from her child but will inevitably torment her with the conviction that he will be taught to hate her rubbishy cause. I hope myself that he will not need to be taught that; I hope that he will conclude, when he is old enough to think about such things, that a cause which leads to such empty, beastly behaviour as his mother was involved in must be a cause to shun, though I hope he does not go on from that conclusion to shun his mother, too.

It may be, of course, that he will grow up to be a credit to her in a sense different from that which she would understand, and instead of being a guerrilla will be the instrument of rescuing her from the mental morass in which she wallows; perhaps he will, through example if not through argument, show her, in the most literal sense of the old words, the error of her ways. Perhaps; yet the only thing of which we can be certain is that anyone who will undertake to say certainly what a newborn child will become is likely to be confounded; there is no reason to suppose that Dr Dugdale is any exception to that proposition, and therefore her son, though he may indeed turn out as she hopes, is much more likely not to. 'He's going to be a guerrilla', is he? Has Dr Dugdale thought of the ultimate horror, the possibility that he might be a priest?

The Times December 18th, 1974

A mug at Ascot

I SUPPOSE THEY must have suspected right from the start that horse-racing is something with which I am less than entirely at home (which reminds me that I once read an article, in a series on collecting, that began with the memorable words: 'Pewter is not everybody's cup of tea'), because when they rang up to ask if I would care to come to Ascot last week, I replied, 'Is that something called the Derby?', and their suspicion must have turned to certainty when, in my letter confirming my acceptance of so promising an invitation, I inquired – wishing, as ever, to do the right thing – whether they would be kind enough to let me know at what points I should shout, respectively 'Up the Gunners', 'Out of court' and 'Oh, well bowled, Sir', though having regard to the likelihood that unpleasant rumours are even now getting about – or, even more probable in view of the company I found myself in, being put about – I must make it clear that I did not arrive enveloped in an enormous red-and-white muffler and carrying a wooden rattle and a case of stout, despite the fact that, in view of the perishing cold, the muffler would have come in handy, though as against that I have to admit that the same could not be said of the stout, as my host's assurance that there would be any amount of wet available was handsomely lived up to throughout.

My host and hostess, knowing how keen I am to remain comfortable at all times, assured me that we would be under cover throughout, whereat I envisaged some kind of canvas awning to keep the rain off, and was therefore pleasantly surprised to discover that my destination appeared to be a vast block of flats, which was said to be the Grandstand, and was fully grand enough even for my exacting tastes.

One of these flats was where I was to watch the racing, and the windows commanded a splendid view of everything that was to be seen. Someone kindly pointed out to me the various sights, explaining their various functions; thus I learned to distinguish 'bookies', 'punters' and 'horses', and gathered that the first, whenever the second said correctly which of the last would win a given race, were obliged to pay out substantial sums of money, though when I remarked that all the bookies seemed to be stout and prosperous gentlemen, whereas the punters for the most part seemed lean and anxious, I was complimented on my percipience, and told that I had independently discovered an important truth about racing, several more of which, in the course of the afternoon, I was destined to learn, including the full import of a song that used to be sung by the late Jerry Colonna, the refrain of which ran:

> Horses don't bet on people,
> And that's why they never go broke.

When I had thus grasped the principle on which the occasion was based, the drinking began, and continued for some time, as did the eating. After a good deal of this, it was time for the betting. It was here that I felt my lack of experience most keenly, for there seemed to be no way of ascertaining which of the many horses engaged for each race (as you may imagine, they all looked alike to me) would win it. I proposed to inquire of the bookies, and in particular one whose stand was immediately below me and who, in view of the fact that his name was Levy, I felt might be sympathetic, but I was told that such an inquiry would be met with, at best, a good deal of brusqueness; I felt vaguely gratified in consequence when, shortly after it had come on to rain torrentially, Mr Levy's umbrella was blown down.

'Form' (as I was told it was called) being no use to me, I fell back on divination. In the chief race of the meeting, for instance, the prize for which included a trophy of, to judge from its photograph in the programme, exceptional, if not entirely unique, hideousness, there was a horse by the name of Charlie Bubbles.

As a dear friend of mine had starred in the film of that name, I determined to back it, despite the fact that it was what is called the favourite – a term indicating, if I understood the explanation correctly, that the bookies, should it win, would be obliged to pay out to each successful punter a sum considerably smaller than would have been the case in the event of any other horse succeeding. No sooner had I determined on this course of action, however, than my eye fell upon the name of another horse in the same race, bearing the name of Questa Notte, which seemed suitable in view of the fact that I was due to go to *Il Trovatore* at Covent Garden the same evening – a circumstance which also seemed to cover yet another horse in the same race, this one hight Gracious Melody. Nor did even this exhaust the possibilities of the third race, for Liberty Lawyer seemed to have a certain attraction, since I have been recently devoting a good deal of attention to one who is undoubtedly a lawyer, and no less undoubtedly guilty of what in popular speech is referred to as a diabolical bleeding liberty.*
If you add to this list Mrs Tiggywinkle, which had for me romantic associations which are no concern of yours, and King Oedipus, which seemed appropriate in view of the fact that I had also gathered that certain races are called 'classics', you will see that the number of favourable omens I had at my disposal was almost embarrassingly large.

I determined to follow my varied luck wherever it might lead, and backed them all, but to my astonishment not one of the enormous list of beasts I had backed was among the first three past the post, and my distress was made all the greater by the company's assurance that in no circumstances would those with whom I had struck the bets entertain a suggestion that they should regard the entire transaction as void *ab initio* and return my money. (I was to some extent mollified, however, by being assured that I was a 'mug' – a term which I took to be one of approbation.)

I will not bother you with the full details: suffice it to say that,

* I think this referred to the Attorney-General; I cannot recall which one, nor does it much matter, as it could have applied to any.

in the interstices of the eating and drinking I backed horses called, among other things (and some of the things I called them are unfit for publication in a respectable newspaper), Temple of the Sun (did not shine), Abide With Me (abode with the starter), True Lad (false), Run Tell Run (walked), Master Petard (hoist) and Comet Kohoutek (fizzled out), and only the fact that I had to leave before the last race prevented me from attempting to recoup my losses by plunging heavily on Fair Georgina, which I assumed is what must be meant by a 'dark horse', and which for all I know is running still. The drinking and eating did my liver no good, I got soaked to the skin between the grandstand and the car park, and my accountant assures me that the losses I incurred are not allowable against income tax. All in all, Ascot seems a long way to go for cirrhosis, indigestion, pneumonia and bankruptcy, and I cannot imagine why they call this ridiculous business the 'sport of kings', if indeed they do. But I got to Covent Garden in time and *Trovatore* was splendid.

The Times May 6th, 1975

There was an old Bishop of Birmingham ...

IT APPEARS THAT some people in Birmingham view with alarm
concern and despondency (not necessarily in that order) the
possibility that the Right Reverend Hugh Montefiore, at present
Bishop Suffragan of Kingston, may be translated to the Birmingham See, from which the present incumbent has announced that
he is to retire. They feel that the attitudes and views of the Bishop
of Kingston leave much to be desired; closer inspection of their
reasons for feeling as much, however, reveals that it is not, by and
large, his theology that seems to them suspect, for no criticism is
offered of his position on the Real Presence, nor is it suggested
that the Monophysite or Arian heresies will flourish unchecked
throughout Birmingham should he be installed in the palace. He
is charged neither with Romish practices on the one hand nor
with Congregationalism on the other; his sermons, in the ears of
the disquieted faithful, have sounded no unacceptably Latitudi-
narian note; he has not been heard to speak disrespectfully of the
Epistle to the Thessalonians.

No; the Bishop's sin, which in the opinion of the godly folk of
Birmingham unfits him for the episcopal care of their souls, is that
he is opposed to Concorde* and that he may well look with no
kindly eye on motor cars themselves. 'This is an aerospace city',
says one of Bishop Montefiore's critics; 'we could not view with
equanimity anyone who is so strongly opposed to Concorde.'
'He could apply to the internal combustion engine', says another,

* He was one of those who gave evidence before the American court charged
with ruling on the British application for Concorde to be allowed to fly to the
United States; he opposed the application.

'what he said about Concorde.' (He does, as a matter of fact.)

Anathema sit. The Bishop's critics do not claim that they have biblical support for their hostility to him (though they could in fact cite, if they were so minded, the passage from the Sermon on the Mount which runs 'Blessed are they who make whacking great piles of money out of the white heat of the technological revolution, for they shall probably appear in Sir Harold Wilson's resignation Honours List', and the hardly less significant passage in St Matthew, in which Christ, responding at the Last Supper to the toast of 'the Lord Mayor and Corporation of the City of Birmingham', observes, 'He that dippeth his hand with me in the dish, the same shall betray me, probably by encouraging the unrestricted import of Japanese motor cars'); but they insist that he is not suitable material for the Bishopric of Birmingham.

As I have had occasion to say before, when venturing to dip a toe into the turbulent waters of Christian controversy, an agnostic Jew of mixed Bessarabian and Lithuanian descent is perhaps not the ideal champion of Anglican orthodoxy, or for that matter the best possible critic of it. I am emboldened to participate in this particular debate, however, first by the fact that Bishop Montefiore was born, like me, into the Hebrew persuasion (though I believe a rather more *soigné* corner of it), and second by my uneasy conviction that if I don't nobody else will.

The question is: ought a bishop to be a devoted advocate of increased production in the factories of his diocese, irrespective of the nature of the goods produced, and ought he to be barred from enthronement if he thinks that the goods in question, so far from providing the closest possible earthly approximation to the Kingdom of Heaven, fall most decidedly within the province of the devil and all his works?

I could point out, though I agree that it would not be a conclusive argument, that if the bishop's critics were to press their case a little too far they might find themselves insisting that their pastor should give his episcopal blessing to those Birmingham concerns which turn a penny or two by producing large numbers of exceptionally ugly brass ashtrays stamped 'Made in Benares' on the underside of the rim. But there is a rather more fundamental point which seems to have escaped those who think a bishop should be in favour of Concorde if it brings employment and prosperity to the city over the spiritual life of which he is, partly by the workings of the Apostolic Succession and partly by those of the Crown Appointments Commission, appointed to preside. It is that there really is a very considerable difference between Jesus Christ and Mr Gerald Kaufman, and that it does not lie only in their respective spiritual qualities, though there may be substantial differences in that respect, but also in the fact that the functions allotted to them by history are quite distinct.*

Now Mr Kaufman, I am sure, is well aware of this, and would never think of suggesting that Bishop Montefiore is unworthy of promotion in the Anglican hierarchy because of his views on Concorde. Unfortunately, not all those with the well-being of the aerospace industry at heart take so modest a view; whence the present commotion. Biblical exegesis has taken us far; but it has not yet taken us to the point where 'My kingdom is not of this world' is taken to mean that it is. A bishop may be a supporter of Concorde or an opponent thereof, just as he may be a collector of matchbox labels or allergic to mint sauce, but none of these things will affect one way or another his ability to exercise his ghostly functions.

And it is, after all, for the exercise of his ghostly functions that a bishop is appointed. That, at any rate, has been the general view until now, and if Birmingham wants a public relations officer for the aerospace industry, it is very unseemly of Birmingham to expect him to double the job with that of their bishop, and not much less so to declare him unfit to be their bishop at all if he won't. And one of the bishop's critics in this matter has added a further reason for dismay at such an appointment; it is that 'he would carry our name – Birmingham'. I suppose it could be argued that a bishop carrying the *laissez-passer* of the Holy Ghost should none the less be mindful that he also carries a rather more

---

* Mr Kaufman was, at the time, the Government Minister in whose province Concorde fell. Jesus Christ needs no introduction.

important form of imprimatur if his office bears the name of England's second city, but again, I cannot help feeling that he has got other fish to fry, and that keeping Birmingham's chromium plating bright ought not to take priority over the saving of souls.

'Render unto Caesar', said one of the principal figures in this dispute, 'the things that are Caesar's; and unto God the things that are God's.' It is a pity that no specific allocation of Concorde into one or the other of those categories was undertaken at the time; these makers of general statements little know the trouble they cause when it comes to their interpretation for practical purposes. But since there is now no way of settling the point, other than waiting for the Second Coming and asking for elucidation, I think Bishop Montefiore is entitled to hold, and even to propagate, the view that Concorde is not a good thing without thereby rendering himself ineligible to serve as bishop in a city where they think that it is. For all I know, the Bishop of Burton-upon-Trent doesn't like beer, the Bishop of Stilton hates cheese, and the Bishop of Yarmouth is sick at the thought of a bloater, yet they seem to be secure in their seats, and I hope will long remain so. If it comes to that, the Bishop of Bristol, in whose diocese Concorde is actually made, may share Bishop Montefiore's views on the device, and has, so far at any rate, escaped stoning. And quite right too, for such views would not make him any the less admirable a bishop.

On the other hand, he may think that Concorde is the greatest boon to this country since the Dissolution of the Monasteries, or at least since the New English Bible, but that would not make him any the better a bishop, either. I do not know whether it is true that Bishop Montefiore is about to be offered the rumoured preferment,* but if he is not, I hope that those who might otherwise have offered it to him have not changed their minds because some people in Birmingham – or the entire population of the place, if it comes to that – think it unacceptable for their bishop to oppose Concorde. No doubt some people think that Christ

* He was, and accepted it. Nothing untoward happened.

said 'in my father's house are many mansions, all of them ideally placed for the occupants to hear some lovely sonic booms', but I think that the Bishop of Birmingham, whoever gets the appointment, is entitled to have reservations on the authenticity, or even the validity, of the second half of the proposition without actually being crucified.

The Times October 4th, 1977

The falling mountain

O N FRIDAY THE 21st October, 1966, at a quarter past nine in the morning, the village of Aberfan, in the valley of the River Taff, which runs through the heart of the coal-mining country of South Wales, was going about its normal business. The first shift of miners was below ground; the children of the junior school were already at their lessons; those of the senior school, whose day started half an hour later, were on their way there; the wives, after seeing their menfolk off to work and their children to school, were getting ready for the shopping or the housework; and Mr George Williams, the local hairdresser, was making his way to open his shop, which stood at the north-west corner of the village.

The day was misty, though it had started fine, so when Mr Williams heard a sudden roaring sound, like a jet-plane coming in very close, he could at first see nothing to explain the loud and frightening noise. Then, as he looked at the street ahead of him, he saw the houses crumple and fall towards him, as though they were being pushed over from behind, which indeed they were.

A few minutes later the roaring stopped, as suddenly as it had begun. Mr Williams remembers noticing the extraordinary silence which followed: it was, he said, like turning off the wireless suddenly, and he added 'in that silence you couldn't hear a bird or a child'.

The dreadful aptness of Mr Williams's words was soon to be apparent. For a mountain had fallen on Aberfan, and dead beneath it lay 116 children and twenty-eight adults. One hundred and nine of the children were from the junior school that had lain in the path of the avalanche; five of the adults were their teachers.

Now the mountain which fell was made by men. It was composed of the rubbish inevitably attendant, everywhere in the world, upon the industry of coalmining. These piles of waste products are known by various names; in Wales they are called 'tips'. The first tip in the vicinity of the village had been started during the First World War; when it had grown too large for any more tipping of waste to be done on it, a second one was started, then a third, a fourth, a fifth, a sixth.

And then a seventh. The seventh Aberfan tip was begun in 1958. By October 21st, 1966, it was about 110 feet high and 1,000 feet long, and contained some 300,000 cubic yards of waste. And at 9.15 a.m. on that day, roughly half of that material slid away from the rest of it and came roaring down the natural hillside on which it had been deposited. It overwhelmed two farm cottages that stood in its path, crossed a disused canal and a railway embankment, and swept on to the village. In the village it destroyed a school and eighteen houses and damaged many more.

That which is made by man is accountable for by man. A tribunal of inquiry was set up in the wake of the disaster to discover why it had happened, and whether it could have been foreseen and prevented. That tribunal has just produced a devastating and damning report, telling of 'ignorance, bungling, ineptitude and failure', and pointing the finger of a terrible accusation at nine individuals and an organization.

The story is heavy with ironies of all kinds. There was – and is, and will be for some time – the irony of the fund opened for the stricken village. Contributions poured in from all over the country, from all over the world; in a few weeks it had reached nearly £2,500,000, at which point it was discovered that nobody had begun to think what should be done with it. You cannot compensate with money a family that has lost a child; the disaster of Aberfan was not like most mining disasters, in which it is the miner, the family breadwinner, who is killed; and the destroyed buildings are to be replaced free by the municipal authorities. A good deal of bitterness has tragically grown up in Aberfan as the argument continues.

Then there is the irony of the position which Aberfan holds in the present state of the mining industry in Britain. The local Member of Parliament, in his evidence before the tribunal, explained with remarkable candour that for him or anyone else to have expressed fears about the safety of the tip might have led to the mine being closed. For coalmining, in Britain as in other lands, is a declining industry; pits are closing almost every week, and the number of men in the industry is shrinking fast and will shrink still faster, as oil, natural-gas-fired electricity and ultimately perhaps atomic power, replace coal as the fuel which drives the wheels of British industry.

Aberfan, like many other marginal mining villages, lived in fear of an announcement to the effect that its collieries were no longer economic to work, and were to be closed down, bringing unemployment to a place which, over the years, has had more than its fair share of it. So, according to the Member of Parliament's testimony, those across whose minds had passed the thought that the tip might not be safe put it from them.

There is the irony of Lord Robens. After a sound but not spectacular political career with the Labour party, Robens was appointed six years ago to be chairman of the National Coal Board. In his period of office, he has fought tremendously on behalf of the industry – even to the extent that manifestly unproductive pits are being kept open, and the modernization of Britain retarded; a recent government proposal that coal should produce only 140 million tons a year by 1970 was fought by Robens, and the government, fearful of facing the possible political consequences of adding to the unemployment figures, agreed to raise the figure to 155 millions.

But now the Aberfan tribunal has turned a powerful and revealing light on the organization that Lord Robens heads. Its criticisms of the National Coal Board are savage; it tells of incompetence and ignorance, of men being appointed to jobs for which they were not qualified, of slackness and casualness, of a total breakdown of communication and the chain of command within the organization, of a cumbersome and inefficient bureaucracy.

It goes further. Though absolving Lord Robens from any personal blame for the disaster, it criticizes him sharply for his and his officials' evidence before the tribunal; the Coal Board maintained stubbornly, for week after week, until broken down by relentless cross-examination, that the disaster was entirely an accident and could not reasonably have been foreseen.

Coalmining in Britain has a bad history. For a century and more before nationalization, the private mineowners were probably the worst body of employers in the country. Now their inhumanity has gone, but it is clear that their inefficiency lingers on, and may even have got worse. The end of an industry which compels its workers to burrow underground like moles, and whose product scars and begrimes our land, cannot come too soon. And the final and most tragic irony is the way in which the dying giant, writhing in its death-throes, fell upon Aberfan and devoured its own children.

International Herald Tribune August 8th, 1967

C

Vintage Montgomery

Now that the obituaries have all been written and read, and we are on the eve of his funeral, I think I may presume to add my own memories of Montgomery: those of my readers who are surprised to find that I have any such memories may be assured that they are not half so surprised as I am.

It began a good many years ago, when I was conducting a series of television interviews, in which I had talked about their life and work to such people as Robert Bolt, Orson Welles, Enoch Powell, Michael Tippett (who claims – rightly, I am sure – to be the only man in the world with a refrigerator named 'Bernard Levin', thus entitled because he bought it with the money the television company paid him), Joost de Blank, Rebecca West, John Huston and Alexander Kerensky. (This was one I had set my heart on, for the reminiscences of the man who overthrew the Tsars, and was himself overthrown by Lenin, could hardly be anything but fascinating, and so they may have been, though since not six words of what he said were in a language that even roughly corresponded to English, I was hardly in a position to judge. It was never screened.)

Anyway, although Monty had appeared quite frequently on television at that time, he was always invited to address his mind to such matters as homosexual law reform or South African race relations – subjects on which, to put it as kindly as possible, his views were of no great significance or originality. What I suggested to my programme's producers was that I should ask him about war, generalship and allied matters, on which, after all, he might be presumed to know what he was talking about.

They rang him up (he always answered the telephone himself) and put the suggestion to him. 'I'll have to see this chap Levin first,' he barked; 'tell him to come down here and have tea with me.'

He came out to greet me. Before we were inside the house he had explained that he had insisted on our meeting 'to see if we got on'. 'You might not like me,' he said cheerfully, adding (and it really was said as an afterthought), 'or I might not like you.' But we liked each other from the start, and it was clear that we were going to have a good programme.

He was completely without pretentiousness or self-consciousness. In the programme I asked him — after discussing his well-founded reputation for never squandering a single life — to tell me how he felt about the fact that, when all the preparations for the battle had been made, and all the care and foresight expended, he nevertheless knew that within a few hours many men, perhaps many thousands, would be dead. 'D'you know,' he said, 'I've never really thought about it like that', and then and there, while the very cameras held their breath, he thought about it on-screen, and then answered with a soldier's directness and simplicity that the important thing was to ensure that the troops knew that if they were killed their bodies would be 'reverently collected and reverently buried'.

After that I used to go down to see him at his home in Hampshire, and grew very fond of him indeed; I don't know why he liked me, though I suspect it was partly because I teased him and partly because he could ask me about things of which he knew nothing and concerning which he would not pretend to knowledge he did not have — books, for instance, and much of politics, and people in the news whose names meant nothing to him. But I know why I liked him; it was because, so far from being the narrowly Puritan egoist of popular legend, I found him warm, touchingly innocent and vulnerable, full of a crisp, positively sly, humour, and quite extraordinarily thoughtful. (Once I was visiting him while he was working, on his *History of Warfare*, with two young researchers. One of them, he felt, looked tired and jaded. 'I know what you need,' he suddenly said to the young man; 'invite your girlfriend down here for the weekend.')

He used to go to Bournemouth for a fortnight every year, in the early spring, where he found himself in the company of Basil Liddell Hart, whom I had known for many years and who showed me great friendship and kindness. I would visit them both there, and at lunch saw it as my duty to posterity to provoke them into combat over military history and theory. Their disagreements had once been real, and touched by some feeling, but by then it was all battles long ago, and I would only have to mention Eisenhower or Churchill to have them spluttering at one another in mock-rage. Basil was very touched when, in my television programme with Montgomery, I led the Field-Marshal into acknowledging his military debt to the Captain – something he had never done before.

Once, in front of the fire at Isington, I asked Montgomery what was the biggest row he had ever had with Churchill, and after his ritual protest (we were both used to it by then) to the effect that he had never had any rows with anybody, he told me. It seems that Churchill had been looking through some lists of equipment landed on the beaches almost immediately after D-Day and found among the stores 'Two dentist's chairs'. Next time he saw Montgomery, he demanded to know why, at such a perilous moment, precious space had been found for such luxuries. 'I told him,' snapped Monty, 'I told him. I said "Prime Minister, a soldier with toothache's no use to me – he can't fight. Good morning."'

He had that old man's habit of telescoping the generations below him, so that to him I was the same age as the village children. But it brought out yet more of his solicitude: he would pause to ask, 'You know who I mean by Wavell?' or even 'by Attlee?' And the solicitude went into all sorts of odd corners, belying again the picture of a vain and selfish man; whenever we ate together he would insist, though he was of course notoriously teetotal, that I was supplied with wine of my choice, and would anxiously inquire whether it was really to my taste. (One of my happiest achievements, I may say, was persuading him to drink an entire glass of champagne, on his birthday, to the stupefaction of the *sommelier* at Claridge's.)

He reminisced endlessly, and with endless fascination for me. And constantly he would return to the questions through which he wanted to fill in the gaps in his own mind: 'E. M. Forster, now,' he would say; 'is he a good writer? What sort of things did he write?' Always he was scrupulously courteous, escorting me to the garden gate, making unnecessarily sure I had complete instructions for the journey. I can see him now, his eyes piercing and kind at once; I can feel his hand on my arm as we negotiated steps; I can hear his voice, clipped and warm. Of his generalship I am not qualified to form an opinion; as a man I felt for him admiration and a great affection. I am glad I knew him; he added a glowing strand to my life, and anyone attacking him in my presence is in for an unpleasant surprise. May the earth lie lightly on a soldier's bones.

The Times March 31st, 1976

The blood trial revived

O N MONDAY NEXT, in the little Ukrainian town of Vinnitsa, there begins a criminal trial the like of which has not been seen in the civilized world for some five or six centuries. Indeed, the matter is so horrible and the manner so fantastic that even I, whose regard for the Soviet political and judicial system is not at all high, would have found it difficult to credit had the details not come to me from sources of unquestionable authority, backed with a massive array of references.

The prisoner is a Jewish doctor, Mikhail Stern, and some idea of the standards of Soviet justice may be gained at the outset from the fact that although he was arrested six months ago, and has been held incommunicado ever since (for three months in an underground cell), and that the trial, as I say, is due to begin on Monday, the charges he will face have not yet been revealed. Unless the Soviet authorities lose their nerve at the last minute, however, and invent stories of espionage or financial speculation, it is likely that he will be charged with the murder by poisoning of Soviet children, of which he has already been accused in print.

Dr Stern, who is fifty-six, graduated as a doctor in 1944, and began to specialize in goitrous diseases, being put in charge of an endocrinological institute; in 1952 he was invited to found a similar centre in Vinnitsa. He lost this job amid the anti-semitic persecution of which the 'Doctors' Plot' trial was the focal point; but managed to continue to organize medical services in Vinnitsa, despite continual harassment by the authorities.

Another wave of Soviet anti-semitism broke in the Ukraine in 1961, among the victims of which were local Jewish doctors; Dr

Stern protested against this, and for this became one of the victims himself. Scurrilously and insanely anti-semitic articles appeared in the local press, accusing him of being an unqualified quack
and a poisoner whose method of going about his murderous
work was to persuade his patients to consume great quantities of
sugar and thus bring on diabetes. The only one of his supposed
victims to be named was a girl called Liubochka Belinskaya; I
have the text of a letter written in November of this year, by
the girl who was supposed to have been murdered in 1961, and
her mother, to Dr Stern's wife: it expresses gratitude, affection
and admiration for him. They also wrote to the editor of the
paper in which the charges were published as well as to the
municipal and medical authorities and the local Communist
Party, but no retraction of the mad accusations has ever been
made. On the contrary: the authorities responded with repeated
searches of Dr Stern's house and the digging up of his garden.

From some time in 1963, until his arrest in May of this year,
Dr Stern worked as a consultant at the Vinnitsa Endocrinological
Centre: he was clearly loved and trusted by his patients, who
came from far away as well as from the town itself.

In November last year Dr Stern's younger son August, a
psychologist, applied for permission to emigrate; Dr Stern was
pressed by the authorities to dissuade his son from this intention,
and refused. From then on he and all his family underwent a
series of interrogations. On May 29th this year he was arrested;
his apartment, and those of his two sons and of the sister-in-law
of one of them, were ransacked by the K.G.B. who committed
numerous violations of Soviet law. Among the property of the
family that was taken was 1,500 roubles of Mrs Stern's savings,
the car of one of their sons, and various scientific papers. Dr Stern
was held under close arrest, his family being refused all access to
him, as indeed they have been to this day; he is a very sick man,
suffering from, among other things, tuberculosis, ulcers and
stenocardia. During the three months in which Dr Stern was kept
in the underground cell of the Vinnitsa prison, the authorities
sought, but failed to find, evidence of any kind of wrong-doing

by him. They therefore set about fabricating it, and suborning the appropriate witnesses.

All the patients who had consulted Dr Stern during the past ten years (some thousands) were questioned by a special group of twenty-five interrogators. The interrogators demanded that they testify to Dr Stern's guilt as a child-murderer; complaints made by his family against the nature of these proceedings were rejected, and in addition, in violation even of Soviet law, the rejection came from the very person named in the complaints, who was the man in charge of the interrogations, Procurator Kravchenko. When the family applied for a Moscow lawyer chosen by them to be told the nature of the case, this was refused, the excuse being that Dr Stern had said he wanted only a Vinnitsa lawyer; it is impossible for the family to check this as they have all been refused permission to see him, his sons being told that they may not do so until sentence is passed.

Many of Dr Stern's patients, displaying high courage, have been writing testimonials on his behalf; it is clear that he is widely loved. Some of them have demanded that their testimonials should be admitted in evidence at his trial. Meanwhile, August Stern and his wife, who had been given permission to emigrate, have had it withdrawn, and Dr Stern's other son, Victor, a distinguished physicist, has been dismissed from his job and allowed to work only as a telegraph boy, his wife (a qualified chemist) being unable to get work of any kind at all.

On the day of Dr Stern's arrest, and during the search of the family's homes, Procurator Kravchenko said in the presence of witnesses that the preparation of charges against Dr Stern was connected with the expressed wish of members of his family to emigrate. The same admission was made by another official, Procurator Poznyck, to Victor Stern in August.

On October 21st, the family filed a series of requests and complaints concerning the treatment of Dr Stern and the violations of Soviet law that have occurred in the preparation of the case against him. The family have asked for a lawyer chosen by the family to take part in the case, for permission for them to visit

Dr Stern in prison, for an inquiry into the basis of the case and for the investigation into the breaches of the law committed by investigating and other officials. Procurator Alexandrov rejected all the family's requests out of hand and without giving any reason.

Those in charge of the fabrication of the case against Dr Stern have ignored the favourable testimony of thousands of patients: they have so far persuaded some forty people to give evidence against him. At present, the identity of only one of these is known: she is a woman named Overchuk, who is apparently prepared to testify that he has deliberately poisoned children and spied for Israel.

It should be added that Mrs Stern has been subjected to a continuous campaign of vilification and persecution, including threatening telephone calls by night and day. On the 6th of this month, she requested the Soviet Procurator-General Rudenko to put an end to the persecution of her husband and their family; in reply it was made clear that he fully supported the actions taken by the local authorities.

Soviet anti-semitism has, of course, a long and terrible history. It recently suffered a striking exposure in an extraordinary episode in Paris where the Soviet Embassy had published a pamphlet containing the crudest anti-Jewish scurrilities. Since, under the law of France, nothing may be published there unless a French citizen makes himself legally responsible, it was possible to bring a case against a high official of the French Communist Party, who was the nominal publisher of the document. (The transcript of the trial has been published in English, by Wildwood House, edited by Mr Emanuel Litvinoff under the title *Soviet Anti-Semitism: The Paris Trial*. An account of it appeared in the *Guardian* under the headline 'Jewry verdict prejudiced'; the writer's chief complaint seems to be that the book might have the dreadful effect of encouraging prejudice against the Soviet Union.) In the course of the trial, which resulted in the conviction and fining of the defendants on charges of incitement to racial hatred, there was a sensational revelation. The text of the offending Soviet publication was shown to contain forged passages, falsely said to be from the Talmud and other Jewish writings, which were taken word for word from an anti-semitic pamphlet published in 1906 by the notorious 'Black Hundred' organization, which organized pogroms against Russian Jews; the only differerence between the two documents in these passages was that the Soviet version had replaced the word 'Jew' throughout by the word 'Zionist'.

Now, the Soviet authorities have gone one step further, and appear to be about to return to the even earlier practice of the 'blood trial', in which Jews were accused of ritual murder of Christians, together with such activities as poisoning of wells. I should add that Dr Stern's trial was due to start on December 9th, but was abruptly brought forward by a week when there were signs of a campaign on his behalf starting in this country (an appeal for signatures of support was to be sent out to doctors all over Britain this weekend). We know the name of the President of the Court, which is Savchenko, and of the Judge, Orlovsky; we know nothing else except that only immediate international publicity and protest can save Dr Stern.

The Times November 28th, 1974

The bloody trial concluded

LAST WEEK, DR Mikhail Stern was sentenced to eight years' imprisonment in a concentration camp, after a show trial in the Ukraine town of Vinnitsa, on false charges of swindling and corruption. Before discussing some of the aspects of the court proceedings, I think it is worth considering the motives of the Soviet Government in deciding to hold such a trial, in selecting the charges on which he was to be convicted, and in having so severe a sentence imposed.

In a grim sense, Dr Stern is lucky; the original intention, as is clear from the preparation of the case by the authorities, was to charge him with child-murder, of which he had already been publicly accused some ten years before, during an anti-semitic purge in the Ukraine. Patients were pressed by prosecuting officials to give false evidence in the case, the Deputy Procurator of the region insisting on 'the necessity to save the lives of the children who have been deliberately poisoned by Dr Stern'. (A Mrs Soloveichuk, with astonishing courage, made a formal complaint about this attempt to suborn her; it was, of course, ignored.) However, though at least one witness was prepared to testify that Dr Stern was a murderer, the authorities decided (presumably because even a Soviet show trial might come unstuck with such charges, and even their most slavish followers in the West would be unlikely to swallow them) not to proceed along these lines, and when after Dr Stern had already been in solitary confinement for over six months, he was finally allowed (a few days before the trial opened) to know what he was accused of, the capital charge had been abandoned; he was to be convicted on charges of financial extortion and taking bribes.

What Dr Stern was tried and sentenced for was, of course, the desire he and his two sons have expressed to emigrate from the Soviet Union. The Soviet authorities have not, for some time now, charged would-be émigrés with 'political' offences; it is obviously easier for them to deflect or minimize protest in the West if they can portray their victims as ordinary criminals. Thus, when Alexander Feldman, who had been active in the emigration movement, protested against the refusal of his application for an exit visa, he was arrested and charged with 'malicious hooliganism' (he was alleged to have knocked a cake out of a woman's hand), and Leonid Zablishendky, who had bravely withdrawn testimony against another would-be émigré, Vladimir Markman, was charged with 'parasitism' (which is the Soviet Catch-22, used to punish for not working people whom the authorities have prevented from getting work).

In a more direct sense, Dr Stern was doubly unfortunate. In the first place, he was a permanently marked man after the anti-semitic campaign of the early sixties in the Ukraine, in which he had not only defended himself against the medieval blood charges, but had protested vigorously against the whole campaign. In the second place, the authorities have clearly decided that, if they are to keep their side of what may be called the Jackson Agreement – trade advantages in return for permitting emigration – they must in advance so terrorize those who might consider applying to leave that their numbers will be substantially reduced; the Soviet Government also feels obliged, clearly, to demonstrate to the Soviet people that it is not bound by any agreement entered into with the West. Dr Stern, therefore, was chosen as the victim, and the sentence (the heaviest on a would-be émigré for many years) clearly decided on *pour encourager les autres*. The stage was now set; the actors rehearsed; Mr Boris Antonov chosen and instructed as the instrument to be used for disseminating the official handouts; and, after a number of postponements (the last – a fine touch of comedy – when it was realized at the eleventh hour that the trial was due to open on Human Rights Day) the performance began.

Curiously enough, the script was published in advance. On November 29th – almost a fortnight before the trial started – the Soviet Embassy in the Netherlands put out an account, 'by' Mr Antonov, of the charges, the witnesses, the testimony they would give and the general course of the investigation and trial, and I earnestly appeal to him, should he be selected for this job in another such case, to prevent a good deal of anxiety by also revealing what the sentence is to be. (The Soviet statement put out over Mr Antonov's name also included a claim that 'The personnel of the Vinnitsa procurator's office are being harassed by various persons ... who ring up and send telegrams demanding that Stern should be released on the sole ground that he is a Jew ... ' This was a plain lie; I have copies of the protests and appeals sent on Dr Stern's behalf, including a particularly fine one by Dutch doctors, and of course no such demand is made or implied in them.)

The scenes, as is customary in Soviet show trials, generally followed the lines laid down in advance, so that those responsible for the accounts of the trial sent to this newspaper by Mr Antonov clearly felt that they needed to do little but repeat the advance script, sometimes word for word. As is by no means customary in Soviet show trials, however – as, indeed, is literally unprecedented – a number of the performers, when they got on to the Vinnitsa stage, withdrew the testimony they had been obliged to give the investigators before the curtain went up. Though some of the witnesses recited their lines as required, nearly a score retracted, and denied that Dr Stern had demanded or extorted payments or bribes from them.

It is worth pausing here to consider the courage required, and shown, by these people – courage of an even higher order than was displayed by that vast majority of Dr Stern's patients who had refused to give false evidence against him throughout the months of the preparation of the case. That courage is the most heartening aspect of the case, and indeed one of the most heartening signs to be seen in the Soviet Union for many years. At first, the brave ones were men who would obviously have been outstanding in any society – the Sakharovs and Solzhenitsyns, the Bukovskys and Gluzmans, the Fainbergs and Chornovils. These were reinforced by the Jews who wanted to leave their vast Soviet prison-house, and were willing to risk everything in making their plight public outside it. For the first time, the Stern case has produced a substantial number of 'ordinary' Soviet citizens (but there is nothing ordinary about a Soviet citizen who refuses the demands of the State), themselves neither leaders of society nor would-be émigrés, who refused to tell lies when ordered to, and a few who went further and insisted on telling the truth. Though Soviet society inevitably produces Boris Antonovs, let us never forget that it also produces men and women in whom humanity and honour survive. Let us also not forget that these are from now on marked for vengeance whenever – and as we have seen in Dr Stern's own case, it may be a decade or more – the Soviet cat stretches out a paw.

Meanwhile, Dr Stern abides, and faces what, for a man in his state of health, is almost certainly a death sentence, in a concentration camp. Only a widespread and continuing campaign of protest can save him. For the moment, let him have the final word. After the verdict last week, he faced his persecutors and said, 'I stand before the court with a completely clear conscience. The sentence is a disgrace to all those who sow hatred against the Jews.'*

The Times January 7th, 1975

---

* After a persistent campaign outside the Soviet Union, Dr Stern was released some time before the expiry of his sentence, and he and his family were allowed to emigrate.

From my hammock

S HOULD YOU HAPPEN to come across me in the near future and
hear me muttering things like 'Sheep be nesting high this year,
'twill be a hard winter', or 'Blossom on bough, go milk a cow',
or 'I don't hold wi' all this manure on the land – 'tis against
nature – give me Fisons every time', please evince no surprise.
The fact is, I have acquired a window box and gone spectacularly
horticultural overnight.

I have not hitherto, to put it mildly, taken much interest in
such matters. I am aware that God, having arranged that the
earth should bring forth grass, the herb yielding seed, and the
fruit tree yielding fruit after his kind, saw that it was good, and
had I been present at the time I would have raised no objection,
particularly since I would only have had to wait another couple
of days for the bit about the fowls of the air going forth and
multiplying, presumably in order to ensure a regular supply of
Père Bise's *poularde braisée à la crème d'estragon*. (Mind you, though
you might not think it to look at me, it was I who grew the
largest cucumber in the history of the world; I was away at
school during the war, and what with being exhorted to Dig for
Victory, and what with being obliged in chapel to insist from
time to time that I ploughed the fields and scattered the good
seed on the land, I got quite carried away and, with two friends,
applied for what was then called an allotment, a patch of land
about the size of a grave, which we cultivated assiduously, obtaining from it astonishing quantities of lettuces, carrots and toma-
toes. The cucumber section, however, which was my special
concern, presented a problem; the planting and tilling seasons for

these friendly beasts took place before the summer holidays began, but they came to maturity long before we returned, and we had to rely on nature to do the best she could. Well, one year she surpassed herself; having left the cucumbers as veritable minnows, I came back to find them as vegetable marrows, one of them being so vast that it was a mercy it had not been requisitioned for housing evacuees; I seem to remember – though the details are a little hazy – that it was eight yards round the middle and weighed two and a half tons.) All the same, my view of the countryside has always been that it would be better for an ample covering of asphalt, and of flowers that they are things found in florists, for giving to pretty ladies.

Imagine, therefore, my astonishment when, the other day, a pretty lady, no less, came tottering up the stairs with a helpful taxi-driver who bore one end, as she the other, of a magnificent window box, some five feet long and made of stout and handsome oak. It was filled with rich black earth and planted with a profusion of bulbs, which clearly needed only the slightest twitch of spring to burst into a dazzling array of bloom. I had a moment's unease when the donor told me that she had even remembered to put some worms in (it seems that these are necessary to the proper functioning of agriculture and similar processes, though I cannot imagine why), for the obvious place for my *jardinière* was the window sill of my bedroom, and I did not much care for the thought that the worms might slither into the room in the middle of the night and catch me by the big toe. Assured, however, that worms are home-loving bodies, never roaming from the earth in which they live, I settled back to await the coming of spring and with it the disclosure of what I had in my window box – for promising though the display of greenery was, it was also disconcertingly anonymous to one who had hitherto recognized hardly more than three kinds of flowers, viz, daisies, buttercups and those-pink-things-over-there.

Daffodils! That, from end to end of my window box, was what appeared, in such crowded plenitude that it seemed from the street below as though someone had painted a shining yellow stripe beneath my window. Ten thousand, I tell you, saw I at a glance, tossing their heads in sprightly dance; fluttering and dancing in the breeze, they were, and continuous as the stars that shine and twinkle on the Milky Way, to boot; a poet, my goodness, could not but be gay in such a jocund company.

They positively lit up the room, and I watched, fascinated, as from day to day they ripened (I watered them, as instructed, occasionally). When they came to full maturity I could hardly do other than reap and return them, *en bouquet*, to the Ceres who had planted them in the first place, whereupon she arrived with a capacious plastic carrier bag of fresh earth (and, no doubt, fresh worms), and a further supply of flowers. These last came already in bloom, and were of two kinds; unfortunately, I have forgotten the names of both. I think she said that one lot were primroses, but I have always believed that these are invariably yellow, and although some of them are, others are a kind of pale mauve, and still others reddish; experts whom I have consulted suggest that they might be primulas, easily confused, at any rate where the names are concerned, with primroses. A similar difficulty arises with the other variety, lovely floppy things with an exquisite velvety texture and two-tone petals; peonies, I think these are supposed to be, though I am assured that from my description they cannot be, and among emendations suggested the most likely seems to be pansies.

Anyway, whatever they are called they make a brave show, though they are much more thirsty than the daffodils; I am thinking of getting one of those jolly miniature watering cans. Indeed, I am thinking of equipping myself with a whole range of gardening tools; a trowel, and a mini-hoe, and a rake, and even a spade, though probably not, at any rate to begin with, a combine harvester. (The spade might enable me to fulfil a lifelong dream; if I could find a man called Wilkinson who had a used one and would sell it to me, I could address it with that unbelievable but genuine first line of a sonnet of Wordsworth's: 'Spade! With which Wilkinson hath tilled his lands.') With these I shall go in for things like mulch, loam, tilth and other agricultural monosyllables, of the meaning of which I am wholly ignorant, but which I understand are good things to have in, or perhaps do to, gardens. As you would, I fear, expect of me, I already have gigantic plans for the further extension and elaboration of my window box; I look forward to the day when deer roam through the branches, parakeets nest in the leaves, and voles – or possibly, assuming that they are not in any case the same thing, moles – burrow among the roots. My opposition to blood-sports will not permit me to give the local hunt (the St Marylebone, I suppose) leave to pursue foxes across my land, which may therefore in time come to acquire the character of an animal sanctuary; the question of riparian rights does not arise, though I shall later install some ornamental fountains and, of course, a sundial, and advertise for a game warden, a verderer and a woodman. Meanwhile, she has planted some nasturtiums (I wrote the name down), and I patrol the territory daily looking for signs of their appearing through the subsoil. Nothing to report yet, but I think I heard a skylark the other day. An entire flock of skylarks, I mean, of course.

The Times April 11th, 1974

The joy that passeth all understanding

LET US NOW praise famous men, and our fathers that begat us. Not that the man I am to praise this morning begat anybody, or indeed had much time to, for he died a couple of months before his thirty-second birthday. He died, moreover, 150 years ago this year, and although the anniversary does not fall until November, the celebrations have already started, as well they might have, so I shall lay my own tribute of words on the grave this morning. Those who wish to lay a floral offering on his real grave will find it in the Währing cemetery in Vienna, a few feet from the last resting place of one of the only two men in all history to whose spirit and achievement his own can be seriously compared; his great neighbour's name was on his lips in the last hours of his life, and his brother understood him to be saying that that was where he wanted to be buried. (His only other peer lies, alas, in a grave forever lost.)

He was bespectacled and curly-haired, and the ladies adored him, their feelings being quite warmly reciprocated, though nothing ever came of it. His real passion was his work, and passion is the right word, for even when there was no possible purchaser for his wares, he could not stop turning them out, flooding an already saturated market; he could no more give up working than he could give up breathing, and he did not, indeed, cease from the former till he finally abandoned the latter. But his industry was prodigious; the list of the things he made takes twenty-one pages in the standard work of reference, and is exceeded in length only by the register of the products of that other of his equals who is buried no man knows where.

His brief life is sometimes said, by the less perceptive bio-
graphers, to have been unhappy, but that is great nonsense, for
apart from the fact that he had within him, and expressed in his
work, a divine light that nothing could possibly extinguish, and
that carried him through inevitable sorrow, not to mention
poverty, his nature was so sweet and noble that he never lacked
true friends, and there is solid evidence that he revelled in friendship and drew great strength and comfort from it. If you don't
know who he is by now, I am sure that you won't find the
answer in the curious and touching fact that his last request, made
on his deathbed, was for some more of the novels of Fenimore
Cooper. But I shall now bring your frustration to an end by
quoting the noble epitaph that a poet friend wrote for him:

> The art of music has
> entombed a great
> possession,
> but far fairer hopes.
> Here lies Franz Schubert.

Schubert is a mystery almost as great as Mozart, and more so
than Beethoven. If you try to explain him – try, that is, to
imagine how the music got into his head – you will find that your
hair begins to stand on end in terror lest you might think of the
answer. It is possible to comprehend Bach, Beethoven, even
Wagner; imagine respectively the human qualities of reverence,
optimism and originality, and multiply them by a figure roughly
equal to the number of atoms in the universe. You will then have
some idea of what drove those three giants down their giants'
causeway. But when we come to Mozart and Schubert, there is
no means by which we can turn them into even infinitely magni-
fied versions of ourselves; not merely their bodies, but their
minds – their very souls – are useless in the search for the truth
about their genius. Schubert, like Mozart, was a conduit, through
which music poured out into the world's lap, and the only
question worth asking is: who or what was putting it in at the
other end?

But that is the question that each of us must wrestle with, and perhaps the wrestling is best done in private. What can be achieved *coram populo* is everything short of that, and in particular a celebration of the fact that Schubert lived and wrote, and 150 years ago died. He should have lived hereafter; and yet, as Gilbert, of all revolting Philistines, put it:

> Is life a boon?
> If so, it must befall
> That Death, whene'er he call,
> Must call too soon.
> Though fourscore years he give,
> Yet one would pray to live
> Another moon!
> What kind of plaint have I,
> Who perish in July?
> I might have had to die,
> Perchance, in June!

We think of Schubert, rightly enough, as the spirit of song incarnate, and not merely because he wrote well over 500 of them. For even in his orchestral works, he is to be heard singing; the inexhaustible fecundity of his gift for melody, in which he surpasses all other composers who ever lived, not excepting Mozart, turns even the richest musical texture into the heartsease of song.

Not that Schubert should be thought of as a mere tunesmith (though any man who could claim to have written, say, three tunes as good as any of his thousands would earn immortality for the feat); the depth of feeling and insight that he reaches without the aid of words – perhaps most of all in his chamber music – is as great as that plumbed by Mozart, and comes very close to what Beethoven achieved in the last quartets and the Hammerklavier Sonata.

But I must not fall into the opposite trap either; Schubert, though he touches us more deeply than almost any artist who ever lived, and is therefore often grave, is never solemn, and the title of the Tragic Symphony, though his own, is a misnomer. If you take, as I do, the C Major Symphony to be his masterpiece, you will be in great danger of misunderstanding it, and him, if you think of it in the kind of architectural terms applicable to, say, the *Eroica* or the symphonies of Brahms. Even Beethoven's Ninth is not the right analogy, and the didactic glories of the Fifth are not Schubert's affair. But if you will listen to the last movement of Beethoven's Seventh, or the duet 'O Namenlose Freude' from *Fidelio*, or the final pages of *The Marriage of Figaro*, or the amazing fugue with which Verdi closed *Falstaff* and his life's work, or for that matter the Hallelujah Chorus, what you will hear is what you hear in the C Major: spontaneous, uninhibited, all-embracing, God-lit but utterly human, joy.

If, then, we wish to sum up the life and work of Franz Schubert, it seems to me fitting that we should keep this, his supreme quality, in the forefront of our minds. Joy, in Schubert, is indeed unconfined, and it is for this reason, I think, that he is the only composer who can succeed in making me happy when I am sad. I find that it is no use turning to Beethoven for that purpose; he only makes me ashamed of myself for giving in. Nor Mozart, for all I can then hear is the D minor throb of his own awareness of pain. Nor Wagner, for I can hear him shouting 'It's your own fault' in everything but *The Mastersingers*, and in that I feel that I am intruding unpardonably on his characters' happiness with my long face. Only Schubert can sweep me along in his own shining certainty that nothing bad matters, and everything good does. And now, I think, though I am not at all unhappy at the moment, I shall go and put Schubert's Octet on the gramophone, and raise a glass, and thanks, to his memory.

The Times May 19th, 1978

Truth or consequences

How rarely heroes live up to expectation, and how satisfying when they surpass it! That is what, last week, I felt after meeting Alexander Solzhenitsyn for the first time – that, and the familiar and inexplicable feeling of exhilaration that comes from talking to those who know what it is to live in hell, and who, although they can say only

> I tell you naught for your comfort,
> Yea, naught for your desire,
> Save that the sky grows darker yet,
> And the sea rises higher

nevertheless radiate a kind of invulnerable optimism that comes from within, and is the mark of those who are eternally secure in the knowledge that their tormentors are not only wrong but doomed. This was said some time ago in the form: 'He that findeth his life shall lose it; and he that loseth his life for my sake shall find it', and it is still true today.

I remember this feeling very vividly from my only visit to South Africa; all the misery and cruelty and despair I could see around me, which were in themselves almost unendurable, were transmuted into a kind of joyous hope by the indomitability of those I talked to who were resisting evil with a serene gaiety and a courage that it is fortunately beyond our necessity to measure. I felt the absence of this feeling more strongly than anything else in my life on my only visit to the Soviet Union, because I was there before either the dissident movement or the emigration movement had broken surface, and the cruelty and misery and despair all around me were unrelieved by anything that might suggest, however irrationally, that there was cause for hope. But I have experienced that uplift of the spirit whenever I have met any of those, from Valentin Prussakov to Viktor Fainberg, who have managed to get out, and I also felt it intensely the night before I met Solzhenitsyn, when I met Garfield Todd. The gentle Rhodesian and the Russian Titan could scarcely be more different, in the experiences they have undergone, the situations in which they find themselves, or the nature of their lifework; yet the same current of delight ran through me as I met them, and the same lightness of heart accompanied me as I left. Good, brave men, it seems, are the same the world over, and their goodness and bravery can no more be hidden than they can be counterfeited.

Alexander Isayevitch Solzhenitsyn came into the room smiling, and that was the first surprise, for he is one of those people whose faces are frozen by the camera, and he is consequently almost always portrayed looking solemn, if not actually seeming to scowl; in fact, he smiles very readily, and laughs a great deal. The next surprise was also physical, and I have not got over it yet. I am a very unobservant man, but we sat side by side on a sofa, our faces only a few inches apart, and I could not have been mistaken; I tell you that this man of fifty-seven, who spent eight years in a Siberian concentration camp in torments that we can hardly even guess at, and then spent something like twenty years doing unceasing battle with the foul thing that has stolen his country from its people, has not a single grey or greying hair on his head or in his beard, and his blue eyes and the skin of his face are as clear and smooth and young as those of an untroubled child. Even as he spoke, in halting English (which broke constantly into torrential Russian, while our interpreter struggled to keep up), of his despair at the folly, nervelessness and lack of imagination and understanding the West now displays in the face of Soviet imperialism (he blames Europe more than America, saying that Europe has not had the excuse of America's thankless and debilitating struggle in Vietnam), his demeanour was that of a man in a state of grace. There was no need to ask him where he gets such inner strength and intensity; this is a man who walks with his God, and makes one understand what 'Holy Russia' once meant.

That was a private occasion. But last night, in an interview for Panorama (admirably conducted, with self-effacing tact, by Michael Charlton), Solzhenitsyn mounted a public indictment of the supine inattention of the West that rang like the blows of the hammer with which Luther nailed his manifesto to the doors at Wittenberg. 'For nearly all of our lives,' he said, 'we worshipped the West—note that word worshipped; we did not admire it, we worshipped it.' (Beneath the simultaneous translation you could hear the stabbing emphasis of the Russian word.) But now?

My warnings, the warnings of others, Sakharov's very grave warning directly from the Soviet Union—these warnings go unheeded ... We realized with bewilderment that the West was ... separating its freedom from our fate, and before I was exiled I had already strong doubts whether it was realistic to look to the West for help ... And when I came here unfortunately my doubts increased very rapidly ... During these two years the West ... has made so many concessions that now a repetition of the angry campaign which got me out of prison is practically impossible ... the campaign to get Sakharov to Stockholm was almost as strong, but it didn't help, because ... Moscow now takes infinitely less note of the West.

And then, just as he so often speaks in the accents of Tolstoy, he spoke in the voice of that other Russian giant whose philosophical descendant he is, the man who saw as clearly into the heart of man a century ago as Solzhenitsyn does today. Is this not Dostoevsky writing about Peter Verkhovensky and his wretched father?

One can say that this is what forms the spirit of the age, this current of public opinion, when people in authority, well-known professors, scientists, are reluctant to enter into an argument ... It is considered embarrassing to put forward one's counter-arguments, lest one becomes involved. And so there is a certain abdication of responsibility, which is typical here where there is complete freedom ... There is now this universal adulation of revolutionaries, the more so the more extreme they are! Similarly, before the Revolution we had in Russia, if not a cult of terror in society, then a fierce defence of the terrorists. People in good positions, intellectuals, professors, liberals, spent a great deal of effort, anger and indignation in defending terrorists.

Then the hammer ceases to be Luther's, and becomes Thor's:

It would be more appropriate if it were not you asking me which way the Soviet Union will go, but if I were to ask you which way the West is going. Because at the moment the question is not how the Soviet Union will find a way out of totalitarianism, but how the West will be able to avoid the same fate ... I am surprised that pragmatic philosophy consistently scorns moral considerations ... one should not consider that the great principles of freedom finish at your frontiers, that as long as you have freedom, le the rest have pragmatism. No, freedom is indivisible and one has to take a moral attitude towards it ... The West is on the verge of a collapse created by its own hands. This quite naturally makes the question one for you and not for us.

Once only, in the course of the interview, did he become excited; the pencil in his hand became a conductor's baton or a rapier, and his voice rose towards a shout. This was when he told the truth about what '*détente*' means to those being persecuted in the Soviet Union.

What does the spirit of Helsinki ... mean for us ... ? The strengthening of totalitarianism ... Someone went to visit Sakharov; he went home by train and was killed on the way. No, it wasn't you, *he* was killed ... Someone knocks on the door of Nikolai Kriukov; he opens the door. They beat him up nearly to death in his own house because he has defended dissidents and signed protests ... They let Plyushch out and they are putting others in lunatic asylums ...

What can we do about the presence in our midst of such men as Alexander Solzhenitsyn? We turn away in embarrassment, an embarrassment that rises to act as a protection against the pain of admitting both that he is right in his analysis of evil and that his very existence is a reproach to our society, embedded as it is in the granite of his faith. I do not believe (though presumably he does) that faith has to be a religious faith to be effective; but what is wrong with the West – and one can sense in his condemnation of us that it is this which excites his anger and contempt, more even than the strategic, political and moral retreat in which the West is engaged – is that we do not even have the courage of our secular convictions, we do not seem to care enough about our liberty to be willing to consider that it is under assault and to think about ways of sustaining it, indeed to consider that it ought to be sustained. Is it any wonder that a man who has dragged logs all day in a temperature of minus 30 degrees Centigrade has to make an almost visible effort to stop himself spitting in the face of a society that refers to *Oz* as the 'underground' press, persuades half a government that the Shrewsbury Two* are martyrs, and runs howling to the Bar Council and the correspondence columns of *The Times* when Sir Robert Mark† says that there are crooked lawyers who are helping crime to flourish?

So what can we do with Solzhenitsyn? Well, if I may conclude with a modest proposal, I suggest that the West, when he has provoked it a little further, should, possibly under the auspices of the United Nations General Assembly, formally condemn him to death, and execute him either by obliging him to drink hemlock or by crucifixion. After all, the two most noted figures in history

* Convicted of conspiracy to intimidate with violence non-striking building workers.

† Then Commissioner of Police. See p. 157.

who respectively experienced those fates were condemned, whatever the ideological niceties involved, principally because they told their own societies truths that made those societies uncomfortable, and since our own society is even more averse to discomfort than those were, it seems only fitting that the man who is doing much the same thing to us should suffer a like fate. Meanwhile, at any rate, I can look at the hand that shook the hand of the man who shook the world, and if he will allow me, say: 'Alexander Isayevitch, do not despair just yet. We understand.'

The Times March 2nd, 1976

The people will listen

IT WAS NOT necessary to borrow the crystal ball of Madame Zaza, the celebrated clairvoyante, to predict the public reaction in this country to the appearance on Panorama of Alexander Solzhenitsyn. Indeed, I predicted it with the utmost exactitude myself, and the only thing I know about tea leaves is my mother's conviction (perfectly correct, for all I can say) that they are good for cleaning carpets with. 'What do we do with such men?' I asked, and I answered my own question thus:

> We turn away in embarrassment – an embarrassment that rises to act as a protection against the pain of admitting both that he is right in his analysis of evil and that his very existence is a reproach to our society, embedded as it is in the granite of his faith.

As a description of the whinnying, sniggering, piddling response by the very people whose like have made Solzhenitsyn's indictment of wickedness and folly so urgent, necessary and unanswerable, I cannot better that even with hindsight. (The response was epitomized, as you would expect, by the tittering editor* of the tottering New Statesman, whose only contribution was to complain that he had not been invited to meet Solzhenitsyn, and to rebuke the Russian colossus for this act of impiety by sneering at him as 'Spengler Mark 2'. Depend upon it, we shall yet see the New Statesman carry an article by Mr Dev Murarka†

* Not the present one.

† Then (and still, as far as I know) the magazine's Moscow correspondent; he had recently written an article belittling the Soviet dissidents, including Solzhenitsyn.

explaining that Dr Sakharov is much overrated as a scientist.)

The note that has run through so much of the public comment on Solzhenitsyn's philippic has been one of fear. The phenomenon is entirely understandable; the spiritually weak always fear the spiritually strong, as the foolish fear the wise, the petty the great, the timid the brave, the small the big, the trivial the significant. Since Solzhenitsyn is strong, wise, great, brave, huge, significant and right, Lilliput's fear of Gulliver is thus many-faceted and therefore the more intense. And fear, in these circumstances, takes the form of nervous laughter, as is demonstrated twice nightly in a different context, at any cinema showing *Jaws*. The reason for the fear in the case of a man like Solzhenitsyn is that even as he speaks of external dangers he forces his hearers to look within themselves for the ultimate causes of those dangers, and since that truth is unbearable (like, alas, most truth), the only defence available is the belittlement of the accuser. Fortunately, I have good reason to know that Solzhenitsyn also touched another nerve altogether. The exceptional number of letters I have been receiving since I wrote about him, and the strangers who have been approaching me in public, in greater numbers than I have previously known, have all had the same purpose in mind, which has been to tell me that they understand what he is saying, which is that men who do not value freedom, and who divorce it from morality, will not long possess it.

It cannot, I think, be healthy for a society to be flawed by a massive gulf between what is felt by those who do not have to offer any public comment and those who are professionally obliged to say something and who, having nothing of their own to say, rummage through the tired fashions of our tired time to find some pat, pert comment with which to sustain in themselves the fading illusion that they are still alive. Yet that is what has just happened in the case of the Solzhenitsyn interview. To find anything comparable to the effect his words and personality have had on those who saw the programme it is necessary to go back to some of the early Churchill wartime broadcasts, and the parallel is also apt in the breadth of the effect. Now Churchill, after all, was talking to a nation at war, which already had one mind, one will and one purpose: what he was doing was to articulate that unity to reflect it back to those who already felt themselves part of it. What I sense most strongly in the private response to Solzhenitsyn is precisely that: not a feeling that he was offering revelations or suggesting previously unconsidered ways of thought, but that he was opening the sluices of the dam that had for so long held back the lifegiving, rounded human response to the truth – the truth being that there is a difference between right and wrong.

It is, of course, that response that has for so long been stifled by the bloodless *fainéants* who occupy so large a number of the tin thrones of public comment. They are the beavers who have built the dam across the feelings of people better than themselves, until they have made feeling itself suspect. (I have lost count of the number of times that some cringing idiot in charge of a television or radio discussion in which I have expressed myself passionately on such matters as liberty and tyranny has deflected the embarrassment he feels – though I have yet to find the audience sharing the embarrassment – by saying, with that special mirthless laugh they have, 'Well, well, Bernard certainly seems to feel strongly on the subject.') And the giggling with which the beavers have greeted Solzhenitsyn's appearance indicates that they are uneasily aware of the sound of the dam cracking.

Wherever I have gone in the past fortnight I have found the human feelings of human people pouring through. Everywhere, people of all sorts and conditions have been speaking of the effect Solzhenitsyn had on them, and adding that wherever they have gone they have found the same reaction among others. I have never known so many people to speak of finding tears in their eyes as part of their response to the words and personality of a single individual who was, after all, doing nothing more dramatic than answer an interviewer's questions. And remember that because of the conditions of secrecy in which the interview was filmed there was no publicity until the last minute (the *Radio Times*, for instance, had only a general note about Panorama, with no hint of what the content of this particular edition was to be). It is very good indeed to know that the B.B.C. has already committed itself to repeating the programme in its entirety within the next month or so; this time I am sure that the audience will be very much larger, and the response more overwhelming still. (The B.B.C.'s decision is particularly welcome in view of the fact that it has not always been willing to resist Soviet pressure, and that the official Soviet protest in France at the showing there of another programme about Solzhenitsyn has been followed by an unofficial one here, which will obviously be repeated in the hope of making the B.B.C. lose its nerve and cancel the second showing.)*

Of course, it is perfectly possible for a reasonable man to disagree either with Solzhenitsyn's analysis of the world's condition or with the conclusion he draws from that analysis. There was, for instance, a massive and dignified reply to Solzhenitsyn in the *Observer* by Mr Edward Crankshaw. But Mr Crankshaw has earned the right to disagree with a man who speaks from such experience by his own unswerving dedication to the ideals of freedom by which Solzhenitsyn lives, his relentless denunciation of the denial of those ideals by those at whose hands Solzhenitsyn suffered, and the breadth of understanding and knowledge that he brings to his dissent. It is quite another matter when we who have just seen the greatest man now alive, and have found ourselves responding to him immediately and without equivocation, on the level at which he was addressing us, then find our mood so ludicrously misjudged, and the measure of the man so signally missed, by most of those who have, so to speak, accidentally been entrusted with the task of speaking for us; it is a precipitate descent indeed to go from Solzhenitsyn's demand for a moral content in politics to the spectacle of such a giant being patronized by Mr Peter Lennon, instructed in clarity of thought by Mr Clive

* There was more to this paragraph than met the eye. The B.B.C. had *not* when it was written, decided to repeat the programme, and there was opposition within the Corporation to the suggestion that it should do so. My words were designed to add a straw's weight to the pressure for such a commitment.

James, compared with Ronald Reagan by Mr Mervyn Jones, and offered suggestions for the improvement of his character by Mr James Cameron.

But the people know better. Whenever before did the *Listener* (it carried a substantial chunk of the interview) have to be reprinted to meet public demand? When did Panorama serve as such a focus for the feeling of millions and such a trigger for their release? When, if it comes to that, did a single man, commanding no armies and disposing of no votes, last compel the world to listen to him, to take him seriously, and to wrestle with the dark angel he has raised among them – an effect achieved by nothing other than the force of his character and the iron strength of his moral purpose?

Never, I think. And what is so heartening is that, clear and bell-like above all the febrile jeers and the expressions of incomprehension, has come the people's voice. I wrote my own column about Solzhenitsyn's interview, and my meeting with him, on the day the programme was shown, before I had had any opportunity to gauge the reaction of others. Yet it is already clear that I was speaking for a vast army in the words with which I concluded, and which I find even more apposite for my conclusion today: 'Alexander Isayevitch, do not despair just yet. We understand.'

The Times March 19th, 1976

D

Ah, so

As a LIFELONG collector of significant conjunctions, I was delighted to find the other day, in an unobtrusive paragraph, a specimen (in excellent condition) of that rare form the Apparent Contradiction. 'Americans', it read, 'are using the post more and more, so stamp prices will not rise as fast in coming years as previously predicted.'

So. Not 'but', you notice, or 'however', or even the neutral 'and'; a full-strength 'so' links the fact that Americans are using the post more to the conclusion that the stamps they buy are cheaper than they might otherwise be.

The Apparent Contradiction will be apparent only to the British. Here, if we are told that more letters are being posted, we brace ourselves for the inevitable announcement of an increase in the price paid for posting them, and even for a massive campaign by the Post Office to persuade us to write fewer.

That is because of the well-known Post Office principle that the best way of responding to an increase in the use made by the public of any of its services is to seek ways of reducing demand rather than increasing supply. The easiest way of doing that, of course, is to raise prices; the Post Office dreams of a day when the cost of a stamp will have reached infinity and the number of customers nil; as the customers are well aware, satisfying progress towards achieving both these laudable intentions has been made in the last few years.

Now the Post Office is not alone in this attitude; if it were, I would hardly bother to bring the subject up. In fact, it typifies an entire range of practices and instincts in the commercial life of

Britain which contrast strikingly with those of the United States, and, increasingly, the rest of the world. America practises the precept that if you are in business to make money, it helps to find out what people want and then sell it to them at a price they can afford, and also that the lower the price the more of it they will buy, and the more money you will therefore make.

How many times have you been told in a shop in this country that you cannot have the object you are seeking, not because the shopkeeper does not like your face, or because he fears that you will ill-treat it when you have got it home, or because he is too distracted by the fact that his wife has just run off with the milk-man, but because 'there's no call for it'? Well, I assure you that if an American shopkeeper said that to a customer, the customer would literally be quite unable to discern any meaning in the words, and would conclude that he was being addressed in some unknown tongue.

This variety of *vice anglais* can be seen in a particularly vivid symbolic form in restaurants of the less sophisticated kind. If the menu, for instance, includes roast beef with brussels sprouts and roast lamb with peas, it may take you anything up to forty minutes to convince those in charge that you want the beef with the peas, and even at the end of that time you will as like as not be unsuccessful in your request, possibly even being told that there is no call for it.

The American attitude, when faced with an eccentric or even hitherto unknown demand, is to seek first to understand exactly what is being asked for, and to seek next a way of providing it. I have often asked in the United States for something that was either unknown there, or was known under a name that was un-known to me. The response has always been to try to elicit what I am talking about, and then to find something as close to the specification as possible.

In Germany this is taken still further; if you go into a restau-rant – not just a café, but a real restaurant – and order only a bowl of soup and a glass of wine, they will not only serve it to you without demur; it will never occur to them to think your request is in any way odd. Nor, of course, is it; they are there to sell you food, and what items of food they sell you depends only and entirely on your wishes in the matter. (And I have never, to my recollection, been refused service in a restaurant or café in Germany, Austria, France or Italy if the door was open and the lights on, whatever the hour of the day or night. I could not count the number of times I have entered a British establishment, and been met only with a snarl of 'We're closed'.)

What all this amounts to, of course, is the difference between the respective attitudes to competition held in Britain and the rest of the world. It can be seen with limpid clarity in the motor car industry; the British driver having expressed a liking, by his purchases, for Japanese cars, large numbers of these are imported to meet the demand. It did not occur to the British manufacturers to meet this competition by making their product more attractive to the customer; they simply squealed 'unfair, unfair' and Mr Edmund Dell* was sent to Tokyo to beg the Japanese to export fewer cars to Britain. The Japanese are a notoriously polite people, but even they must have been hard put to it to go on bowing and smiling when what they wanted to do was to throw him down the stairs.

It's no good saying that Britain is the nice place it is precisely because we are not imbued with the spirit of competition and hustle and push and ambition and commercialism. In the first place, since we live in an internationally competitive world, we have to sell our goods and services competitively, and cannot now turn ourselves into a kind of Gandhian peasant economy, with the good men of Didsbury, Handsworth and Claygate sitting before their semi-detached doors clad in dhotis and plying spinning-wheels. In the second place, we actually have all the worst forms of envy without any of its good effects. (Indeed, another example of what I am talking about, and that perhaps the most terrible of all, can be seen in the widespread reaction to the discovery that somebody else has got, or is earning, more

* Then Minister for Trade.

money than the discoverer. The response is not, as it would be in America, to strive to catch up and surpass the rival; it is not, as it would be if Britain really practised what the simple-lifers preached, a complete indifference; it is a sour determination to ensure that the other man is so penalized, weighted, taxed or even – in the case of trade unionists, for instance, putting in more hours of overtime than the union specifies – actually fined, that the balance will be redressed. If you want a specific example, go and read some of the comments made about Mr Don Revie when he signed his lucrative contract with the Saudi Arabian government.)

And so – so indeed! – the Americans can look forward to cheaper stamps as a reward for posting more letters, while if we dared to emulate them we could expect only fewer collections and higher prices as a punishment for our temerity. It has been pointed out that if the Post Office introduced a special cut-rate postage for Christmas cards, not only would this please many people, but so many more cards would be sent that the Post Office might actually make more money than it otherwise would. But the Post Office will not heed the suggestion; and when I say 'but' I mean 'so'.

The Times November 23rd, 1977

The bomb and the rope

IN THE DEBATE, renewed after the Birmingham murders,* over the restoration of capital punishment for such acts of terrorism, one important point is being neglected or misunderstood, and before the gallows are swept back into use on a tide of public anger at the killing, I think it is necessary to examine it. For I believe that that tide ought to be turned.

One of the most important tasks in war is to discover what the enemy wants, and deny it to him; the corollary, of course, is that the enemy will seek to disguise his true wishes. In the discussion of the correct response to the latest outrages, this is the vital principle that is being ignored. Some say that the restoration of capital punishment would deter the murderers, some that it would not; I am not sure that anybody has yet suggested that one of the main purposes of the Birmingham bomb, if not indeed the only one, was to stampede Britain into bringing back judicial executions. Yet that seems to me very clear. Indeed, it is nothing but an extension of the policy unmistakable behind the I.R.A.'s actions for some time now. Every time there has been an approach by the British Government to abandoning the use of internment or releasing a substantial number of those interned, the response has been a fresh wave of bombings and shootings, designed to make it politically impossible for such intentions to be carried out. When the Home Secretary made it clear that the Price sisters† would be returned to Northern Ireland if there was a diminution in the terrorist activities, there was an immediate

* By a bomb, placed by terrorists who were subsequently caught, convicted and sentenced to long terms of imprisonment.

† Also guilty of terrorist activities.

increase in them. And if it were now to be announced that a bill to provide for the execution of convicted terrorists would be prepared but not introduced if there were no further large-scale killings, there would at once be a series of large-scale killings.

Why should this be so? Why should the leaders of the I.R.A. want to see their followers hanged? Why should the O'Connells and Twomeys, the 'Chiefs of Staff' and 'Army Councils' (how this weedy gang do love to give themselves high military titles, like 'Field-Marshal' Dedan Kemathi of the Mau Mau and 'General' Idi Amin!) seek to ensure that the British Government responds with the utmost severity to their campaign? That question was, in my opinion, answered incorrectly in the main leading article in this newspaper last Saturday. The relevant passage read:

It is argued that the death penalty would create martyrs and would thereby strengthen the I.R.A. cause. The I.R.A. already has a string of martyrs whom they recall in their sentimental moments; it is difficult to believe that the addition of further martyrs, which must in any case happen from time to time, adds significantly to their popular appeal.

Alas; 'those who cannot remember the past are condemned to repeat it'. The Easter Week rising in Dublin had virtually no popular support, and was led by men largely unknown to the general public. But when the leaders were executed, they instantly won an immortal crown in that mythology by which Ireland lives.

> Come all you young rebels and list while I sing,
> For love of one's land is a terrible thing;
> It banishes fear with the speed of a flame
> – And it makes us all part of the patriot game.
>
> My name is O'Hanlan, and I'm just gone sixteen,
> My home is in Monaghan, there I was weaned;
> I was taught all my life cruel England to blame
> – And so I'm a part of the patriot game.

'Tis barely two years since I wandered away
With a local battalion of the bold I.R.A.;
  I read of our heroes and wanted the same
  – To play up my part in the patriot game.

They told me how Connolly was shot in the chair,
His wounds from the battle all bleeding and bare,
His fine body twisted, all battered and lame
  – They soon made me part of the patriot game.

So now as I lie with my body all holed,
I think of those traitors who bargained and sold;
I'm sorry my rifle has not done the same
  – For the quislings who sold out the patriot game.

Anyone who has ever heard Dominic Behan sing that song
will not need to be told of the compelling power of Irish repub-
lican hagiography. But it is unfortunately true that a stale martyr
is not nearly as useful as a nice fresh one; it may be 'difficult to
believe that the addition of further martyrs adds significantly' to
the I.R.A.'s popular appeal, but the effort must be made, for it
does. If we start hanging I.R.A. murderers, we shall have Napper
Tandy telling us all over again that 'They're hangin' men and
women for the wearin' of the green', and most of Ireland persuaded to believe it. Of course, most of the Irish do not approve
of the I.R.A. killers, and even among those who do, most will
not take any direct part in their activities; most do not do so now,
preferring their various equivalents of the character in a post-
O'Casey Irish play about the Throubles who is forever boasting
about his heroism in those days, until his wife says rather sharply
that he had been entirely occupied, during Easter Week, in
'fetchin' things out of Woolworth's window'. But the I.R.A. fish
need a lake of public sympathy, however inactive, to swim in,
and they will get it, in full flood, from the execution of their
killers. For:

There's nothing but our own red blood
Will make a right rose tree.

Nor is it even an answer to say that, although the leaders who live beyond the reach of the British authorities would certainly not be deterred at all by the chance of being hanged, and the 'hard men' who organize the killings on the spot scarcely more so, there would be a significant deterrent effect on 'the landladies, lookout and drinking companions', without whom the bombers could not do their work. It might indeed be true; but the truth leads inescapably to an even more terrible trap. No doubt someone who knowingly and with premeditation harboured a killer would be just as guilty, in law, as the killer who went out to plant the bomb and returned to the harbourer. But let us just think for a moment what propaganda effect could be made from the execution of one who had done no more than that, or who had received, and got rid of, incriminating evidence, or who had even supplied explosives and played no further part in the outrage. It would be easy for the I.R.A. propaganda machine, not to mention those in Britain who sympathize with its aims, to paint such people as innocent martyrs, guilty of nothing worse than devotion to a loved one or enthusiasm for the liberty of Ireland.

Ira furor brevis est. It is right that we should feel anger and revulsion at such slaughter as took place in Birmingham, and express those feelings. But anger and revulsion are not the ideal conditions in which to decide on the best course of action. The best course of action is that course of action which is most likely to achieve the effect desired. The effect desired in this case is the defeat of the terrorists, one crucial element in which must be to ensure that they are deprived of sympathy among those to whom they look for support and assistance. I do not think that hanging them will help to diminish sympathy for them in the minds and hearts of those who are not permanently alienated from them by their actions, and consequently I do not believe that hanging them will contribute to their defeat. I am not interested in taking revenge, though I understand the feelings of those who demand it for the bombers; I am interested in ending the bombings. I believe that those two aims – the exacting of vengeance and the defeat of the I.R.A. – are incompatible, and I believe that to mistake the first for the second is dangerous. And that is why I remain of my opinion that we should not restore the death penalty.

The Times November 26th, 1974

With apologies to Edgar Allan Poe

I HAVE OFTEN maintained, as my readers will be aware, that anything disastrous that is going about looking for someone to happen to happens to me. If a man eight feet high should take it into his head to go to the theatre, it will inevitably turn out that his seat is directly in front of mine. If another man, at a party, wishes to spend several hours explaining to somebody his unique theory for curing inflation, it is me he picks on for the honour of serving as audience. I sometimes think that if the Russians should ever decide to drop the H-bomb, it is me they will drop it on, and though this may be a somewhat extreme view, I certainly believe that anyone caught in a thunderstorm would be very ill-advised to stand anywhere near me.

That I am as a man marked out by fate is, therefore, no news to me. But what has happened to me now is so absolutely outrageous, so atrociously unfair, so entirely unique even in the long and tragic story of the Doom of the Levins, that I feel I have cause for complaint far exceeding anything experienced before.

I was sitting quietly reading when I became aware of a faint, irregular, but unmistakable tapping sound. I went into my study and looked at my typewriter in case a poltergeist, or possibly Archie the Cockroach, was trying to leave me a message; all was still. I returned to the sofa and tried to believe I had imagined it; five seconds listening and I knew I had done no such thing. I toyed with the idea that it might be a bomb – bombs tick, I believe; or that the clock, normally inaudible from even a few inches away, had suddenly developed a bizarre and unprecedented imperfection; not so. I considered the possibility that I had added yet another to my extensive collection of hallucinations; I had not. I began to fear that it was a plot to drive me mad, engineered by my relatives – to be precise, by my Uncle Reb-Leser, who has already, over the years, driven the rest of the family mad, or at any rate such few members of it who were not mad to start with; but I murmured *hypotheses non fingo*, and dismissed the theory. All the same, there was a tiny but persistent tapping sound coming from somewhere in the room; what was it?

It is notoriously difficult to trace the source of a sound too faint to be obviously coming from one particular direction. I tiptoed about the room, stopping to judge whether I was getting warmer. After a time I was; the sound was gradually beckoning me into one particular corner. The books at that point are biography, and as I closed in, held my breath and listened, there was no doubt about it; the sound was coming from the end of the fifth shelf up, where the last book in the row was E. F. Benson's *Life of Alcibiades*.

I have been in some tight corners in my time, Carruthers, but I don't mind admitting that I was by now pretty close to panic. What in the name of Apollo and Pallas Athene was going on around here? The sound did not move, and when I took *Alcibiades* down, and the books next and next but one to him – Plutarch and Suetonius – it stayed in the shelf, getting louder. To steady my nerves, I took Suetonius back to the sofa and read him on Caligula ('Besides his incest with his sisters, and his notorious passion for Pyrallis, the prostitute, there was hardly any lady of distinction with whom he did not make free'), but still it cried 'Sleep no more!' to all the house.

It was at that point that, without any further thought, the explanation leapt into my mind, and I can tell you that even when it did I did not feel a whole lot better than before. So help me, ladies and gentlemen, I have got death-watch beetle.

This gloomy beast, which gets it name from the belief that it presages death (oh yes, I am having a very cheerful time, thank you) is, as you will no doubt be aware, a wood-boring beetle of the genus *anobiidae*, a division of the order of *coleoptera*. Its full

name is *Anobium striatum,* to distinguish it from *Anobium pani-*
ceum, or biscuit-weevil (oh good God, wait a minute while I go
and see if the biscuits are all right), and the ticking sound is
caused by its head tapping against the wood, an activity which
it appears to enjoy. (My compliments to the one behind *Alci-*
biades, and if he will only come out and show himself, I will give
him a bang on the head that will satisfy his craving for that
particular sensation for a very long time indeed.)

A diligent search has revealed nothing very much among my
books in the way of a do-it-yourself guide to pest extermination;
I had momentary expectations of Pliny when I came upon a
paragraph headed 'An insecticide', only to find that this is all the
old fool has to say on the subject:

> The tendrons of the elder, incorporal with goat's tallow, and
> reduced into a liniment, are singular good for the gout, if they
> be applied to the grieved place. The water of the infusion, if it
> be cast or sprinkled with the decoction of the leaves, it will not
> leave a fly alive.

A volume by H. L. Edlin in that excellent Collins series, *The*
New Naturalist, called *Trees, Woods and Man,* was the next to
raise hope, but the author breaks off just where I wanted him to
start, saying: 'Consideration of such timber-destroying fungi, and
insects, would take us a long way from the forest'; if it comes to
that, the little bleeder in my bookshelves is a long way from the
forest. Gilbert White asserts that: 'In the dusk of the evening,
when beetles begin to buzz, partridges begin to call', which is
about as much use as Pliny. Herodotus says that according to the
Thracians the country beyond the Ister is possessed by bees, 'on
account of which it is impossible to proceed farther', and the
editor of my edition of the Rawlinson translation insists, I know
not on what authority, that when Herodotus said bees, he meant
mosquitoes, though even if he did I do not see what use the information is to me. There is Macbeth's shard-borne beetle with his
drowsy hums, of course, but the noise mine is making could not
by any exercise of the imagination be described as a drowsy

hum. If it comes to that, there was a song in my youth which went:

> Oh, there's a maggot in the cheese,
> Crawling on his hands and knees,
> Can't you hear the beggar sneeze,
> Itchy-koo, itchy-koo.

But that can hardly be said to help, either. I suppose it will have to be Rentokil, though I must remember not to imply, when I ring them up, that I am the owner of Blenheim and that the roof is about to fall in, but only a humble flat-dweller with a single uninvited guest in his library.*

The Times September 19th, 1974

* Rentokil read this column and most kindly came without invitation and indeed without fee. I have heard no more from my little friend in the bookshelf.

The practised and the imperfect

ALL PROFESSIONS, SAID Shaw, are conspiracies against the laity, but the laity rarely gets it hands on such solid evidence of this truth as has just been provided by Dr John Taylor, secretary-designate of the Medical Protection Society. This body acts as a kind of insurance company for doctors, so that when a surgeon who has been engaged to correct an in-growing toenail absent-mindedly removes two-thirds of the patient's stomach (a trifling error which could be made by anybody and for which it would be absurd as well as unjust to think of actually blaming the practitioner) and then for good measure leaves a pair of forceps nine inches long in what remains of the unfortunate sufferer's interior (another paltry mistake which has been known to occasion extraordinary hostility on the part of the subject's surviving relatives), the Medical Protection Society takes up, in any legal proceedings arising out of the operation, the defence of the operator, and even pays the damages if he should lose (always provided, I take it, that he is up to date with his subscription). Such surgeons are substantially helped, no doubt, by the extreme difficulty said to be experienced, on the part of those who want to sue a surgeon, in obtaining a qualified medical opinion critical of another medical practitioner – a difficulty second only to that reputedly faced by an aggrieved litigant who tries to find a solicitor willing to undertake a case against another one, more than which I cannot well say, other than that any letters I receive from the British Medical Association or the Law Society, indignantly denying that their members are reluctant to act against their professional brothers, will be returned marked 'Dead' and 'Bankrupt' respectively.

Dr Taylor was complaining that court awards against doctors and surgeons in negligence cases are now getting so high that they threaten medical advance, by making the medicos reluctant to undertake new techniques. He gave the example of a deaf woman upon whom a doctor tried a 'novel' (Mr Taylor's word) operation which failed, leaving her suffering from noises in the ear and some infection; a court awarded her £19,000 though 'the surgeon's lawyers thought that settlement should be around £6,000'. Well, no doubt the happiest arrangement for the medical professional would be for a defendant doctor being sued by a patient to fix the damages himself after consultation with lawyers engaged by the Medical Protection Society, but exceptionally suspicious fellows (me for instance) might feel that this was not perhaps the most entirely bias-free way to arrive at a figure which would represent adequate compensation.

Moreover, Dr Taylor complained that, if the courts went on shelling out such enormous sums as damages in medical negligence cases, doctors would soon begin to practise what he called 'defensive medicine'. This strikes me as the best news I have heard for years; there has been far too much aggressive medicine practised for some time now, and an end to the tendency of some members of the medical profession to regard their patients as little more than raw material on which to impose the latest medical fashion is long overdue. In the long and immensely varied history of medicine there have been few things quite so disgraceful as the way in which no sooner had Mr Louis Washkansky (Professor Barnard's first heart-transplant patient) died, a few days after sitting up in bed to broadcast a tribute to the good doctor, than surgeons all over the world began merrily to whip hearts in and out of other people's bodies, almost every single one of the recipients (to say nothing of the 'donors') suffering a severe attack of death in the process; it seemed like a kind of international sporting contest, and I got a distinct feeling that the thing was stopped* only just before it would have involved an attempt to

---

* It started again later.

see whether heart-transplanting could be included in the Olympic Games. Heart-transplanting was, and for that matter is, a 'novel' technique, though not necessarily of the kind Dr Taylor has in mind; but playing about with novelties, though it may be nice for the doctors, may be less so for the patients, and the more important aspect of that now discredited operation* lies in the fact that medical science was, and still is, years away from solving the problems that made it, as one very distinguished British surgeon called it, 'the only method yet devised of killing two patients at the same time'.

A little defensive medicine would go a long way in areas like that, and a little of the same would help in some of the cases the existence of which Dr Taylor frankly admitted, with no attempt to excuse the doctors involved, such as that of the man who went into hospital to have a ganglion removed from his wrist, and instead underwent a vasectomy, which was no doubt bully for the population explosion but less so for the man's peace of mind, not to mention that of his wife – and he still presumably had the problem with his wrist.

Dr Taylor was also at pains to draw attention, very properly, to what he called some paradoxes in the law relating to medical negligence and compensation. One of these was the case of a boy who suffered irreparable brain damage during an operation, owing to 'an anaesthetic error', and was condemned to live the rest of his life as a human vegetable, for which he was awarded £60,000 compensation. But, pointed out Dr Taylor, if the boy had died, his family would have received only £500. It is not clear what moral Dr Taylor was inviting his audience to draw from this case, but I can think of one that certainly had not occurred to him; if in doubt, kill your patient, as it will be much cheaper in the long run.

But the juiciest part of Dr Taylor's argument was his claim that negligence is 'mainly a legal, not a medical, concept'. Well, it is a legal concept when it gets into court, of course, but I am not at

* But see previous footnote.

all sure how it can be one to start with. The only operation lawyers have been known to perform, as far as I know, is one for the removal of money from the client's pocket, and although this is normally performed without any anaesthetic other than a bottle of sal volatile to bring the patient round afterwards, it is certainly never performed negligently – indeed, the highest skill is invariably used. If Dr Taylor's claim that negligence is not necessarily blameworthy means anything at all, it presumably means that, provided a surgeon is reasonably sober and does not attempt to operate with an unsterilized coal-shovel, his good faith and best endeavours should be protection for him from the consequences of error. But negligence is always blameworthy, and anyone who endeavours to convince doctors that it may not be does nobody any service – not the doctors themselves, not the Medical Protection Society, and certainly not the patients.

'The operation was successful', runs the old medical chestnut, 'but the patient died'. If the spokesmen for the Medical Protection Society, and those who think like them, have their way, the thinking behind that principle will be enshrined in the law. I think it is time the patients started practising defensive medicine themselves. Defensive something, anyway; karate, perhaps.

The Times April 13th, 1972

All those in favour

QUESTION: IS CENSORSHIP always a Bad Thing? Answer: Yes, always. Question: When is censorship a Good Thing? Answer: When it is censorship of what the Socially Committed disapprove of. Question: But if censorship in those circumstances is a Good Thing, how can it be said to be *always* a Bad Thing? Answer: Because a Bad Thing becomes a Good Thing when the Socially Committed approve of it. Question: Is not the speaker a socially committed humbug? Answer: That is the sort of remark that ought to be censored.

With which exchange the catechism ends and the explanation begins. It begins in the world of the public library, once thought of—rightly, as a matter of fact—as a place of quiet learning, giving access to all the knowledge of the world and all its entertainment, a fountain with the miraculous property of satisfying every taste it is possible for the human race to imagine. What is more, it used to be the public library's proudest boast that it did not discriminate between tastes, so that the reader who wanted nothing but Agatha Christie could find her works there, and the reader who sought Shakespeare could find his, while the seeker after the views of Karl Marx was not frustrated by a ban imposed by the followers of Disraeli, and those who wished to slake their thirst for knowledge with the pages of Arius did not find those pages firmly closed to them by edict of those who admire St Athanasius. So at least it was in Britain; let dictatorships adopt other practices, let ecclesiastical anathemas fall upon the heads of other peoples, in this country the public library existed to serve all, and the only words not to be found echoing among the shelves were: Thou Shalt Not Read.

Nous avons changé tout cela, as close students of that indispensable journal, the *Assistant Librarian,* can testify. For some time now its correspondence columns have contained appeals to librarians to censor the material on their shelves and to exercise a similar censorship in their selection of new books. Except for those of you who have spent the past decade undergoing deep-sleep therapy, there will be no difficulty in guessing what is coming now. The books the censors wish to censor are not those which, say, express unqualified admiration for the policies of Stalin or the present rulers of Cambodia, which declare that we should at once adopt the ideas of Trotsky and of Mao Tse-tung, of Fidel Castro and Che Guevara, which espouse the doctrines of the Socialist Workers' Party, the Workers' Revolutionary Party, the International Marxist Group or the Communist Party of Great Britain (Marxist-Leninist). Not at all; proposals to censor such books would be received by the people I have in mind with the same horror and indignation that they would occasion in me (though I dare say for somewhat different reasons). No; as you would expect, the call for censorship comes from those who want to ban right-wing opinions, and who insist that what they call 'racists and fascists' should be denied a place on the shelves of Britain's public libraries.

Those who think of librarians as quiet, gentle people will be surprised to learn that this demand is sometimes coupled with an appeal for physical violence against the same enemies, as in the case of the fierce Laura Schwitzer, who not only declares that librarians have a duty 'to censor all material which is racist' but also insists that 'violent opposition to these individuals ... does prevent the racists from using the streets to voice their views ... It's not enough just to say that N.F. marches should not be allowed to take place ...'

Well, well; the suppression of books that the suppressors don't like, and the bashing in of the faces of those who do like them, is not the kind of thing librarians used to advocate. I recognize, however, that we must move with the times, and no doubt Miss Schwitzer is a notable advance, intellectually, aesthetically and morally, on Montaigne. All the same, I cannot help wondering why it should be she and her friends who are to decide what views are sufficiently right-wing to be suppressed ('free speech for all but ...'). I mean, suppose she really is as ignorant and as foolish as her letter suggests ('If we as librarians agree ... even racists have a right to their opinions ... and "so-called racist literature has its place in any British library" ... we are condoning racism ... and excluding many of the immigrant population from using our libraries'): might she not get it wrong from time to time, and put on the suppression list someone who ought not to be on it? Or even leave off it someone who should be there?

No doubt such questions worry me more than they worry the members of an organization called 'Librarians For Social Change', and they also worry a correspondent who cleaves to the quaint idea that, as he puts it, 'as a librarian I should not allow my personal views to influence my book selection policy'. But 'Librarians For Social Change' do at least define themselves, saying in one of their manifestos that

> LFSC is a forum for the reappraisal of getting information to the people ... Our readers are active in ... fighting the isms – capitalism, fascism, racism, sexism, and other oppressive ideologies ...

– a statement which almost tempts me to offer a small prize for anyone who can name one particular oppressive ideology that 'Librarians For Social Change' are *not* active in fighting, though it certainly ends in 'ism'.

Another such organization (the indefatigably fissiparous nature of these bodies would make an amoeba envious) is called 'Librarians Against Racism and Fascism', and it recently held a 'Day School', the conclusions of which made as repellent a case for suppressing free speech as has been heard for a considerable time. As, for instance:

> We as library workers agree that it is a major function of librarianship to actively combat racism and fascism, and we advocate the following: That stock selection for libraries should

be guided by anti-racist and anti-fascist principles ... That staff recruitment should reflect a similar policy ... That local authority buildings should not be used by racist or fascist organisations.

And before you dismiss such stuff as mere dust in the wind, of no significance in the real world, take note that in one Lambeth branch library the only party political publication on display is the *Socialist Worker*.

Nor is that all. In the *Assistant Librarian* for March 1978, there is an article which not only comprehensively expresses the views to which I have been drawing attention, but is such a magnificent compendium of mental sludge that it sums up to perfection the kind of notion that is running through our society today like a science-fiction bacillus for which there is no known cure. It is in fact by a senior librarian; his name is Keith Harrison, and his article appears under the innocuous title 'Community Stock'.

Mr Harrison begins by declaring that 'it's books that I'm into' and goes on to make clear that he is interested in what his local community 'is all about and where it's at' – a statement of faith which hardly leads to a belief that it is literacy that Mr Harrison is into or that the English language is where he's at. Nor is this a trivial point; I have rarely read anything that made as clear as Mr Harrison's article does the connection between the corruption of language and the corruption of thought.

Mr Harrison first attempts to define his attitude to books (them things what he is into, remember) and their selection:

Good book selection surely means selecting materials which directly relate to the wants of local people. Good book selection is surely selecting materials which are intended to improve the quality of life ... For community librarians, this quality of life we should be trying to improve is nothing to do with sterile and reductive systems of formal education. What a lot of dry textbooks and unimaginative project material that gets rid of!

Yes, indeed; including most of the world's literature and scholarship, which Mr Harrison would leave, in words that Goering himself might have found a trifle too anti-intellectual, to 'schools, colleges, and other seats of so-called learning'.

But if Mr Harrison would sweep away all the old-fashioned stuff that is only fit for 'seats of so-called learning', what would he put in its place? He tells us:

> We should be actively pushing our own vision of a more enlightened, more humane and more caring society than that which exists today ... If we carefully review and criticize all the new books which we could buy, *then reject the many which for professional and political reasons we shouldn't buy*, we are left with a spiky hardcore reflecting a committed and socially motivated point of view ... our non-fiction stock will be much smaller in number and range of titles, but very much larger in its strength of purpose and potential social effect. (My italics)

Now for a butcher, a baker or a candlestick-maker to display such ignorance of what literature, education and libraries are, or what the function of a librarian is, would be deplorable enough. But Mr Harrison is himself a public librarian, and a senior librarian at that. And in what I have so far quoted, I can assure you, he is only warming to his work. His scorn is next applied to the Dewey system of classification for books:

> Dewey leads you into terrible dangers. Not the least of these dangers is a so-called 'balanced stock'. Each ... subject must ideally be represented by authoritative documents which carefully sift every point of view, and then (if the readers' request system works properly) give you a judicious and possibly even liberal conclusion. Holy Mother! Help us to be less balanced in the future!

I must say here, without claiming any special knowledge of the attitude of the Holy Mother, that I cannot easily see how she could help Mr Harrison to be any less balanced than he already is. 'Public Librarians', he tells us, 'have a long and rather depressing

history of impartiality' – a history of which he can certainly claim
not to be part. 'Impartiality is O.K.', he goes on, 'if you don't
believe any one thing very strongly.' I always thought it was
O.K. if you did believe things very strongly, provided one of
those things was that views opposed to your own should also be
heard. But Mr Harrison seems alternately amused and outraged
at such an attitude. The 'quality of life' which he seeks to improve, after all 'is about open-ended enlightenment rather than
restrictive formal education', so that he advocates 'deliberate
entertainment rather than gently philanthropic culturizing'.

And having heard the word culture, he reaches for his gun.
'How easy is it in your local library', he asks indignantly, 'to find
quickly a colourful and fun paperback of jokes, cartoons, puzzles
or quizzes?' Not easy enough, it seems, for Mr Harrison; but
stocking the shelves with comics is only a start; we must also remove literature (he calls it 'literature', the quotation-marks being
there to make clear that it is something to be despised) and replace
it with material which, as well as being politically acceptable, will
not be of 'lasting literary merit', since 'Novels of lasting literary
merit can be scant in pleasure-potential'. For, after all, 'spreading
worthwhile human values is surely more important than promulgating tedious literary worth'. By now we have an alarmingly
clear picture of Mr Harrison's mind. Political judgments should
dictate which non-fiction books are stocked; one of the worst
dangers in a library is a balanced range of opinions; impartiality
is only suitable for those with no opinions of their own; those
equipped with strong views have the right and indeed the duty
to suppress views they do not themselves hold; literary worth is
tedious; and 'as socially committed community workers, we are
surely responsible for the human values and attitudes reflected in
the novels we buy'.

It is with that last remark that the abyss opens before our feet.
There is a public librarian in this country who really does believe
that he has, and ought to have, a responsibility to ensure that even
the novels, let alone the non-fiction works, on his shelves should
express only views of which he approves. Beside so stupendous

an absence of any understanding of what a library is, his direct call for censorship becomes almost modest:

> In novels and other materials, picture books for example, what we must try and control are the more despicable manifestations of injustices such as racism, sexism, and ageism. To exercise this kind of control over our materials requires a high degree of social and political awareness.

Actually, it requires the tolerance of a *Gauleiter*, the humility of Narcissus and the intelligence of Neanderthal Man, but the truth is that the expressed contempt for knowledge displayed by Mr Harrison is exactly equal to his unconscious contempt for the people, who cannot be trusted, and therefore cannot be allowed, to read books he disapproves of, so that these must be removed from the shelves before the people are allowed in. And his contempt for knowledge extends to those who possess it:

> ... librarians ... may indeed know a great deal about books, but is this really the right basis for deciding what to buy and what to tear up?

Well, I would have thought it was a good start; Mr Harrison, however, puts his view clearly when he insists that those in charge of reference libraries should purchase 'materials intended to inform local people about their rights and opportunities rather than informing them about the "universe of knowledge" ', after which few readers will agree with him when he says: 'It may seem surprising that in an article which claims to be about book selection I have not quoted any authors or titles'. On the contrary, it would be surprising, to anyone who has followed him this far, if he *had* quoted any, and anyone who follows him just one step further will discover precisely why he does not:

> Books and authors come and go ... Ideologies go on ... for quite a long time ... the ideas and emotions which motivate and politicize us are far more important than the formulaic and

bookish criteria which have been drummed into us by traditional librarianship.

There is a good deal more of this sort of thing, but I think I have quoted enough to provide a picture of what our public libraries will be like when Mr Harrison and his political friends take over. No 'tedious literary worth', no 'universe of knowledge', no range of books expressing more than one, approved, point of view, no books chosen by people who only 'know a great deal about books', no 'culturizing', no books which do not form part of 'a spiky hardcore reflecting a committed and socially motivated point of view'. Instead, there will be books 'intended to inform local people about their rights and opportunities' and many a 'colourful and fun paperback of jokes, cartoons, puzzles or quizzes'.

It seems an unduly restricted diet. But then, by 'it seems' I mean 'it seems to me'. It doesn't so seem to Mr Harrison, whose own Burning of the Books seems likely to be a good deal more comprehensive than the one most of us have heard of. If illiteracy, cant, totalitarianism and ignorance seem to you to be the best criteria for guiding library stock selection, Mr Harrison and his friends are clearly the librarians for you. If not, you would do well to practise keeping your views to yourself, against the day when they compel you to.

The Times May 30th and May 31st, 1978

Cats out of the bag

The Cecil King Diary, 1965–1970*

THE FIRST THING I did after finishing this astounding and devastating book was to make a note that, should I ever be invited to lunch by its author, I would listen much and say nothing. I would say nothing because it would not be safe to do otherwise; Mr King simply writes down not only what he thinks of the people he meets but also what the people he meets think of other people. Having written it down, he quotes it, verbatim. Indeed, so outrageous, unlimited and appalling is his indiscretion, which makes Lord Butler seem a Trappist and Mr Crossman a deaf-mute, that he really ought, for decency's sake, to have his invitation cards embossed R.S.V.P. in one corner and 'You are not obliged to say anything, but it is my duty to warn you that anything you say will be taken down and may be given in evidence' in the other.

Let the galled jade wince; those who have never been invited to lunch by Mr King may sit back with unwrung withers and enjoy what is not only (we will come to this in a moment) perhaps the most revealing and valuable political record yet published in post-war Britain, but an account of the actions and thought processes of the public figures of the time (mainly Labour politicians) written with such monstrous, overwhelming and unmitigated candour that any reader who is not actually named in the book, and who has any feeling for the finer sensations of malice, *Schadenfreude* and hate can savour these in unlimited quantity and concentrated dosage, despite the remarkable fact that the book is written entirely without them.

* Cape, 1971.

I think I am right in saying that there is not a single page anywhere in the book that will not make somebody profoundly unhappy, and I can only faintly convey my feelings on this aspect of it by saying that there is a passage in it, in which Mr Richard Marsh reports what Mr Robert Mellish told him about Messrs Crossman and Greenwood, that not even I can bring myself to quote, the full force of which reluctance will perhaps be seen when I append some of the things I *can* bring myself to quote. As:

> At 4.30 to see Wilson ... at his request ... very friendly, relaxed and ... confident ... Cabinet changes ... Soskice is ill and slowly seizing up; Frank Longford quite useless ... mental age of twelve.

> Callaghan ... did not impress. He says the Government is definitely going into the Common Market and that the pledges were only given to keep Barbara Castle and her friends quiet until after the election.

> Wilson, when he was Leader of the Opposition ... liked leaving the Mirror office in my car, a Rolls-Royce, but always got out before he reached the House and on the journey wore spectacles!

> A long talk with Maurice Allen [Executive Director of the Bank of England] ... Allen says (1) the latest figures coming up are worse than ever and (2) that our reserve figures are faked.

> Denis Hamilton came to lunch ... Wilson ... had Denis to lunch and specified four members of *The Times* staff who were to be dismissed.

> Lunch today with Vic Feather ... He regards Barbara Castle as ready to go to any lengths to get herself publicity or acclaim.

> I am a great believer in Marsh ... he certainly has all the right ideas (including contempt for George Woodcock).

> Blankenhorn, the German Ambassador, came to lunch ... he says Erhard is a weak man, a bad politician and will not last

long ... Blankenhorn came to lunch ... he never thought anything of Chalfont ... A hilarious lunch with Blankenhorn ...
He assumes Ted Heath will take office and within two years
will be a manifest failure.

The staff at No. 10 is weaker than ever—a dim little secretary,
Wigg, and an inadequate press man called Trevor Lloyd-
Hughes.

Lunch American Ambassador David Bruce ... Bruce expressed
contempt for Gordon Walker, and said he could not make out
what Gore-Booth did.

Max Aitken talked complete nonsense. It is hard to see what
can be done with such a man. He had two themes: one was
how right Ian Smith was and how wrong H.M. Government
was over Rhodesia, and the second was Booming Britain. I
know these are the themes of the *Express* just now, but it never
occurred to me that he actually believes this nonsense.

Parker, the Lord Chief Justice ... surprised me by saying that
the Conservatives have no one in politics ... fit to be Lord
Chancellor, Attorney-General, or Solicitor-General.

Lunch today with Arnold Weinstock ... He believed in equal
pay for equal work, but the men's wages should be brought
down to that of the women.

There is more—much more—very much more—of this, but
the book, if this were all, would only be enjoyable. It *is* enjoyable—oh, my paws and whiskers, it is enjoyable!—but it is something else besides. It is a portrait of the Labour Government, or
more precisely of Mr Wilson's conduct at the head of it, which
surpasses, in its merciless depiction of chicanery, duplicity, nervelessness, incompetence and sheer political squalor, anything at all
previously written or even hinted at.* Again and again, from

* But it was as nothing compared to what has been emerging—sometimes
almost hourly—since Wilson finally retired as Prime Minister.

Wilson's own lips, from those of his colleagues, from civil servants, journalists, Bank of England officials, foreign observers, trade unionists, from every quarter, there comes the same evidence – evidence of Wilson's unfitness to be Prime Minister, of the almost insane recklessness and irresponsibility he displayed in his pursuit of short-term political ends, his subordination of everything to his one goal of staying in office until tomorrow, and then until the day after, and then until the day after that, and then ...

King tells this dreadful story as he records the indiscretions of others; plainly and straightforwardly (his excellent, dry style reminds me of Attlee, as his breathtaking candour and honesty – though not his indiscretion – remind me of Woodrow Wyatt), with simple common sense and without any apparent sense of grudge or resentment.

His judgment, too, is both good and consistent (there is no evidence that he has been tidying the diary up with hindsight); his main theme – that the country is moving inexorably towards financial and economic disaster and that only some kind of Government of National Unity will save it – is deployed with vigour but without fanaticism (but is still not convincing); his shrewd realization that politicians see everything from inside the House and that that is the principal trouble with our politics, is well argued. But all this, like the indiscretion, comes second to his implacable determination to make known the uttermost truth about Harold Wilson and so help to prevent him from ever again being allowed to get his hands on supreme political office. It is a worthy cause, a necessary cause, and Cecil King's concern with it quite clearly springs from the most straightforward of patriotic motives; he thinks Wilson's return to office would be disastrous for our country.* Some inkling of why he thinks so can be gained from this passage:

Had 45 minutes with Wilson ... I came to tell him about my trip round Europe and, in particular, to warn him that ... de

* It was.

Gaulle was determined to keep us out of the Common Market if he could ... Wilson ... spent 40 of the 45 minutes saying what a wonderful relationship he had established with Kosygin; how he had missed a cease-fire in Vietnam by a hair's breadth. Later, he ... went into a long account of how well he had handled de Gaulle, and how friendly he was ... You cannot break through Wilson's façade of buoyant optimism. His vanity is quite astonishing – each failure is hailed as a brilliant break-through; realism never shows up. One must just wait for events to reveal to the world that the emperor has no clothes.

Events did reveal it, just in time. But if the country should ever again delude itself that the emperor is after all, fully dressed, the result would be national catastrophe. If Cecil King's book helps, by however little, to avert that catastrophe, he will have deserved the thanks of us all. And if it does not, I shall be very surprised.

Observer October 19th, 1975

Pray you undo this button

THERE LIVE NOT three good men unhanged in England, and one of them is fat and grows old. Sir Bernard Miles is one of the most astute publicists in the history of the theatre, and unlike some of that breed the stunts he has devised have always been directed not towards his own vainglory, and still less his own pocket, but to the upkeep of his precious Mermaid, to whom he has been so loving that he might not beteem the winds of heaven visit her face too roughly.

But now, I fear, there is a very ancient and fish-like smell coming from Puddle Dock. There has of late (but wherefore I know not) been discovered in London the extraordinary fact that people are willing to pay good money to look at unclothed ladies, with the result that there has been a great flood of these upon our stages and screens, though in the meantime some necessary question of the play be then to be considered.

At times, it has begun to seem that there would soon be no dramatic work, however inappropriate, not decked out with its ration of naked players, and that nude house-party guests would enter through french windows (uncurtained ones) to extend invitations to tennis in the buff, while housemaids without a stitch would explain on the telephone that the young master was expected home from Oxford on the morrow with no clothes on, and grave butlers in their birthday suits would enter to announce duchesses similarly unattired.

Eventually, of course, it had to spread to Shakespeare, and actresses at auditions have found themselves being asked not if they are able to speak the speech trippingly on the tongue but whether they are willing to expose themselves in a manner which, were they to do it without the licence of dramatic art, would render them liable to prosecution under Section 81 of the Public Health Acts Amendment Act 1907.

And now the Mermaid has succumbed, and a lady, attended by the greatest quantity of publicity Sir Bernard Miles can devise (which is no little), has declined to play Desdemona in Sir Bernard's forthcoming production of *Othello* because the production called for her to go to bed without benefit of pyjamas; another lady, presumably less inhibited, has taken her place.

Well, sit we down, and let us hear Bernardo speak of this. Taxed with the irrelevance of the scene, Sir Bernard defended himself by drawing attention to the exchange between Emilia and Desdemona:

> Shall I go fetch your night-gown?
> No, un-pin me here.

Sir Bernard, of course, had his tongue in his cheek: all the same, I feel bound to draw attention to Desdemona's words to Emilia only eighteen lines earlier, 'Give me my nightly wearing, and adieu', which disposes of what might be termed, stretching a point, Sir Bernard's argument.

As a matter of fact, Sir Bernard had no need, if all he wanted as an excuse to ask his players to strip was textual authority, to stop at Desdemona, for later in the next act Othello says:

> Look in upon me, then, and speak with me,
> Or, naked, as I am, I will assault thee,

which would surely enable him not only to have Othello play the last scene as naked as Desdemona, but in addition to do several things made illegal by Section 13, Sub-section (a) of the Sexual Offences Act 1956.

But once Sir Bernard sets his mind to it, there is no need for him to stop anywhere. Richard III's

> And thus I clothe my naked villainy
> With odd old ends stol'n forth of holy writ ...

E

will obviously allow the actor playing the part to camp nude about the stage mock-bashfully holding a page or two of the Bible to his private— or, as I suppose we must now learn to think of them, public— parts, and Lear's

> Poor naked wretches, wheresoe'er you are
> That bide the pelting of this pitiless storm ...

should obviously be accompanied by a procession of them across the stage.

In *Henry VIII*, of course, Wolsey must play his greatest scene in the nude; his words

> Had I but served my God with half the zeal
> I served my king, he would not in mine age
> Have left me naked to mine enemies

admit of no other interpretation but that he has just (symbolically, no doubt, in view of his fall from grace) taken all his clothes off.

I hesitate to guess what Lear has in mind when he says 'Through tattered clothes small vices do appear', though I have no doubt what could be made of it by a sufficiently intrepid producer with a sufficiently compliant cast. As for *The Tempest*, an all-nude production is surely overdue in view of the fact that Prospero describes the play's setting as 'this bare island'. Launce, in *The Two Gentlemen of Verona*, refers to 'a bare Christian', which would provide the opportunity to have a naked clergyman pass across the stage (there is no clergyman in *The Two Gentlemen of Verona*, of course, but that would not worry the kind of producer I have in mind).

I am not sure quite how Sir Bernard Miles would fit *The Rape of Lucrece* into his theory, since Shakespeare makes it clear in the lines

> For with the nightly linen that she wears
> He pens her piteous clamours in her head ...

that she, at any rate, does not go to bed in the nude, and if a lady can be raped with a nightie on, it can hardly be maintained that it is improper for her to be suffocated except without one.

Pish and tush. 'These rough uneven ways,' says Richard II, 'draw out our Miles and make them wearisome', and that is the point. Sir Bernard has his own ways, and fine ones they have always been; he, of all people, ought not to ape the cheaper and sillier ways of lesser men. And before the usual nonsense about 'artistic necessity' is heard, let the defenders of irrelevant stage nudity answer this question: why is it that the actresses who are asked to strip in the cause of art are invariably the prettier ones?*

The Times September 9th, 1971

---

* Not quite invariably; in 1978 the lot fell upon a quite exceptionally ill-shaped *actor*.

Testimony to the lies of tyranny

THE PORTUGUESE REVOLUTION is almost two months old, and its future course is still uncertain.* At present, there looms the hideous danger that Portugal may fall into a communist dictatorship, which would make the overthrown regime seem nothing worse than a mild and benevolent form of paternalism. But one aspect has still not been sufficiently explored, and since whatever happens will not affect it, it seems to me worth exploring in some detail.

The distinguishing fact about the coup was not that it was successful, for many coups have been successful, nor that it was rapid, for some have been equally rapid, nor almost bloodless, for a few have been entirely so; what set this apart from so many seizures of power, even from obviously justified ones like the overthrow of Farouk or Nkrumah, was that in the space of a single day – no, in the space of a few hours – it demonstrated that the Portuguese dictatorship had absolutely no support in the country at all, that apart from the dictators themselves – the handful of rulers and their jailers and spies and torturers and gunmen – nobody in Portugal accepted the regime voluntarily, so that the instant the people realized that they no longer had to accept it under compulsion, there was the sound of a great crumpling of paper, and before the sun went down on the first day of the new

* In April 1974, the dictatorship of Dr Caetano, who had succeeded Salazar, was overthrown in an overnight coup led by General Spinola. The infant democracy of Portugal remained precarious for a considerable time after this was written, and is by no means fully secure yet. But the worst dangers seem to have receded.

era, the entire edifice of a regime that had existed without serious internal challenge for over half a century had vanished as though it had never existed at all. By Joshua and Gideon, and for that matter by the child who pointed out that the emperor had no clothes, that was a good day's work.

I own to a certain personal satisfaction at what happened, in addition to my pleasure that a brutal and corrupt tyranny has been swept away and that a people of ancient and admirable lineage has been freed from its oppression. For the truth that the Portuguese revolution demonstrated is the one I have spent my entire adult life proclaiming, and which I will be proclaiming even as my eyelids close for the last time; contrary to the assertion of the slave-master, the slave does not love his chains.

I am aware that in the modern world many people have been rendered apparently incapable of believing that fact, and – what makes it all the stranger – these include many who know very well that they would hate chains if they found them on their own wrists. There is no tyrannous regime so vile, so entirely without redeeming features, that it lacks defenders: South Africa and the Soviet Empire, Duvalier's Haiti and Ho's North Vietnam, Batista's Cuba and Castro's Cuba – all have had their toadies and their sycophants, their apologists and their defenders. And the song is always the same: the slave loves his chains. See the smiling Hungarian factory worker, so loyally devoted to cautious, patient Mr Kadar! Imagine, in East Germany the standard of living is constantly rising! Just think, in Spain the peasants pray for Franco's health! All together now, in the key of C major, 'It wouldn't do for us, old man, but they certainly seem to like it.'

And what General Spinola and his associates demonstrated in about twenty minutes is that that age-old claim is a lie, that it has always been a lie, and that it will always be a lie. People living under a dictatorship speedily learn to dissimulate: they vote the right way in the plebiscite, they line the streets for their rulers and cheer as these go by. After they have learned such techniques, a new stage is reached: they learn to endure what they cannot cure, and knowing that they cannot get the heel off their necks, they live as best they can in a recumbent posture. Pretence; resignation; the final stage is acceptance.

But that stage is never reached. In 1968, when for a few glorious and tragic months Czechoslovakia was free, it became apparent—as it had in Hungary in 1956—that out of a population of many millions there were, quite literally, only a few hundred people who supported the regime under which they lived. And yet I had read, in the previous decade, miles and miles of column-inches in the British press by trans-Curtain travellers who insisted that although of course they held no brief for communist tyranny, there was no denying that the Czechs—or, as it might be, the Hungarians—were solidly behind their leaders. At the very first shot in Budapest, at the very first announcement in Prague, the whole rotten edifice of propaganda and subornation, of doped dupes and flattered fools, disappeared instantly. Alas, in both cases it was restored by force of arms, and now you can scarcely buy a helping of fish and chips without finding it wrapped in a glowing account of the widespread popularity of Herr Honecker in East Germany, the liberal outlook of Mr Ceaucescu in Rumania, or the delightful smartness of the girls' clothes in Poland.

I am not so foolish, or so optimistic, as to believe that the great rush of air let out of this gigantic bladder of lies by General Spinola's needle will have blown away tyranny's apologists for ever. But it will have served to strengthen those of us who refuse to accept apologies for tyranny. For a little while, at least, we can reply to the claim that the black man in South Africa is generally content with his lot, that the vast mass of the Chinese people are true believers in the communist system, by pointing out that until the 24th April, the eve of the second Lisbon Earthquake, that is exactly what was being said about the people of Portugal and Dr Caetano. One day, even the greatest of living tyrannies will fall.

> And like the baseless fabric of this vision,
> The cloud-capped towers, the gorgeous palaces,
> The solemn temples, the great globe itself,
> Yea, all which it inherit, shall dissolve,

And like this insubstantial pageant faded
Leave not a wrack behind.

And if you think otherwise, answer me this before we go our
ways today: why do you suppose that when Senator Edward
Kennedy visited Moscow University, the Soviet authorities con-
cealed the fact of his presence from the students, locked off the
part of the institution he was in, filled the hall with elderly hacks,
and closed the meeting the instant the Senator asked the audience
a question about their own Government's policy?

The Times July 2nd, 1974

My secret dread

A YEAR OR SO ago, staying with some friends in France, I was reading in bed, in a room separate from the main house, when something caught my eye as I turned the page. Whereupon I got out of bed and set about wrecking the room, with considerable success. I dragged and hurled the furniture about; I tore down the curtains; I threw jugs of water in every direction; I flung the rugs into the bathroom; I found a carpet-sweeper and produced an ocean of mud by emptying the dust out of it on to the soaking floor. Then I went back to bed; but not to sleep. In the morning, I crept up to the house under the necessity of telling my hosts that their guest room was virtually a total write-off, and of explaining my appalling conduct. This, in the circumstances, might seem a formidable task; but they are old friends and know me, and I only had to pronounce one word for everything to be understood and forgiven.

A few of my readers will already have arrived at the solution to the mystery; these are my fellow-sufferers. The rest are presumably wondering what on earth I am talking about, and concluding that at the time of the episode I have described I must have been temporarily deranged; and as a matter of fact they are not far wrong. For what ails me and that minority who suffer with me is acute arachniphobia; the word I said to my friends in France was 'spider'. Berserk with panic, I had smashed up the room in an effort to kill one without having to go near it. And above all without letting it come near me.

Here we approach a paradox. I know that there is nothing I would not do, in the way of, say, trampling old ladies to the ground, to get away from a spider. Yet at the same time I am capable, in the presence of one, of behaving in a manner which, given the irrational and uncontrollable basis of my panic, is nevertheless perfectly directed, with all possible economy of effort, to removing the spider from my presence, or my presence from its. I had hurled the furniture and rugs about to deny the enemy a hiding place (the ultimate horror is the knowledge that a spider is lurking out of sight), I had torn down the curtains because I had seen it scuttle behind them, I had flung the jugs of water in an effort to drown it, which is in many ways the best method of all, for it relieves the victim of the necessity of making even the indirect contact involved in hitting it with a weapon (such as the carpet-sweeper with which I eventually beat it to death).

That is to say, though my impulse is irrational in the extreme, it does not drive me to behaviour in itself irrational, as would be the action of someone trapped in a fire who in panic rushes into the flames instead of through the door to safety. Indeed, spider-phobia seems to sharpen the ingenuity to a remarkable degree; I once found one in the handbasin in my bathroom, and after turning the tap on and leaving it running for some time, found that the spider, though drowned, was stuck in the cross-bars of the plughole. I got a pencil to dislodge it with; but my arm refused to obey the orders from my brain, and I stood there paralysed. Then I had an idea; and just before the second soda syphon spluttered empty, I squirted it loose.

Tee-hee; the spectacle of an adult unable to go within two feet of a dead spider, and compelled instead to Schweppesorcize it, must indeed cause hilarity. Not to me it doesn't; at the end of that episode I was *weeping* with fear and humiliation; and I trembled uncontrollably for an hour.

Very well; I have a horror of spiders, you of mice, he of enclosed spaces, she of birds, they of cats. I know people who believe in astrology, in ghosts, in the banshee, in leprechauns, in the nationalization of the means of production, distribution and exchange. We all are more or less crazy; what's so special about a man who is reduced to a gibbering idiot at the sight of eight hairy and harmless legs? Nothing, of course; but I want to know why. (I also want to be cured, but although I am sure that the good Doc Eysenck could remove my spider-phobia and replace it with a fine upstanding boot-fetishism at the drop of a reflex, I have no real hopes of ever being rid of my secret dread.) Let us consider.

I believe that orthodox psychiatric opinion offers me the choice of two basic explanations.* The general one – that my horror is the irrational defence I have built around a real, buried horror (did I try as a child to murder my sister?); and the particular one – that the hairy spider suggests subconsciously the forbidden mysteries of the private parts, and that a lack of naturalness about proffered explanations of such things in childhood has somehow got mixed up and come out in this way since. Perhaps; but then it would take psychoanalysis to provide even a chance of finding out for sure, and the attendant risks seem to me greater than those of my being driven to jump out of a high window in an effort to get away from *Tegenaria domestica*. Come not psychiatry. Entomology, I may say in passing, is no help either. My spider-phobia extends to many other creepy-crawlies, too, with different degrees of intensity, but I can trace no pattern sufficiently logical to provide any help. The daddy longlegs, for instance, arouses only a very mild horror, and the tiny 'money spiders' just do not excite any kind of feelings at all. Beetles I fear in exact proportion to their size; moths I don't care for, but do not actively dislike; caterpillars – small ones, anyway, I find positively attractive. On the other hand, I could not bring myself to touch a live crab, and if I had been the chef I read of who opened the refrigerator door to find that someone had presented him with an Alaskan King Crab (two feet across), I would have dropped dead on the spot. (He cooked it.)

The mythology of spiders has an astonishingly long lineage, but it is no help to me. Spiders have been venerated as repositories of wisdom (Bruce's spider is presumably a late stirring of this

---

* Three, actually. But if the third psychological explanation is the correct one in my case, it also inhibits me from writing about it. *Noblesse oblige*.

attitude) and rejected as demoniac; I can find no trace of spider-revulsion in folklore, however, though it occurs in history, of course (the Cardinal spider is so nicknamed because Wolsey very nearly died of shock at the sight of a large one scuttling from beneath his chair). Appearances I cannot disentangle from my feelings; a geometrically composed web strung between bushes and glistening with hoar frost I find very beautiful, but only if the tenant is out. If he is in, the whole thing becomes unbearably loathsome. (Spiders always strike me as dirty, incidentally, an admission which may perhaps strengthen the psychiatrists' case against me; I am anyway beginning to think that I have already said enough to get myself certified.) Similarly, the power of words and images – suggestive or mystical – is very strong on me in this area, but I am unable to distinguish with certainty between cause and effect; the word 'spider' (and 'scuttle', for that matter) sound horrible in my ears, and although I can read books about them I cannot without discomfort look at drawings or photographs.

Psychology, mythology, history, entomology, aesthetics, philology – all these I have ransacked for the clue to my behaviour, and an end to it; in vain. I fall back, of course, on philosophy, which never fails. I use my weakness, as Montaigne used his (the kidney-stone, and a variety of others), to remind myself that the perennial philosophy is the true one, and the materialist versions false. 'Men are unwise, and curiously planned'; they are irrational, immeasurable, unpredictable, uncontrollable. Rousseau was right, Hume was right, Heisenberg was right; Pope was wrong, Jefferson was wrong, Stalin was wrong. It is tiresome for a grown man to be afraid of spiders, but I am; it is inconvenient for men to act irrationally, but they do.

This is not just a quibble. That an area of my behaviour is not subject to the control of my mind, that even my body, in certain circumstances, refuses its subjection – this is at first sight dismaying; we all like to pretend, even if we are not judges or schoolmasters, who are inordinately given to the habit, that we act only according to the evidence and the appropriate balancing of interests. My spider-phobia is there to remind me that we lie; that our actions are dictated by eternally inexplicable impulses. Dismay turns to relief and gratitude, as failures, depressions, actions bitterly regretted, all loom less large, less awful and inevitable.

And on the other hand, fresh hope is engendered in all sorts of places where it might be thought to have died for ever. You have no idea how useful a morbid horror of spiders can be, for instance, to a man contemplating the political scene. For it teaches the contemplator that anything can happen, and probably will; if we spider-phobes can behave the way we do, and yet survive and thrive, the world will survive its apparently implacable determination, governed by the most rationally ordered motives, to come to an abrupt end. Go to the spider, Mao Tse-tung; consider her ways, and be foolish. Why, even Mr Crossman, viewed from between the legs of *Aranea cucurbitina*, takes on a harmless aspect. Nay:

> H. G. Wells has found that children play
> And Bernard Shaw discovered that they squall;
> Rationalists are growing rational,
> And through deep woods one finds a stream astray
> So secret that the very sky seems small—
> I think I will not hang myself today.

Not, at any rate, unless I meet a *very* large spider.

New Statesman September 30th, 1966

An ideal way to clear the mind

I SPENT PART OF the weekend at Olympia, at the Festival for Mind and Body. It is the strangest fair I have ever been to, a gathering of the guilds such as no medieval assembly could have rivalled, let alone the Motor Show or the Ideal Home Exhibition. Nor is it easy to define: the organizers say of it that it is a 'meeting place for all those concerned with living creatively, economically and responsibly', but I could draw up a list of a dozen gatherings that could be so described, none of which would have anything in common with any of the others. And if I say it is peopled by those who seek paths different from those along which our century has so far progressed, it will convey little more to those who do not already know what the festival is. And if I simply list some of those who have taken space at the festival – and they include the Aetherius Society, the Atlanteans, Esoteric and Occult Productions Ltd, Cranks Health Foods, the Fellowship of the Inner Light, the Followers of the Way, the Grail Foundation, Granary Health Products, Human Potential Resources, Interorientation Ltd, Lotus Foods, Pyramid Energy Products, Solar Quest, the White Eagle Lodge, the Universal Church of God and the Vegetarian Society of the United Kingdom – it will be written off as an assembly of more or less harmless lunatics, some of whom probably believe that there is a man who can and does walk over red-hot coals without either feeling pain or experiencing burns, merely because it is true.

The published comment on the Festival has been very interesting. This is the second year it has been held, and the organizers now intend it to be a regular annual event; last year, the coverage, both in advance and while it was actually happening, consisted almost entirely of giggling in a superior tone. There is no lack of that approach this year (we shall come to the implications in a moment), but it is now accompanied by something that can best be described as a reluctantly serious curiosity, and even an uneasy respect.

For what is common to almost all the exhibitors – whether what they are exhibiting is a range of foods free from chemicals or a philosophy of life – is a conviction that what the world lives by at the moment just will not do. Nor will it; nor do very many people suppose any longer that it will. Countries like ours are full of people who have all the material comforts they desire, together even with such non-material blessings as a happy family, and yet lead lives of quiet, and at times noisy, desperation, understanding nothing but the fact that there is a hole inside them and that however much food and drink they pour into it, however many motor cars and television sets they stuff it with, however many well-balanced children and loyal friends they parade around the edges of it, however much contentment they place between it and their own consciousness, it aches.

Apart from a few of the sillier scientists and the more bone-headed survivals of nineteenth-century anti-clericalism, almost everybody today reacts to an assertion that the materialist explanation of the universe is obviously inadequate, and indeed ridiculous, in one of two ways. Either they assent to a proposition too obviously true to be worth discussing except as a starting point for a discussion of what *is* worth talking about, or they display the kind of panic reaction that I predicted for Brian Inglis's *Natural and Supernatural*, and that, when the book was published, fulfilled my prediction ninety times over and then nine more.*

The panic is a healthy sign, not an unhealthy. After all, to take

---

* The book is a history of the paranormal from the earliest times to the First World War. I predicted a terrified rejection of the evidence by those unable to face the fact that there are things in the Universe that they are unable to understand.

an obvious and familiar example, if extra-terrestrial beings exist, these phenomena may lead to undesirable consequences; the beings may land on earth with hostile intent. But the mere existence of the creatures from space is not, rationally considered, a frightening thought. What frightens those who are frightened by the very idea is inside themselves: it is the insistence, by the higher part of their own personalities, that there are more things in heaven and earth than are dreamed of in their philosophy. And the closer they approach to the moment when that insistence breaks through to all the parts of their mental psychological and spiritual constitution, the more fierce their resistance becomes. That, surely, is why the very distinguished scientist I met soon after I wrote about Brian Inglis's book attacked me and it (he had not read it, of course) in a voice that was shrill and unsteady and with the sweat breaking out on his forehead; not because he knew he was right, but because the most important part of him knew he was wrong.

The Festival for Mind and Body begins where that attitude ends. For those who know that our present way of life is unsatisfactory, and cannot be made satisfactory by repeated applications of the principles and policies that have made it what it is, there is on show at Olympia an almost unimaginably varied range of suggestions as to what we might do about so depressing a state of affairs.

What *we* might do about it. No government enterprises are here represented, nor any political parties. Economic institutes have no stand; United Nations agencies do not beckon the visitor; amid the showers of leaflets and brochures, the roaring torrent of courses and exercises, our universities are as silent as our great industrial companies.

It would be astonishing if it were otherwise; for if they had not all failed us, the festival would not exist, or need to. Take, at random, this note from one of the organizations represented at Olympia. It offers

... a highway to those in search of peace of mind by helping them to understand the God force and showing them how to use it creatively. Dormant forces, stilled at the Creation, are awaking and changing the universe; we offer you guidance to change too.

Now that is the theme that runs right through the Festival, and its characteristics are those of the Olympia gathering as a whole. It is undogmatic; there is no proselytizing; and the offer is not of something outside the individual, which is to be supplied, but of something already inside us, which can be released. Take, again, the organization that exists to disseminate the teaching of a very remarkable Indian sage, Rajneesh: 'We have', they say, 'a wide range of meditation and group techniques to support your Quest.' To support your Quest, note; note also the words of the Association for Humanistic Psychology, which is 'concerned with enabling people to grow to their full potential as human beings', and the attitude of the group around the Buddha Maitraya Sangha, 'who has assumed the title to imply the realization of the Buddha nature within himself and all of us'.

The crowds were vast; there was not a stand without a stream of visitors. And the crowd was even more interesting than the exhibitors, the most interesting thing about them being their ordinariness. Here and there, of course, there were individuals dressed in a style that the gigglers would thankfully recognize; men with long plaited hair and women with flowing robes and flapping sandals. (It was, though, noticeable that many of these also bore on their faces the visible signs of an exceptional serenity.) But most of the throng looked like the people you could see in the street outside. And the question therefore presents itself: why were they inside?

That is the easiest question of all to answer. They were all seeking something, something that would give them not certainty (for the belief in that mythical beast died out long ago) but understanding; understanding, that is, of themselves and their place in the universe. At Olympia they could find any amount, and every kind, of suggestions as to where they might start to look for themselves, but almost every path on view began in the same place: inside the seeker. Whatever the answers, that is the question, and it is being asked more insistently today than ever before in all history, while the traditional answers of ideologues and politicians sound more and more obviously absurd. The crowds pouring through the turnstiles at Olympia are only the first drops in the wave that must soon crash over the ideologues and the politicians, and drown their empty claims fathoms deep in a self-confidence born of a true understanding of their own nature and that universal nature which is so much more than the sum of all its parts.

The Times May 3rd, 1978

Return from a long journey

HERE ARE TWO statements by the same American:

With all of its faults, the American political system is the freest and most democratic in the world. The system needs to be improved, with democracy spread to all areas of life, particularly the economic. All of these changes must be conducted through our established institutions, and people with grievances must find political method for obtaining redress.

What's left is force: fuel for the fire that will rage across the face of this racist country and either purge it of its evil or turn it into ashes ... I say it to racist America, that if every voice of dissent is silenced by your guns, by your courts, by your gas chambers, by your money, you will know that as long as the ghost of Eldridge Cleaver is afoot, you have an ENEMY in your midst.

The clue lies in the respective dates of those expressions of two strikingly different attitudes. The second is the earlier, having been written in April 1968, as the concluding words of a first-hand account, in the form of an affidavit, of the shooting incident in which one of Cleaver's fellow members of the Black Panther group was killed by police fire. Cleaver was then on parole from prison, where he had served nine years for rape; he was immediately returned to prison, and after a legal struggle, obtained bail. He never surrendered to it, but went into exile, first in Cuba, then for some years in Algeria, finally in France. The statement was published in a volume of his writings and speeches.

The first of my two quotations from Cleaver was published a fortnight ago; it comes from an article by him in the *New York Times*. In it, he tells why he has decided to return to the United States despite the unexpired prison sentence and the subsequent, extra charges outstanding against him. It is in its way as moving and convincing a credo as any of the pieces in his book *Soul on Ice,* which was a work of astonishing, burning power in its cry of rage and hate at the society that for so long had denied his people equality.

Eldridge Cleaver's exile lasted seven years, and they were bitter ones. For a time, he held court in Algiers, trying to convince himself and others that his followers in the United States were about to achieve revolution, and encouraged in this fantasy by the dreadful white apostles of radical-chic, who have done so much to retard the cause of black equality; some of them had even gushed approval of Cleaver's earlier insistence that his rapes of white women were justified as 'an insurrectionary act' ('It delighted me that I was defying and trampling upon the white man's law, upon his system of values, and that I was defiling his women ... '), and were probably disappointed when he repudiated that terrible philosophy ('I had gone astray from being human ... I also learned that it is easier to do evil than it is to do good ...'). But after a time he was forgotten, and the pedlars of radical-chic moved on to newer fashions, such as the one which ended so horribly in Trinidad with the pathetic Michael de Freitas.* Eventually Cleaver had to leave Algeria, and settled, devoid of fame, fortune or followers, in Paris.

Many a man, in that situation, with that history, would deteriorate. Cleaver, instead, awoke. For those with eyes to see, the ground in which his new self grew had been long since prepared; in *Soul on Ice* he had shown himself, beneath all the hate and the calls for violence, a man searching for answers less simple and less untrue. For they were untrue, and untrue in two senses; first, the violent solution in the United States would not and could not

* See p. 273.

lead to the end – full racial equality – desired, and second, the army of blacks ready to follow where the Black Panthers (with their 'Minister of Information' and 'Minister of Defence') led was almost entirely imaginary. In a penetrating comment on Cleaver's change of heart, Bayard Rustin, a black American derided as an Uncle Tom by the revolutionaries, but who has done more to advance the black American than all the revolutionaries put together, had this to say:

> Cleaver's imposing style camouflaged the shallowness of his political thought. It was clear that behind the articulations of anger and frustration was a conception of society which had little relation to the concrete situation of the majority of black people. He shared a sense of rage with many black people, but he did not understand their aspirations ... it was predestined that Cleaver, like all others whose philosophies were rooted in extremism and hatred, would either alter his views to conform with socio-political realities, embrace an opposite or equally-as-extremist doctrine, or, refusing to change, suffer that worst of fates – to be ignored. It is to Cleaver's credit that he is open-minded and honest enough to have learned from his experiences in exile.

It is more than that, though; in the interview (in *Newsweek*) on which Rustin was commenting, Cleaver had cautiously implied that it was seeing the reality of communism in action, on his visits to China and the Soviet Empire, that had persuaded him that his earlier belief in an American Marxist revolution, with sympathy and support from the communist word, was misplaced. 'The Russians', he said (and it is better that such a man should learn such a thing late than that he should not learn it at all), 'would really prefer that the United States cease to exist. I came to the conclusion that they were capable of launching a surprise attack.' From this, he concludes that America needs strong armed forces; he added the final repudiation of his earlier self by saying that America is 'anti-colonialist'.

What now? One of Eldridge Cleaver's tragedies was that in his earlier existence amid the rhetoric and the brandishing of guns, he was written off by much of white America as just another black thug. He was nothing of the kind; or rather, he was something of the kind, but it was a small part of him, and the rest was far more important. His rage, for all its lack of sustenance and of aim, was creative, as indeed was he; *Soul on Ice* is a book that makes a real contribution to American life and indeed literature (and considering that he was largely self-taught and had spent almost all of his adult life in prison it is an even more astonishing achievement), and if it had been heeded, and carefully distinguished from the sterile stuff with which it was indiscriminately lumped, it and he could have contributed much of value to his country in general and his fellow-blacks in particular.

Yet, what now? 'The slogans of yesterday', Cleaver wrote last month in his *New York Times* article, 'will not get us through the tasks at hand ... '

Each generation subjects the world it inherits to severe criticism. I think that my generation has been more critical than most, and for good reason. At the same time, at the end of the critical process, we should arrive at some conclusions. We should have discovered which values are worth conserving. It is the beginning of another fight, the fight to defend those values from the blind excess of our fellows who are still caught up in the critical process. It is my hope to make a positive contribution in this regard.

I think a man of Cleaver's ability, energy, honesty and intelligence can indeed make such a contribution. But he will hardly be able to do so if he is sent back to jail to finish his old sentence, and if on top of that he is convicted and sentenced on the charges laid against him just before his flight. In the seven years that have elapsed since he screamed for white America's blood, America has moved so far (despite all the setbacks and repudiations) that there is now talk, I see, of President Ford selecting the black Senator Brooke as vice-presidential candidate to run with him next November.* That is the United States to which Eldridge Cleaver has returned, and it was certainly not the one he left. I hope that he will be shown generosity, leniency and respect, and welcomed into American society instead of being driven back into his hatred of it. 'Somehow,' he said, 'man is less grand than I would have thought. He's still O.K. but he is less grand.' The wisdom of that understanding has been hard earned; now it is up to America, with much less pain, to learn the true value of a man like Eldridge Cleaver.

The Times December 2nd, 1975

---

* In the end he did not.

From prophet of violence to apostle of brotherhood

THE EXTRAORDINARY STORY of Eldridge Cleaver, on which I reported here in December 1975, has grown more extraordinary still. Before I go on to describe the latest development, a brief recapitulation of the salient facts in his life so far may be useful as background.

Cleaver was, with Huey Newton and Bobby Seale, one of the founders of the Black Panther movement in the United States, and an active leader in its most extreme and violent phase. Brought up in poverty and despair, he drifted early into petty crime, from which he progressed to the more serious (and violent) kind. He spent many years in prison, became convinced that the black people of the United States would never achieve their goal of an end to exploitation and discrimination unless they were prepared to use force, used it, was charged after a violent affray between Black Panthers and police in Oakland, California, in 1968, with various criminal offences, and fled the country. He wandered the world for a long time, living for a while as an honoured 'refugee from oppression' in Algeria, and last year returned to America and gave himself up. (The disgrace of American legal delays – one of the darkest stains on that country's system – means that he has still not been tried, and there is no saying when he will be.)

What makes Mr Cleaver's story so interesting and important is that it is not just one of a man, sick of wandering, coming home to face whatever consequences his trial may bring. During his long exile, he experienced a radical change of heart, coming to the conclusion that his crude Marxism was untenable, that the

United States, for all her faults, is and was the true home of liberty, and that the communist systems, which had once seemed to him to offer the hope of liberation for his race, threatened black and white alike with totalitarian despotism.

These things, on returning to America, he said; I imagine he has not, since he returned, been invited to many gatherings of the radical-chic, who, from their comfort and affluence, used to applaud and encourage the violence and intransigence of the Black Panthers, and to agree, as they sipped their martinis, that the United States ought indeed to be destroyed.

So much for the story so far; now for its extension. It is clear that Mr Cleaver's change of heart was, or more likely has now become, far more radical than that implied by his new-found political maturity. He has become a full and committed Christian.

In an extraordinary interview with an American religious magazine (of an eclectic and non-denominational variety), Mr Cleaver tells how he came to his present beliefs, and of what they consist. And to help measure the change in him, here is one of the milder passages from his writing in his Panther days:

Malcolm X ... showed us the rainbow and the golden pot at its end. Inside the golden pot ... was the tool of liberation. Huey P. Newton ... lifted the golden lid off the pot and blindly trusting Malcolm, stuck his hand inside ... When he withdrew his hand and looked to see what he held, he saw the gun, cold in its metal and implacable in its message: Death-Life. Liberty or Death mastered by a black hand at last! ... The genie of black revolutionary violence is here, and it says that the oppressor has no rights which the oppressed are bound to respect ... The cities of America have tasted the first flames of revolution. But a hotter fire rages in the hearts of black people today: total liberty for black people or total destruction for America.

And now? What is most interesting in Mr Cleaver's conversion is that he has not abandoned his belief that blacks in the United

States are ill-used, cheated, discriminated against and unjustly treated; what he has abandoned is his former belief that violence is the way to change those conditions. And now, as he faces both ways, he says:

> I don't know any other way of dealing with the past. You can't change it. You can't rewrite it. You can't suppress it or hide it. And you can't do it again. The best you can do is kind of learn from it ... So I criticize us for adding, for importing, ideologies.

Nor does he stop there. Discussing attitudes after American troops finally left Vietnam, he says:

> I saw that the fact that the war was over wasn't really being taken into consideration ... Once that stopped the question arose ... how serious is the situation in the world? Well, the situation was extremely serious. There were other countries in the world who were hostile to the United States. Extremely hostile. Who armed on a par with the United States ...

From revolutionary black violence, inspired by the Thoughts of Mao, to believing that the United States needs a continuing defence capacity against the danger of communist aggression (Mr Cleaver's present belief) is a change indeed. But even that need not imply a spiritual change. The crux lies here:

> A lot of people who didn't go through things like I went through, they'd be going through other things that are just as violent to their being as what I went through ... I find that everybody's talking about the same thing. No matter who they are, or what level they are, they're all talking about the same thing.

And from there, this remarkable man progressed to this remarkable position – remarkable, certainly, for one who professed himself a militant atheist:

I believe in the continuation of life after what we call death. But it's based on kind of an understanding of a life force within us ... When you die, one of two things can happen. The charge can cease to exist, or it can be somewhere else ... And the evidence that I see indicates that you don't destroy it, that kind of energy ... It's the force that's able to do a curious thing, like father a child. And you pass on that life force and that life force, then, can outlive you ... And people all down through history have thought about this ... I can't handle the idea of something coming out of nothing ... To me, it has to be something eternal, that always was and always will be ... there's a point on the frontier of our knowledge where you can choose to just be a sceptic ... But there are other joys involved with other people when you share a belief ... One says 'Okay, I'm willing to undergo this. I'm willing to say that I want to be a Christian. I want to believe in Jesus.' And then practise ... That, it seems to me, is how it works ... in the past I would just look at things as political or economic, without a moral or ethical dimension ... I see that that is the ultimate failure in dealing with human ... affairs. That the moment you throw out the moral and ethical considerations, you have reverted to the jungle.

When I previously wrote about Eldridge Cleaver, just after his return to the United States, I said that I hoped he would find clemency in his judges; it would be monstrous to waste such a man, and the contribution he can make to American society, by putting him back in prison. But now my hope is even more urgent, for Mr Cleaver has demonstrated a truth more fundamental, and potentially far more fruitful, than that contained in the social and political truth of his changed relationship in his country. He has, by his life and in his beliefs, shown that no one is inevitably lost, that no error is so deeply buried in darkness that the light can never break in upon it, that no amount of hate can fill any individual so completely as to leave no room for love. Eldridge Cleaver left America as the apostle of violence and revolution. He has returned as the avatar of brotherhood and reconciliation. May his witness be recognized.

The Times October 7th, 1977

Fleet Street-walkers

MOST OF THE comment on the role played by newspapers in the Lambton-Jellicoe affair has concentrated, rightly enough, on the conduct of the *News of the World* ('All human life is there, and if it isn't we'll arrange for it to be') and the *Sunday People* ('Forward with the *News of the World*').* But what caused me to stop what I was doing and to stare for quite a long time out of the window, contemplating eternity, was the less serious (in both senses of the phrase) conduct of the *Daily Express* and the *Daily Mail*.

It seems that, by thorough and speedy action, the *Daily Mail* managed to track down, and to buy for ready money, photographs of Mr and Mrs Levy on their wedding-day:

> 'E was warned agin 'er –
> That's what made 'im look;
> She was warned agin 'im –
> That is why she took.
> Wouldn't 'ear no reason,
> Went and done it blind;
> We know all about 'em,
> They've got all to find!

---

* The affair involved admissions by both men, who were government ministers, that they had been resorting to prostitutes; both resigned and left public political life. One of the two Sunday papers, having learned about these activities, had arranged with one of the prostitutes and her husband and pimp to catch the erring politicians *in flagrante*; the other had bought photographs of the activities.

Now the *Daily Mail*, having spent time and treasure on these vital documents, published them. The bride holds a bouquet, the groom has confetti in his hair:

> Now it's done an' over,
> 'Ear the organ squeak,
> 'Voice that breathed o'er Eden' –
> Ain't she got the cheek!
> White an' laylock ribbons,
> Think yourself so fine!
> I'd pray Gawd to take yer
> 'Fore I made yer mine!

This amazing, unprecedented, heroic achievement by the *Mail*, which must have had the nation's breakfast tables in convulsions of excitement ('See, see, Mabel, the *Daily Mail* has secured photographs of the Levys on their wedding-day, whereas the *Daily Express* has failed to do so! Is this not what Sir John Betjeman would call a "scoop"?'), had the *Express* in convulsions of something else. The editorial executive there who had been in charge of the search for the earth-shaking photographs, and on whom was thought to lie the responsibility for allowing the *Mail* to win the vital race, was instantly sacked. Such, he may have reflected as he took his hat, is the power of the printed picture:

> Escort to the kerridge,
> Wish 'im luck, the brute!
> Chuck the slippers after –
> (Pity tain't a boot!)
> Bowin' like a lady,
> Blushin' like a lad –
> 'Oo would say to see 'em
> Both is rotten bad?

Now I simply do not know whether the readers, or potential readers, of a particular newspaper are or are not impressed by the fact that it has managed to secure, in the face of intense rivalry

from a similar newspaper, wedding-day photographs of a prostitute and her pimp, and correspondingly unimpressed by the
failure of the rival sheet. But since I am here to give my own
opinions rather than those of other people, I will answer for myself; when I learned of the epic struggle between the two sides of
Fleet Street, I caught a whiff of mothballs, a memory of bodies
in trunks at Brighton Railway Station, an echo from a faded,
sepia-tinted past, and I remembered the great days of all those
newspapers, like the *Sunday Dispatch*, and the *Sunday Referee*, and
the *Daily Sketch*, and the *Daily Herald*, which also staged great
battles with their rivals, some even giving away encyclopaedias
or complete sets of the works of Dickens, yet somehow amid all
the excitement, failing to notice the hands of the clock going
round.

But a further reflection is prompted by this business. It is possible – indeed, I think it is very likely – that future ages, examining
the conduct and attitudes of this one, will find it odd that in 1973
men could be employed to rush about London in search of
photographs, and that other men could lose their employment
altogether for failing to do such rushing with sufficient vigour
and enterprise, the photographs in question being of prostitutes
and prostitutes' mates on the day they tied, as the saying used to
go, the nuptial knot:

> **See the Chaplain thinkin'?**
> See the women smile?
> Twig the married winkin'
> As they take the aisle?
> Keep your side-arms quiet,
> Dressin' by the Band.
> Ho! You 'oly beggars,
> Cough be'ind your 'and!

If future ages do take the view that such behaviour on the part
of our society was indeed odd, I cannot help feeling that future
ages will be right. A week or two ago, it was widely felt –
certainly I felt it – that some of the revelations of the Lonrho

affair suggested that our society had got its values the teeniest bit awry. I did not feel this at the revelations about the fallen ministers, because men have succumbed to their lusts throughout history; but only in our times have they begun to have large sums of money paid to them in the Cayman Islands,* and only in this age have they thought it proper to spend time, energy and money, in varying but substantial quantities, to secure photographs of women who perform sexual services for cash down.

Blake was of the opinion that the harlot's cry from street to street would weave old England's winding-sheet, and I am just about beginning to suspect that he might have been right. Whoring after strange gods is one thing; but gadding after strange whores is another, whether the whores are made of flesh or money.

The trouble is, our leaders do not talk in these terms. If there is no party advantage to be gained or withheld by comment on these matters, our principal politicians remain silent, and our leading churchmen are so scared of being thought to have any view at all on moral matters that they also have nothing to say. Lord Longford would instinctively feel that both Lonrho and the competition for the prostitute's photograph are wrong (both, of course, are perfectly legal), but his obsessive beliefs about the unique wrongness of pornography have devalued his opinions; St Mugg would take a similar view about both activities, but they would only feed his belief in the vanity and emptiness of the real world. Is there no generally respected, loved, even feared, figure to speak in powerful tones about the values of such a society, and be listened to? Or is England condemned to sink giggling beneath the waves, leaving the resultant desolation to the Maoists on the one hand and M.R.A. on the other?

Not a cheerful prospect; so let us return for a last look – since all the world loves a lover and marriages are made in heaven – at the pictures of Mr and Mrs Levy on the happy day:

* This is what was done for some of the individuals connected with the Lonrho company.

Cheer for the Sergeant's weddin'
Give 'em one cheer more!
Grey gun-'orses in the lando,
An' a rogue is married to a whore!*

The Times June 7th, 1973

* For permission to quote these stanzas from Rudyard Kipling's *The Sergeant's Weddin'*, I am indebted to the National Trust and Eyre Methuen Ltd.

Keeping them in their place . . .

THE DEATH IN captivity in South Africa of John Cheekykaffir, leader of the movement among black South Africans to persuade the government to admit that they mostly have only two legs each, has given rise to a considerable amount of disquiet, controversy, criticism and kicking demonstrators in the head. It will be recalled that Cheekykaffir, who was twenty-two years old at the time of his death, was said by the Minister of Justice, Mr Sjambok-Goering, to have died of old age. Asked at a press conference how a man of twenty-two could die of old age, he said that he was himself a qualified doctor and had examined the body shortly before the murder, and it was quite clear to him that old age was the cause. 'All the signs of old age were present,' he said; 'a broken nose, torn ears, boot marks on his ribs, the lot. Anyway, the inquest decided that it was old age, which settles it.' At this, several reporters pointed out that the inquest had not been held, and the Minister explained that that had nothing to do with it. 'If we are going to wait for an inquest to be held before we announce its findings,' he said, 'our admirable and overworked police force would never have time to murder anybody at all.'

Next day, 417 leading doctors signed a statement saying that it was quite impossible for a man of twenty-two to die of old age, and the Minister was asked to comment. 'I never said he had died of old age,' snapped Mr Sjambok-Goering. 'I said quite clearly that it was a severe cold in the head.' A journalist (actually it was that horrible man Donald Woods,* who has in the past gone so

* Then Editor of the *East London Daily Dispatch;* he was subsequently 'banned' (that is, forbidden to work or write or associate with other people,

F

far as to suggest that it is somehow improper for South African police to throw suspects out of high windows) then reminded the Minister that he had claimed to have examined Cheekykaffir himself. 'Ah, yes,' said the Minister, 'but it appears there was some confusion. The body I examined was that of another man alto-gether – an easy mistake to make, after all, considering that the buggers all look the same anyway. Besides, don't forget I'm not a doctor – I'm only the Minister of Justice. I don't know anything about medicine – or justice, either, come to think of it.' Woods (for it was indeed he) then pointed out that the Minister, on the previous day, had said that he was a qualified physician, where-upon the Minister smiled wearily and explained that he had been trained as a doctor, but was subsequently struck off the register.

Next day, 8,124 doctors signed a statement saying that it was impossible for a man in Cheekykaffir's excellent state of fitness to die of a cold; at the same time, both the Pope and the Archbishop of Canterbury expressed anxiety at the circumstances of Cheeky-kaffir's death. Once more, the Minister was asked to comment, and explained that when he had said that the cause of death was a cold he had had no direct responsibility himself, but had been relying on the report submitted to him by the governor of the prison, Mr Thug-Deadman. (When Mr Thug-Deadman was asked about this, he replied that he had had no direct responsi-bility himself, but had been relying on the report submitted by Colonel Proudly-Swastika, police chief of the district in which the prison lay. When the Colonel was asked about this, he replied that he had had no direct responsibility himself, but had been relying on the report submitted to him by General Jack Bootz, head of the South African security services. When the General was asked about this, he replied that he had had no direct re-sponsibility himself, but had been relying on the report submitted

---

while it became a crime for any publication to quote any of his words) for his part in exposing the truth about the torture and murder of Steve Biko by the South African police, and the subsequent cover-up by the Minister of Justice, Mr James Kruger. It is, of course, to that case that this and the following column refer.

to him by the Prime Minister, Mr van der Scoundrel. When the Prime Minister was asked about this, he replied that he had had no direct responsibility himself, but had been relying on the report submitted to him by the Minister of Justice, Mr Sjambok-Goering.)

The Minister was then asked to comment on the Pope's statement. 'The Pope is a communist,' he replied; 'I thought everybody knew that.' 'But what about Archbishop Coggan?' he was asked; 'is he a communist, too?' The Minister curled his lip: 'Coggan?' he said; 'don't you know his real name is Cohen?' This, as may well be supposed, entirely disposed of the matter as far as all decent and reasonable people were concerned, but it was not enough for the loathsome Woods, who asked the Minister whether an independent judicial inquiry would be set up to examine all the circumstances of Cheekykaffir's death. The Minister first suggested to Mr Woods that he would do well to have himself examined by his own doctor for signs of a serious cold in the head, as well as old age. 'Something tells me', he went on, 'that you are in great danger of dying of one or the other quite soon. I mean, it is well known that people with colds often fall under motor cars, and the number of old people who put their heads in gas ovens without leaving a note – or indeed anything but signs of a struggle – is shockingly large.'* He then went on to take the wind out of the sails of the repulsive Woods by saying that not only would an independent inquiry be set up; it actually had been. 'And what is more', he continued triumphantly, 'it has already reported.'

The Minister informed the journalists that the members of the inquiry had been the Prime Minister (Mr van der Scoundrel), the head of South Africa's security services (General Jack Bootz), the police chief of the district in which the prison was situated (Colonel Proudly-Swastika), the governor of the prison (Mr Thug-Deadman), and himself. 'And in addition', he added, 'the

* No attempt was made on Woods's life by the South African police, but they did injure one of his children, after which he managed to escape from South Africa with his family.

inquiry had two ex-officio members, namely the policemen who actually murdered Cheekykaffir, and were therefore in a much better position to know what happened than any journalist.'

Asked to say how long the inquiry had taken, and what its findings had been, the Minister said that it had been set up immediately before Cheekykaffir had been arrested, and had reported the same afternoon – fully six days before he had died. 'I venture to say', he added, 'that few countries could equal that record of swiftness and efficiency. As for its findings, the inquiry concluded unanimously that Cheekykaffir died of measles – just as I told you.'

The Minister then went on to reveal that, at the time of Cheekykaffir's death, a number of charges against him were being prepared, on which he would shortly have been prosecuted. These charges included: damage to public property, viz, several police truncheons rendered almost useless by Cheekykaffir repeatedly striking them with his kidneys; unauthorized use of electricity, viz, the substantial amounts consumed through Cheekykaffir's genitals during police questioning; and failing to report an accident, viz, falling down three flights of iron stairs at police headquarters.

Stop Press: The condition of Donald Woods was today said by the Minister of Justice to be 'critical'. Asked to comment, Mr Woods said he had never felt better in his life. Asked to comment on Mr Woods's statement, the Minister said that he had been mis-reported. Mr Woods's condition was not yet critical, but was due to become so towards the end of the week.

The Times September 20th, 1977

... *Six feet under*

I REPORTED HERE A couple of months ago on the case of John Cheekykaffir, the South African black leader who was just about to be prosecuted for damaging several valuable police truncheons (by striking them repeatedly with various tender parts of his body) when he died, much to the regret of the policemen wielding the truncheons who, in the words of the Minister of Justice, Mr Sjambok-Goering, 'Hadn't had so much fun since they burnt down the Koffiefontein synagogue.'

At the time I wrote, my readers may recall, the inquest had not yet been held, and Mr Sjambok-Goering's disclosure of its findings, to the effect that Cheekykaffir had committed suicide while the balance of his mind, and indeed of his skull, kidneys and genitals, was disturbed, was therefore, as he was careful to point out, only provisional. 'When', he said, 'the inquest is finally held – and the Prime Minister (Mr van der Scoundrel) and I are working assiduously to find some means of avoiding it altogether – fuller details will be made available, including the magistrate's finding that the two policeman who killed him should be compensated by the surviving members of his family (we're working on the problem of their survival, of course) for the distress caused to them by Cheekykaffir's selfishly dying just when they had found a lovely new way of poking his eyes out.' The inquest was, as readers will know, concluded last week, and the magistrate, a Mr Mosley Bum-Hack, recorded his findings thus:

> I'm very glad about the wonderful election result here. Many of us South Africans are getting pretty sick of criticism from the rest of the world. I tell you, man, why don't they mind

their own business, eh? I mean, they're always complaining about how we don't treat the blacks so good here. Now you and I know that if I sent a couple of big policemen out into the street right now to ask a passing black man how he liked it here, they would come back five minutes later and report that he had said he liked it fine. Anyway, the bastards breed like rabbits. And another thing, man. How would you like one of them marrying your daughter, eh? And don't tell me that's not what they are after – I know better. Don't give me that Christianity stuff, either – what was the Pope's name before he changed it to Montini, eh? Mendelssohn, that's what – you can always tell by the frizzy hair. Case dismissed.

Mr Sjambok-Goering, the Minister of Justice, said after the verdict that he was very glad to have been vindicated in so striking a manner, particularly since the policemen who had actually killed Cheekykaffir had been vindicated in an even more striking manner.

'While I'm on the subject', he added, 'I want to clear up a misunderstanding. It has been widely reported that when I heard of Cheekykaffir's death I said "It leaves me cold".* I would like to make it clear that I have been misrepresented over this, though I think it was the result of a genuine mis-hearing. What sounded like "It leaves me cold", was actually "I am deeply, nay profoundly, distressed to hear of the death of this man in captivity. Of course, a full and searching inquiry must be carried out at once, and I shall leave no stone unturned to see that, if anything improper occurred, those responsible will be brought to book. We white South Africans have our differences with our black brethren – the bastards breed like rabbits, for a start – but I would never condone any ill-treatment of them – no stop it, I'll laugh – and indeed I regard them as my own children, which is hardly surprising since several of them are. But what I really want to

---

* The Minister of Justice, Mr James Kruger, did indeed say precisely that about Biko's death, to a gathering of Nationalist Party members, who greeted his comment with laughter.

stress is that it is the duty of every decent South African to vote Nationalist in the election".'

That, it was generally agreed, cleared the matter up completely. At least, it was agreed among all right-thinking persons, but the depraved and revolting Donald Woods (Editor of the *East London Daily Dispatch*) was, naturally, not content even with so comprehensive an explanation, and went on inconveniently revealing that the Minister of Justice was a liar and an accessory after the fact, until he had to be 'banned'. (This, as the Minister explained, was only a temporary measure; the banning order would be lifted as soon as Mr Woods's suicide had been arranged by the police.)

Another insatiable critic was the horrible Jewish lawyer, Mr Sydney Kentridge, who appeared for the Cheekykaffir family at the inquest, even though it had been carefully explained to him in advance that in the matter of Cheekykaffir's death no blame attached to anyone, except of course the dead man himself, his family and Donald Woods. Alas, some people are never satisfied, and Kentridge insisted on cross-examining various witnesses at the inquest, including the chief medical witness for the state, Dr George Auschwitz-Syringe.

Dr Auschwitz-Syringe, who agreed that he had been affectionately known since his student days as the Hypocritic Oaf, said that he had been called to Cheekykaffir's cell in the middle of the night, when he found him lying on the floor in a pool of blood, with two policemen sitting on him. Examination revealed that he had a ruptured spleen, five broken ribs, a punctured ear drum, extensive brain damage, bullet-holes in his knee-caps and a nasty cold. Asked what treatment he had given, Dr Auschwitz-Syringe said that he had suggested plenty of orange juice for the cold. 'And what about the rest of his condition?' asked the obtuse and malignant Kentridge. 'Oh,' said the doctor, 'I gave him a bang over the head to teach the bugger not to be so cheeky another time.' Roars of applause greeted this reply, which left the loathsome Kentridge, as may be imagined, entirely nonplussed.

Matters hardly went better for him when he cross-examined

the two policemen who had actually killed Cheekykaffir. He began by asking the magistrate to order the attendance, as witnesses, of the Minister of Justice, Mr Sjambok-Goering, and of the head of the South African security services, General Jack Bootz. The applications were refused, as was a similar demand for the production of the local police chief, Colonel Proudly-Swastika. 'These are very important and busy men,' said the magistrate, 'and anyway, what would be the point of calling them? All the necessary lies will be told by the doctors, the policemen and me – what more do you want?' But, protested the odious Kentridge, at the very least Colonel Proudly-Swastika should be called, as there was reason to suppose that it was he who had held Cheekykaffir's arms while he was being clubbed. 'Well, good God, man,' exploded the magistrate, 'somebody had to hold him, surely?'

After this, the policemen themselves had little difficulty in countering Kentridge's ridiculous questions. Asked how their fingerprints came to be on the handle of the truncheons, to the other end of which bits of Mr Cheekykaffir's brain were adhering, one of them replied 'I've no idea'. The laughter that greeted this sally had hardly died away when the other capped it by adding 'Neither have I'. Further questioning was then stopped by the magistrate, who said that asking the witnesses just what had happened while they had Cheekykaffir in their custody was completely irrelevant to the case. 'I must remind counsel', he said, 'that what we are here for is to ensure the maximum vote for the Nationalists in the election.' Then he delivered his findings, as quoted above, and the case concluded. So did Cheekykaffir, come to think of it.

The Times December 6th, 1977

We are the Old Masters now

A LETTER IN THE *Guardian* (alas, where else?), from a Mr John A. Walker, is very severe on Constable. Mr Walker likes Constable's paintings well enough – indeed he prefers them to those of Blake and Turner – but is deeply distressed by the fact that Constable 'was firmly on the side of the ruling classes'. Since, according to Mr Walker, Constable's 'class loyalty is evident in his paintings', there is no need to examine the artist's character, conduct or views for evidence of the claim; all we need to do – or, more exactly all Mr Walker needs to do – is to examine Constable's pictures, for it is well known that 'artworks mediate social relations' (and they not only mediate social relations, the clever little fellows, they also rhyme with 'partworks' and for that matter 'Can you tell me how the *à la carte* works?'), and if any further evidence were needed, it would be found in the 'highly suspect' fact (the suspicion is Mr Walker's, as is the height of it) of 'Constable's present immense popularity with the middle classes'.

Well, then, let us examine the 'artworks' of this capitalist hack for signs of his reactionary bourgeois deviationism. As soon as we do, the evidence springs to the eye – the eye of Mr Walker, anyway. For instance:

> Constable's family owned large tracts of Stour valley. Constable celebrated this property relationship by recording it for posterity: his family possessed the land, Constable took possession of its visual appearance.

Yes, indeed; anyone who has visited the countryside painted by this lickspittle lackey of the reactionary forces, whose present popularity with the middle classes is, rightly, so suspect, will have noticed that there are huge chunks missing from the landscape, where Constable 'took possession of its visual appearance', no doubt in order to deprive the working classes of the pleasure of looking at them. Nor is this an idle fancy, for Mr Walker complains particularly of Constable's attitude to agricultural workers; the hideous truth is that 'he never shows them burning ricks'.

Well, the filthy Fascist sod. There he was, painting agricultural labourers labouring agriculturally – hoeing, and raking, and ploughing, and no doubt even mulching, stooking and threshing – when everybody knows that all that sort of thing occupied only a tiny part of their time, the bulk of which was spent studying the works of Marx, Kim Il Sung and Mr Richard Gott,* correcting the errors of capitalist-roaders, working for the election of Miss Joan Maynard M.P. as Secretary to the Yorkshire Area of the National Union of Agricultural and Allied Workers, liquidating kulaks, fighting for the liberation of South Vietnam, seizing the vast latifundias of the East Anglian ranchers and turning them into collective farms, saving Czechoslovakia from counter-revolutionaries, and above all, burning ricks. (That is where we get the well known countryside rhymes: 'Red sky at night – rick's well alight'; 'Red sky at noon – revolution soon'; 'Red sky at dawn – the fuzz has withdrawn'.)

But that is not the worst of what this notorious hireling of the C.I.A. was capable of. It is, of course, obvious that, in Mr Walker's penetrating words, 'Constable's obsession with the sky can be seen as an unconscious desire to avert his eyes from the real social conditions' (for 'while he contemplated the heavens he could ignore the toilers on the earth'), but what not even Mr Walker knows, and what I can exclusively reveal after reading the suppressed passages from Constable's diary (suppressed by the capitalists as too embarrassing to their cause), is that Constable's

* Parlour-Marxist Latin-American expert of the *Guardian* and Penguin Books, and general chronicler of fun-revolutionary activities. Known as 'Gusher' Gott.

'desire to avert his eyes from the real social conditions' by means of his 'obsession with the sky' was not unconscious at all, but very explicit. Take this entry of June 12th, 1821:

> Goodness, how I loathe the working classes! Such nasty people, with such horrid habits—I'm sure it's their own fault that they're not rich like me. And to think that some silly people expect me to paint pictures of them! How on earth would they pay me? And say what you like—I only paint for the money, after all, just like Rembrandt and Tintoretto and Van Gogh. Oh dearie me, no, you won't catch me putting all those frightful oiks into my pictures—in fact I make a point, whenever I meet one of them, of looking up at the sky to take my mind off him.

Another thing that rightly causes Mr Walker to condemn Constable's failure to join the struggle for the nationalization of the means of production, distribution and exchange is his total lack of appreciation of the importance of the dictatorship of the proletariat. Constable, he declares indignantly, often put workers into his pictures 'to balance a composition', a sin, as I am sure all fair-minded readers will agree, scarcely less indicative of membership of the 'highly suspect' middle classes than a wish to balance the Budget. Worse, the workers in Constable's paintings

> wear red jackets in order to enhance the complementary contrast with the green setting.

No doubt some members of the middle classes (or *Waffen S.S.*, as they are better known) believe, or profess to believe, that Constable tended to put a labourer in a red jacket into a painting of a green field either because when he was painting the scene there was a labourer in a red jacket in the field in question, or because if he had painted a labourer in a green jacket in a green field the labourer might have become invisible. This only goes to show how fitting it is that the reactionary Constable's pictures should be so popular today with the middle classes, so alike was he to them, in his callous indifference to the principles of socialist-realism in 'artwork'.

Mind you, though Mr Walker does not mention it, Constable was by no means alone among celebrated artists in his bland neglect of his duty to the class struggle. Veronese frequently painted members of the aristocracy with pleasant expressions on their faces; van Ostade no less often suggested that members of the working classes sometimes got drunk, without making it clear that this was only because of the capitalists' exploitation of their labour and their consequent misery; Renoir was a member of the National Front; Velasquez was known to speak lightly of the Socialist Workers' Party; Rubens had a bank account in the Cayman Islands and Titian shares in several multinational companies; Giotto was racially prejudiced; Dürer rhymes with Führer; Mantegna voted for Nixon as President in 1968 and Fragonard for Roy Jenkins in the Labour leadership election; Van Dyck was a male chauvinist pig; and as for the Douanier Rousseau, *he was a member of the middle classes.*

To expose all the reactionary activities of all these would be a lifetime's artwork; we are fortunate indeed that Mr Walker has at least made a start by branding Constable as the enemy of the working classes that he was. Incidentally, it is not generally known that 'John Constable' was not his real name; he was originally called 'Engels Toilingmasses', but changed his name to signify his willing identification with the apparatus of state oppression.

The Times June 18th, 1976

Yours faithfully, Disgusted, Q.C.

(So many letters to this newspaper protesting against the editorial criticisms of Sir Peter Rawlinson, the Attorney-General, have been received, that there has been space in the correspondence columns to print only a very small proportion of them. In the circumstances, the Editor has asked me if I could accommodate a further selection of them in my column, and I am happy to accede to his request.)

From Sir Thieving Rogue, Q.C.

Sir,

Your present campaign against the Attorney-General is disgraceful. You clearly do not realize that to criticize lawyers – poor, defenceless, furry little things, unable to answer back or even to raise a hand in their own protection – is akin to treason. Indeed, it is worse than treason, for treason strikes only at the safety of the realm, whereas criticism of lawyers might easily, given the present unsettled state of the country, lead ultimately to a reduction in their incomes, or even to their being held accountable to their customers.

Yours faithfully,

413a Pump Court,   THIEVING ROGUE
EC4

From Mr Conman Peruke, Q.C.

Sir,

Your present campaign against the Attorney-General is disgraceful. I have known him for thirty-seven years, and in all that time I have never known him depart by a hair's breadth from something or other.

I am, Sir, his obedient servant,

911 Paper Buildings,   CONMAN PERUKE
EC4

From Mr Disbard Wigawry, Q.C.

Sir,

Your present campaign against the Attorney-General is disgraceful. I have frequently been present at cases in which Sir Peter has been involved, and on every occasion I was firmly of the opinion that he was rightly acquitted.

Yours faithfully,

2001 Brick Court,   DISBARD WIGAWRY
EC4

From Mr I. M. Wrightly-Briefless

Sir,

Your present campaign against the Attorney-General is disgraceful. At this rate, you'll be attacking Lord Goodman next.

Yours faithfully,

I. M. WRIGHTLY-BRIEFLESS

Eventide Home for Impoverished Lawyers,
Carshalton Beeches,
Surrey

From Mr Moe the Slasher

Sir,

Yore presunt campane against the Atturny-Jenrall is dissgraysfull. Forteen yeers ago e difendid me on a charj of parkin on a yeller line (I shall be gettin out next yeer), and evry yeer e orlways sends me a card at Christmas.

Yores trewly,

1478653209 Parkhurst,   MOE THE SLASHER
Isle of Wight

From the Hon. Sec., the Society for the
Protection of Sir Peter Rawlinson

Sir,

Your present campaign against the Attorney-General is disgraceful. Only a year ago, two leading members of this organization – Sir David Renton, Q.C., M.P., and Mr Michael
Havers, Q.C., M.P. – found it necessary to write you a letter
listing in detail the numerous attacks made upon Sir Peter
Rawlinson during an earlier, no less disgraceful, campaign by
the deplorable Mr Levin. (Mr Havers has since been given a
knighthood and made Solicitor-General: why hasn't Sir David
Renton got anything, eh? I mean, fair's fair, what? You know,
spread it about a bit, see what I mean? Well, then.) Your
readers may care to know that that letter was incorporated into
a paper by Sir David Renton and Mr Michael Havers, read to
the Annual General Meeting of this Society and subsequently
reprinted in the Society's Journal under the title 'Criticism of
Lawyers: Why it Must at All Costs (Preferably against the
Defendant) be Prevented'. So far from this serving to silence
Mr Levin, he has since had the impudence to suggest, in a
column published on November 28th, 1972, that he is in some
way related to Sir Peter, referring to 'my celebrated ancestor,
the Rabbi Moishe Ben-Rawlinson'. And now I hear that Mr
Levin has been going about London making the most dreadful
and defamatory allegations against the Attorney-General,
accompanying them with a recitation of all the previous
charges, and finishing the performance with a series of
extremely indecent limericks, the least disgusting of which
begins

> I cheered on the day that Sir Peter
> Was arrested for feeding the meter ...

It is clear, Sir, from your present conduct, that you have
throughout encouraged Mr Levin in his behaviour, if, indeed,

you did not instigate it. You both ought to be ashamed of
yourselves.

Yours truly,

RABBI MOISHE BEN-RAWLINSON

Honorary Secretary, Society for Protection of Sir Peter
Rawlinson,
Thieves' Kitchen,
Balham Broadway,
SW12

From Mr Jarndyce Pettifogger, Q.C.

Sir,

Your present campaign against the Attorney-General is disgraceful. Some of the things you have said in the course of it
are tantamount to suggesting that he is not only wrong but
impervious to argument as well – charges as unjustified as they
are scandalous. Mind you, I couldn't help laughing.

Yours faithfully,

789 Essex Court, JARNDYCE PETTIFOGGER
EC4

From Mr Pettifogger Jarndyce, Q.C.

Sir,

Your present campaign against the Attorney-General is disgraceful. You are obviously no lawyer, or you would realize
that to criticize a lawyer is conduct beyond the bounds of
civilized behaviour. No lawyer would do such a thing.

Yours truly,

$333\frac{3}{4}$ Lincoln's Inn, PETTIFOGGER JARNDYCE
EC4

From Sir Blackguardly Garrick-Member, Q.C.

Sir,

Your present campaign against the Attorney-General is disgraceful. If you go on with it, I can foresee the day when you

will not hesitate to quote the remark of Lord Chief Justice Parker (see *The Cecil King Diary*, p. 214) to the effect that 'The Conservatives have no one in politics on their side fit to be Lord Chancellor, Attorney-General, or Solicitor-General', and to add that Lord Parker was clearly right. Oh, yes, you would; it is no use your protesting that you wouldn't. 'Lord Parker said that the Conservatives have no one fit to be Lord Chancellor, Attorney-General, or Solicitor-General', you would say, adding 'and he didn't half hit the nail on the head when he said it'. No, no, don't come the raw prawn with me, my man; I know what sort of scoundrel you are – the sort of scoundrel who would quote Lord Chief Justice Parker's remark that 'The Conservatives have no one fit to be Lord Chancellor, Attorney-General, or Solicitor-General' and would go on to indicate your complete agreement with Lord Parker. And even if you yourself shrank from quoting Lord Chief Justice Parker's statement that 'The Conservatives have no one fit to be Lord Chancellor, Attorney-General, or Solicitor-General' and expressing wholehearted agreement with Lord Parker's view, you are certainly capable of egging on the odious Mr Levin to say it instead. And we all know what he would make of it! 'Lord Chief Justice Parker's opinion', he would declare, 'was that the Conservatives have no one fit to be Lord Chancellor, Attorney-General, or Solicitor-General', and he would almost certainly add something like 'and in my opinion the old boy understated the case, if anything'.

Yours faithfully,

472b New Square,   BLACKGUARDLY GARRICK-MEMBER
EC4

From Mr Robin Steele, Q.C.

Sir,

Your present campaign against the Attorney-General is disgraceful. I have been closely acquainted with Sir Peter's professional record for a good many years, and I can assure you that as a lawyer he ranks second, in my experience only to Sir Geoffrey Howe, Q.C., whose brilliant, meticulous and watertight drafting of the Industrial Relations Act 1971 has been responsible for the present harmonious and delightful state of Britain's industrial relations.

Yours truly,

608 Clement's Inn,   ROBIN STEELE
EC4

From Mr Nick Pinchan-Pillfah, Q.C.

Sir,

Your present campaign against the Attorney-General is disgraceful. Is there no limit to the scurrility and baselessness of your charges against this noble and upright public servant? What will you call him next, I wonder? 'A calamity'? 'A disaster'? 'A catastrophe'? 'A right nana'? 'A gurt booby'? 'A member of the Government who makes Mr James Prior look like a combination of Einstein and Gladstone'?

Yours faithfully,

1003 King's Bench Walk,   NICK PINCHAN-PILLFAH
EC4

From Sir Knavely Picquepocquet, Q.C.

Sir,

Your present campaign against the Attorney-General is disgraceful. *The Times* is certainly not a paper I would wish my wife or servants to read.

Yours truly,

c/o Common Serjeants' Mess,   KNAVELY PICQUEPOCQUET
EC4

The Times July 10th, 1973

The letter of the law

(I hope the Editor is not going to make a habit of this, but he has once again asked me, pleading extreme pressure on the space available for correspondence, to accommodate in my column a selection of letters—this time on the recent speech by Sir Robert Mark*—for which no room can be found in the normal position on the page opposite. In view of the importance of the subject, I have reluctantly agreed.)

From Sir Preposterous Attorney, Q.C.

Sir,

When will people like Sir Robert Mark learn that criticism of lawyers cannot and must not be permitted? And the reason is a very simple and practical one. It is not that lawyers are in some mystical way sacrosant (though they are), nor that the slightest criticism of them will almost certainly lead to the total destruction of civilization as we know it (though it will); it is that lawyers, by reason of their training and the character with which they are imbued by it, are simply unable to do wrong. It makes no more sense to talk of a 'crooked lawyer' than it does to refer to a 'square circle'. Just as there is not, and cannot be, such a thing as a square circle, so there is not, never has been, and never could be, any such thing as a lawyer

---

* Then Commissioner of the Metropolitan Police. He had made a speech in which he suggested that some criminal lawyers were criminal in both senses of the word. The response of the legal profession was every bit as ridiculous as my parodies, and in some instances more so.

who would, in any circumstances, do wrong. You do not have to take my word for it, either; ask any lawyer.

Yours faithfully,

333¾ Lincoln's Inn, EC4   PREPOSTEROUS ATTORNEY, Q.C.

From Mr Understandably Shifty, Q.C.

Sir,

The suggestion by Sir Robert Mark that we lawyers should ourselves seek out and deal with the crooked ones among us is absurd; how on earth would we find the time to make money if we carried on like that?

Yours faithfully,

777 Crown Office Row, EC4   UNDERSTANDABLY SHIFTY, Q.C.

From Sir Grand Larceny, Q.C.

Sir,

The attack on the legal profession by Sir Robert Mark is doubly deplorable. In the first place it is, of course, utterly without substance. But even if there were something in it, Sir Robert has no right to attack a body of men who are entirely without the means of reply. It is well known that lawyers are wholly inarticulate, that they are timid and retiring souls who are quite unwilling to engage in any form of public controversy, and that they are in any case precluded from answering back. They are forbidden, for instance, to write letters to the newspapers, to appear on radio or television programmes, or indeed to defend themselves in any way, however serious the charges made against them. Nor can they hope for redress elsewhere; the House of Commons, for instance – usually quick to take up the cause of so many injured or insulted groups – will certainly not say a word, containing as it does at present only some 160 lawyers.

Yours faithfully,

1289 Essex Street,   GRAND LARCENY, Q.C.
Temple, EC4

From Mr Only Line-Pockets, Q.C.

Sir,

A number of my legal brethren have already, faced with Sir Robert Mark's baseless, absurd and defamatory allegations against lawyers, made a devastating and utterly unanswerable reply, to the effect that if he tells us precisely whom he has in mind we will take whatever action we feel like. But this does not, in my opinion, go far enough. Sir Robert should make his specific allegations public, naming names and giving addresses, in the utmost detail; moreover, he should take care to see that the occasion on which he does this is in no way 'privileged', and he should, if possible, make several unimportant but easily detectable mistakes of fact. If he could manage to confuse two lawyers of the same name, so much the better, and if at the same time he would undertake to offend and antagonize a wide selection of High Court Judges, that would be best of all.

Yours truly,

2135 King's Bench Walk, ONLY LINE-POCKETS, Q.C.
Temple, EC4

From Sir Ratlike Countenance, Q.C.

Sir,

Once again it is necessary to explain to the public – this time because of Sir Robert Mark's scandalous and unjustified allegations – just how the legal profession works. Sir Robert insinuates that we lawyers are willing to tell a pack of lies in court for money: but I can refute this charge – as ridiculous as it is false – quite conclusively. Every lawyer is perfectly willing to tell the truth for money, or even to shut up entirely for money. Indeed, some even prefer to, other things (the money, for instance) being equal.

Yours faithfully,

961 Pump Court, RATLIKE COUNTENANCE, Q.C.
Temple, EC4

From Mr Merciless Extortioner, Q.C.

Sir,

I can answer Sir Robert Mark's unjustified attack on the legal
profession, finally and incontrovertibly, in a single phrase:
*Necesse est, qui sibi non sapit, optat ephippia bos piger, sed nobis a
cum semel occidit quas neque lugeri neque plangi fas est in mare fundis
aquas, verbum impelle perit.*

I trust that will put an end to the argument.

Yours truly,

555¼ Fountain Court,   MERCILESS EXTORTIONER, Q.C.
Temple,
EC4

From Sir Unmitigated Swine, Q.C.

Sir,

Once again all the old, exploded, ignorant charges against
lawyers are trotted out; I wonder that Sir Robert Mark actually
failed to repeat the hoary legend that lawyers, contrary to the
rules of their profession, do in fact pick and choose among
cases. Now let him try to find a counsel if he should himself
be charged with a criminal offence, that's all!

Yours faithfully,

999 Middle Temple Lane,   UNMITIGATED SWINE, Q.C.
Temple,
EC4

From Mr Extremely Bent, Q.C.

Sir,

The disgraceful speech by Sir Robert Mark, in which he suggested that some lawyers are little better than the criminals they
represent, shows how little he knows or understands of the
matter. Lawyers are a fine, upstanding body of men, engaged
only in turning an honest penny or—should this be for any
reason unattainable—a dishonest penny, or several thousand

pounds, honest or dishonest, or even more if they can get it, and they usually can, and what's more should, and if you knew the price of wigs you would agree, and as for paperclips you should see what's happened to the price of paperclips lately, and then we're begrudged the right to make money, and when I say money I mean nothing but a lousy sixty thou or so for a really complicated case, and there aren't many crooks about these days who can come across with even that sort of lolly, I can tell you — why, some of the lads have had to take to a bit of safe-blowing themselves to make ends meet, and then there's the risk from the gelignite, you can easily lose a whole hand, and all this bleeding copper can do is criticize, well, let me tell him that one or two of us aren't going to take that lying down, oh dear no, and Sir Robert Nark or whatever he calls himself had better watch it, that's all, a nod's as good as a wink and how can you prove a bloke carrying a razor isn't taking it home to shave with, eh?

Yours truly,

789 Paper Buildings,   EXTREMELY BENT, Q.C.
Temple,
EC4

The Times November 13th, 1973

Broken on the wheel

THE HEADLINES IN which Sir Hugh Fraser has recently found himself clad are not the kind that most of us would feel very happy about wearing, and I do not suppose Sir Hugh has enjoyed them either. (I think I had better pause here for a moment, in view of the extraordinary number of otherwise apparently well-informed people who manage to confuse the two, to make clear that the Hugh Fraser who owns Harrods, who was recently criticized very severely for his share dealings, and who has now told the world that in the last year or two he has lost one and a half million pounds at the gaming tables, is not the Hugh Fraser who is a Tory M.P. and who has borne his own recent appearance in headlines of a different and domestic character with Stoic dignity and fortitude.)*

I am not concerned with Sir Hugh's buying and selling of shares, or his actions and dealings in running his companies, which are not matters that interest me and about which I know little. What does interest me enough to want to write about it is a phrase which you read in the parenthesis above and no doubt dismissed as a misprint. But it was not a misprint; Sir Hugh Fraser has just gambled away *one and a half million pounds*.

This suggests, apart from anything else, an assiduity quite out of the ordinary. Sir Hugh's particular passion was roulette (I shall come to the implications of that fact in a moment), and all roulette tables have rigidly fixed maximum stakes. The higher the odds, obviously, the lower the permitted maximum; thus, you

* This referred to the break-up of his marriage.

can bet substantially on the 'even' chances (in fact, of course, there are no even chances at roulette, which is why it is much better to be a casino operator than a punter), and progressively less as you go down to the *en plein*, in which you stake on a single, unprotected number, and on which, therefore, the highest sum you can stake is comparatively small. But Sir Hugh has also confessed that it was his invariable practice to bet on a single number; he has indeed even told us what the number was – thirty-two. To get, in this fashion, through three times as many jimmy-o'goblins as there are miles in a round trip to the moon and back might be thought a lifetime's occupation; Sir Hugh managed it, as he has also told us, in a year and a half.

Let us do the arithmetic. The rate is a million quid a year, or roughly twenty thousand a week. No doubt Sir Hugh could not play every week; no doubt he could not, in the weeks in which he did play, manage to play every night; no doubt, on many of his nights at the tables, he had other engagements that made it impossible for him to stay long.

It seems impossible. Indeed, it *is* impossible, and Sir Hugh has explained how he managed it; he would play on several tables – as many as five – simultaneously, making his rounds from one to another, to enable him to lose enough, in the time at his disposal, to satisfy his craving.

Which, of course, is what this discussion is all about. Sir Hugh's unassuageable need to lose money (it is the losing that the true sufferer craves, not the thrill, and still less the chance of winning) is a disease in no fundamental way different from dipsomania or heroin addiction, both of which are means of self-destruction to which the sufferer is driven by whatever urges, failings and un-resolved conflicts are buried deep within him, and which he is himself quite unable to recognize without skilled professional assistance.

Gambling-mania is not confined to the rich, though except when one of the less expensive Sunday newspapers is doing a series on housewives who have become addicted to bingo, it is the spectacular losses of people like Sir Hugh Fraser that provide the talking-point. But let us have no moralizing, and above all no political cant. Sir Hugh's addiction led him to throw away gigantic sums; but the nature of his addiction was identical to that of the poor man who gambles away his wage-packet and pawns the furniture to go on gambling after his wage-packet has gone. Indeed, there is no evidence that Sir Hugh's addiction, unlike that of the poorer addict, has hurt anybody but himself. Any temptation to declare that Sir Hugh's losses demonstrate the need for further taxes on the rich should be resisted; he did not gamble because he was rich, but because he was addicted.

'Lord, I thank thee that I am not as other men are'; anybody thinking anything like that as he contemplates Sir Hugh Fraser's fate has understood nothing. The only correct response is the equally celebrated but opposite one: 'There, but for the grace of God, go I'. At which point I step into the witness box myself.

I believe that, except perhaps under the stress of severe mental breakdown or some similar catastrophe, I could never be in danger of addiction to alcohol or drugs. I have two built-in defences against the former, in that I do not like the taste of spirits and that after more than a moderate quantity of any form of alcohol I feel sufficiently sick to be unable to continue; I am likewise guarded against the danger of addictive drugs by my unceasing and limitless wonder at the fact that people should want to take the risks of inhaling or injecting strange substances into themselves, simply in order to experience a momentary feeling of inexpressible well-being, when they could get the same feeling at an even more exalted level, with no attendant danger and for considerably longer periods, simply by putting Act Three of *Parsifal* on the gramophone.

Yet I know very well that, if circumstances (within as well as without) conspired against me, I could fall helpless into the thrall of gambling. Betting on horses is so boring a pastime that I could never get into the clutches of the habit; I go to the dogs about once a year, but I go for an evening's entertainment rather than for the wagering, and am in any case protected against mishap by observing all around me, with the greatest possible hilarity, evidence that there really are people who believe that any one dog has a better chance of winning a race than any other.

But when I walk through the door of a casino, I know that I am in danger, which is why I walk through the doors of casinos very rarely indeed; never in this country, and when abroad only if I am there on holiday and can be sure of being in a light-hearted mood, though even so I take great care to leave behind at the hotel most of the money with me.

To an addict, of course, those precautions would be laughably insufficient. But I am not an addict; only a potential one. And because whenever I get near a roulette wheel I can recognize in myself the urge, the poisoned excitement, the weakening of control, the temptation that drives me towards the cliff, I am the more inclined to sympathize with those who, like Sir Hugh Fraser, have been driven towards that cliff and fallen over.

It has to be roulette; had to, for Sir Hugh. Roulette is one of the few casino games at which it is impossible to win, not just unlikely. Of course, in any form of gambling – horses, dice, *chemin de fer* – the player will lose in the long run. But at roulette, because of the zero, you cannot win even in the short run; a mere hour at the tables is too much. That is why Sir Hugh chose roulette, rather than, say, backgammon or poker, at which it is possible to display greater skill than other players and thus win, or betting on horses, at which it is certainly possible (though very unlikely indeed) to keep ahead of the game for some time, or chemmy, where it is possible (though even more unlikely) to make a giant killing very quickly. Roulette is the destroyer, which is why those who seek this form of destruction play it; turning that principle upside down, I find that in a casino – even an American one, where the variety of games is much larger than in other countries – it is only the roulette room that is of the slightest interest to me, and that one is of far too much interest for my own comfort.

There is an organization called Gamblers Anonymous, and I believe it has achieved considerable success in enabling sufferers to at any rate control their addiction by keeping away from the places and circumstances of temptation: to cure the addiction, by removing the craving itself, is much more difficult. But I believe that, as with other addictions, no treatment will be efficacious for long unless somewhere in the sufferer there is the will, however weak, deeply buried and hard to get at, to break the terrible habit. I do not know whether Sir Hugh Fraser has that will, or whether, if not, he can acquire it. But I wish him well in his attempt.

The Times December 8th, 1976

Growing up with Dada

Revolutionaries without Revolution by André Thirion*

'I<small>T'S THE SURREALISTS</small>!' That was the cry, designed to strike terror into the stoutest heart, that rang round many a fashionable Paris rendezvous when Dada was king, and when the important thing about the game of *épater les bourgeois* was to ensure that they were in no doubt that they were being *épatés*:

> Char went in first, met the bouncer head on, lifted him up, and threw him against the screen ... The screen came crashing down, some windows were broken, and the four of us – Char, Breton, Noll and myself – stood facing the supper guests. The others – Aragon, Elsa, Eluard, Sadoul, Tanguy and his wife – had stayed outside. Supper had already been served at the little tables; the guests were seated, their glasses were filled with champagne. The women were all in evening gowns ... I violently tore the tablecloths away, flinging down the plates, glasses, bottles and champagne buckets, kicking over the tables and chairs ... the Princess's guests took fright and fled screaming ... I hurled a few bottles at the bartender ... Sadoul was methodically pulling the glass fragments out of the door; he realised that in a few seconds we would be thrown through that exit and decided, quite properly, that getting shredded en route wouldn't do us much good ... Char had a knife wound in his thigh; he accused the bartender of having stabbed him while he was trying to shake off his first adversary. Aragon and Eluard immediately pointed out what a dirty trick this was ...

* Cassell, 1976.

This amazing and absorbing book, of which that is an entirely typical paragraph, is by a man who spent the time between the wars patrolling the boundary between Surrealism and Marxism, lurching unsteadily back and forth across it; he has chronicled *la vie bohème* from a unique vantage-point, for he was himself not only one of the founders of the Surrealist movement but also a leading figure in the French Communist Party, and he knew everybody in the world of both the artistic and political *avant-gardes*. Louis Aragon, André Breton, Max Jacob, Tristan Tzara, Jacques Prévert, Georges Antheil, Raymond Queneau, Darius Milhaud, Nancy Cunard, Salvador Dali ('He absolutely needed an expert and loving woman who would remain undaunted by his penchant for masturbation ... ') Man Ray, Maurice Thorez, Marcel Cachin, Léon Blum – all these and literally dozens more rush in and out of the pages, living jumbled up in a kind of warren, dashing off manifestos, devouring (or being devoured by) women, fighting, drinking, and above all talking, though even at the cafés where Aragon and Breton held court there were certain observances:

> There was a hierarchy of apéritifs. All the anises, pernods, and so on, made up the aristocracy; their drinkers periodically re-regretted the long-standing prohibition of absinthe. Bitters were also held in high esteem, especially Mandarin curacao ... vermouths were tolerated with reservations ...

At times the names rain down so thick and fast, and the poems, paintings and politics are so thick on the ground, that the reader is put in mind of the scene at Beachcomber's *La Brebis Qui Tousse*, and it is difficult to remember that what Thirion is describing he saw for himself. But there is never a moment's doubt that he did; this is the testament of a superbly honest man who records his doubts, his compromises, his betrayals, dishonesties and defeats with the same clear-eyed and unsentimental self-knowledge that he brings to the discussion of his triumphs.

But his book is more than a dazzling and obviously authentic portrait of its era; it is also the story of one man's search for truth, a search which took him through years of lies, and led him eventually to the rejection not merely of the odious Stalinism of the French C.P., but of Marxism in all its guises, when he finally 'sensed that the world was less simple than the schemes in which I wish to enclose it'.

The two men who dominate his pages, as they have dominated his life, are Aragon and Breton, and the portraits of both are masterpieces of observation, understanding and charity. This last quality is particularly necessary in contemplating Aragon, whose artistic and political life was one long succession of betrayals – of his art, his principles, his colleagues, his friends and above all himself – all for the privilege of licking Stalin's boots. Nothing does Thirion extenuate, nor does he set down aught in malice; his judgments are almost always implied, not stated, and if they were stated ten times over his judgments on himself would justify them:

> The moral rigour on Rue Fontaine, which grew tougher and tougher, tended to preserve the solipsism of each individual and the purity of the whole group. Nearly all material support was condemned; work was scorned, and journalistic or quasi-artistic activities amounted to treason. Everyone's associations were closely examined, and trouble-makers, spies, or pigs were found everywhere. Max Ernst and Miró were insulted for agreeing to do ballet sets. Artaud was reproached for being an actor, and Vitrac for writing and producing plays ...

That so Balkan a figure should get involved in a real Balkan adventure was inevitable; he went to Bulgaria to abduct his mistress from her husband, and succeeded in a manner *plus surréal que le Surréalisme*. But that was true of everything he did; his war service (in the Middle East), his Resistance activities, even his final apotheosis as a Gaullist local councillor, all seem to have been part of some pataphysical activity on a giant scale. (During the rising by the Paris Resistance, in August 1944, his group's task was to take over the municipal offices in the nineteenth *arrondissement*; they accomplished it, only to find a couple who were waiting there to get married. So the *franc-tireurs* assumed the power to bind and loose, and promptly married them.)

André Thirion seems to have found peace at last, and few readers of this tremendous book will begrudge it him. But one or two might:

Next, according to a well-established Surrealist rite, we went to the church. It was deserted, so we conscientiously pissed into the holy-water basins, filled the collection box with pebbles, and filched all the ornaments on the altar, including the crucifix. Opening the tabernacle, we removed the ciborium, which was filled with consecrated wafers. That was a fine caper. At the general store, we bought the paper, cardboard, and string that we needed to make up a solid package, and we mailed the whole batch to Monsieur Louis Aragon, poet, 54 rue du Château, Paris.

Observer May 2nd, 1976

It takes two to tango

THE IMMINENT ARRIVAL of *Last Tango in Paris* has caused various interested parties to take up prepared positions, tin hats atop and lances couched, and to prepare themselves for dying in the last ditch or rolling in the last gutter, depending on which way you look at it. What the nation wants to know, however, is where I stand on the subject, so I had better make it clear right away that I don't. I may have been known as Reckless Jack Levin in my days on the North-West Frontier, but I know enough to come in out of the rain, and I am therefore writing this column sitting under my desk; that crash of broken glass may have just been somebody dropping a milk bottle, but on the other hand it may not, and I am taking no chances. What is more, I have brought with me under the desk my passport and a small hand-mirror, so that as the bombardment proceeds over my head I can from time to time remind myself of the glorious fact that, since I am British, white and over eighteen, there is no law, actual or conceivable, that can compel me to go and see the film; nor shall I do so.

The fact is, I have always been of the opinion that there was a good deal to be said for the false Etruscan:

> ... who lingers in his home,
> When Porsena of Clusium
> Is on the march for Rome

but I have also long had a good deal of sympathy with the hither-to undiscovered false Roman, who suddenly found himself

G

afflicted by deafness when Horatio started asking who would stand on either hand and keep the bridge with him. That great and good woman, Nancy Banks-Smith,* discussing a play in which a gallant but outnumbered force declared 'If we go forward we die, if we go back we die, so let us go forward and die', was moved to ask, 'Why not go sideways and live?', and I might as well now stop shilly-shallying and say I don't think it matters a damn if *Last Tango in Paris* is banned in Chipping Campden, Barnsley and Alloa or not.

As I have fairly frequently made clear, I am on the whole against censorship of any kind, which is a great deal more than can be said for most of the more outspoken opponents of censorship, who are certainly not against the kind imposed by Section 6 of the Race Relations Act 1965. But I really do not see why I should go down the line for the right of Marlon Brando to simulate improprieties with his trousers on any more than for the right of Mrs Whitehouse to attempt to stop this sight being publicly seen. I have not the slightest respect for either of them, and I am unwilling to pretend that the freedom of true-born Britons will be advanced or retarded in the smallest degree whichever of them wins.

There is, of course, a sense in which freedom is indivisible, but that sense must be carefully defined and not extended unjustifiably. If you ask me simply whether I think *Last Tango in Paris* ought to be banned from our cinema screens, I obviously answer that it should not, but if you ask me whether it should be shown, I answer that I do not care, and if you ask whether I am prepared to lift a finger to ensure that it is *not* banned, let alone that it *is* shown, I answer that I certainly am not, partly because life is too short and energy likewise, and partly because if you go on the principle of leaping into battle every time somebody blows up a paper bag and bursts it, you will finally become, not to mince words, something like Mr George Melly, a fate which, amiable and engaging character though he is, I would not wish on any-

* Television critic of the *Guardian*.

body with a head needed for purposes more exacting than stuffing pillows with.*

Not everything matters. This vital truth has been almost shuffled out of existence, never mind sight, in recent years, and it must be brought back and embroidered on our oriflamme (oriflamme, Mr Melly, not orifice). It is no use saying that if you give the White-houses an inch from Mr Brando they will take a foot from Mr Tynan, and subsequently a yard and a half from Shakespeare. We must pick our battlegrounds with considerably more care and discrimination than has lately been the fashion, because – apart from anything else – if freedom in these matters really is indivisible, it will be damaged in the important areas by a defeat in the unimportant ones.

This, of course, will seem very shocking to the all-or-nothing merchants. But the all-or-nothing merchants have never under-stood the importance of tactics. What matters is victory, not victory by ten points to none; seven-three is quite sufficient. Let us put the case for *Last Tango in Paris* at its very highest – let us say that it is a great work of art, made with the most impeccable integrity and the loftiest ideals, and purging the spectator of anger, pride and self by its compassion for the tragic predicament of mankind (good grief, I'm writing Mr Melly's review for him). Let us say all that, and add that Signor Bertolucci† and Mr Brando are giving every penny they make from it to the Pit Ponies' Protection Society. Now: will anybody really sleep more, or less, easily o' nights because it can, or cannot, be shown at the moment in the Essoldo, Kirkby Lonsdale? Does anybody believe that, even if it is banned, it will remain banned for more than another year or so, or that in the meanwhile countless great artists will be so disheartened by its fate that they will abandon their vocation and start life anew as computer programmers? I leave out of account the other half of the argument – that if it is freely shown nobody

* Mr Melly is a man of many gifts, as jazz singer, film critic, autobio-grapher and art-collector. But a sense of proportion, and an understanding of politics, have never been conspicuous among his talents.
† Director of the film.

seriously believes, for all the yelling and screaming, that there will instantly be a collapse of moral standards so widespread and disastrous that it will end in a mass rape of the Women's Advisory Council on Solid Fuel – because I think it is more important to warn my own side of the dangers of exaggeration than the other. But if we go into the complete *arc-en-ciel* because Mr Murphy* has removed the butter ('I told you butter wouldn't suit the works',)† or even because Councillor Smith‡ has removed the entire film, what valid response, worthy to be taken seriously, shall we have the next time it is necessary to fight for a Zola, a D. H. Lawrence, or an Ibsen? If, that is, there ever are any more Zolas or Lawrences or Ibsens; I have a gloomy feeling that de-valuation of the artistic currency can take more than one form, and that it is not absolutely impossible that at least two forms are involved in the fuss over *Last Tango in Paris*. And that, friends, is my last word on the subject.

The Times February 20th, 1973

---

* Then chief film censor.
† Butter is used in the film for a very rude purpose.
‡ I don't remember who he was; presumably he had wished to ban the film in his municipality.

Goodbye, Mr Clips

YOU WILL THINK I am making a fuss about nothing, but you will be wrong. For today is the day of retirement for the man who has cut my hair for more than a dozen years, and although he has left me in hands which he assures me are no less skilled than his own, an assurance which I have no reason to doubt, I cannot help feeling distinctly bereft.

He first plied his magic scissors about my crown at Fortnum and Mason; before that I had been fickle in my choice of hairdresser, flitting at fairly short intervals from one to another. But when I decided to try Fortnum's, and made an appointment accordingly, fate, through the good offices of the receptionist at the Fortnum's saloon, dealt me Mr Herbert East, 'since when I have used no other'. Nor ever felt inclined to, for Mr East has, with tact as well as art, imposed regular order on my locks in a manner which I have found entirely satisfactory, and when, some seven years ago, he moved from Fortnum's to Truefitt and Hill, I tucked my head underneath my arm and followed him across Piccadilly without hesitation.

You may think, as I say, that a man's choice among hairdressers is of little moment, and that, provided they do not cut their clients' ears off or apply a powerfully corrosive acid instead of lotion, any one is as good as any other. You would be profoundly mistaken, for hairdressers differ as heads differ, and as the characters beneath those heads, too, and the true master of the art matches not only his tonsorial style, but his chairside manner, to the man on whom he is operating; from the first I knew that Mr East was the scissorer for me.

Take the question of talking. King Archilaus of Macedon (*floruit* 400 B.C.) touched on this very point when, in response to his barber's question, 'How would you like your hair cut, Sire?', replied 'In silence' (thus, incidentally, making the earliest recorded joke in human history). But although I generally share that royal response, others do not (David Langdon once drew a cartoon showing a gentlemen's hairdressing saloon, with an individual queue of customers waiting for each of the chairs, over which there hung signs reading respectively 'Politics', 'Football', 'T.V.' and 'Silence'), and the good hairdresser will sense his client's mood and mute his own approach if it meets with taciturnity, making it voluble only if that seems to be appropriate.

Thus, most impeccably, it has always been with Mr East; he may offer a word or two about the political situation (couched in non-partisan terms), an anecdote or incident, something of his family (this year marks his ruby wedding as well as his retirement, and a forthcoming grandchild, too), his garden or his holiday, but he never goes on unless it is clear I want to, and more often than not I sink into a semi-hypnotized silence, and allow the regular snip of the scissors to provide a soothing and peaceful atmosphere in which (I always make the appointment for the early morning) to start the day.

Nor is this meticulous craftsman's discretion limited to the form of his conversation; it also controls the content. A number of his other clients are known to me, and he always mentions it if one of these has recently been in; but if I know which of them likes to touch up the grey with artifice, it is certainly not from Mr East, who would allow himself to be roasted to death by blow-driers rather than breathe to one client a word that another would not like breathed.

He never allows what might be called professional wounds to show; sometimes, if I have been away for a long holiday, and resolutely refused to trust my head to the care of foreign hands, not to mention foreign hairstyles, I have come back with a mop in which you could hide the Crown Jewels and a dozen Beef-eaters to look after them, but he never even winces at the jungle presented to him. (Well, once only; I came back with a beard, and a very raggety beard at that. I thought Mr East was going to fall lifeless at my feet; Jeeves's disapproval of Bertie's new-grown moustache – 'I gave the moustache a thoughtful twirl. It seemed to hurt Jeeves a good deal, so I chucked it' – was nothing by comparison. And when I made it clear that I was not going to take it off just yet, he was as a brave man on the rack, determined not to gratify his tormentors with even a single groan. But it had gone by the time I visited him again.)

One of the oddest consequences of having one's hair done by the same man for many years is that, should he for any reason not be in charge, the patient is quite unable to instruct the locum as to his normal requirements. Once, after a confusion (on my part) about dates, I arrived to find Mr East on holiday, and the firm fielding a substitute. To all his questions – how did I like it, what sort of shampoo did I have, what dressing did I use – I was unable to make any reply at all; Mr East had done it the same way, with the same materials, for as long as I could remember, and I had long since forgotten the details, if indeed I had ever known them. (Some enterprising firm of hairdressers ought to keep photographs, front, back and sides, of their regular customers after treatment, together with relevant data, so that the replacement of regular attendants would not produce such difficulties.)

I have never learned from Mr East how he decided on the calling he has followed for so many years, nor how he acquired such skill in it, though I have gathered that he took it up on returning from the war (some of his clients will be even more bereft than I am, for there are heads to which he has been attending for thirty years, which makes me a very newcomer). No doubt such skill can be achieved by years of hard work, though some gift for it is surely also necessary. But be that as it may, Mr East is one of those who keep the world spinning in its proper orbit by maintaining the essential character of *homo faber*; to cut hair skilfully is not so great a contribution to civilization as to write the Jupiter Symphony, but it is a contribution none the less. Not because it is of great importance that hair should be cut well, for we could all get along without much difficulty if we all looked like frights on emerging from the hairdresser's: but because it is of great, indeed of crucial, importance that there should continue to be men and women who scorn to take their wages for a job ill done, and would do their job well even if there were no one about to see.

Such people are rarer today than they used to be. Prime Ministers rarely meet the test; Gas Board officials who do not answer letters fail it; miners whose output falls concomitantly with every pay rise can hardly attach much weight to it. But fine craftsmen like Herbert East and his sort live by that principle all their lives, and that is why they can retire with honour and satisfaction when the times comes. I wish him and his wife a happy leisure, and many healthy years to enjoy it.

The Times April 15th, 1977

Sense takes a holiday and envy
stays at home

I DON'T KNOW WHO coined the phrase 'the politics of envy', and in any case it has become so worn a cliché as to be now no more than a noise, conveying no meaning. But that we need a fresh phrase in much the same area has just been brought home to me rather forcibly by a copy I have received of a letter sent from, and presumably on behalf of, the North West Thames Regional Health Authority, to the heads of all that body's departments and divisions, concluding with the words 'Will you please ensure that each member of your staff is aware of this'. I do not intend to name the writer of the letter (though he is, to judge from the post he holds, which is recorded beneath his signature, clearly a figure of some weight in the Authority) because I assume that his letter is only promulgating policy rather than determining it, and that the rule he lays down would operate whether he had sent the letter or not. The essential point of the letter (the correspondent who sent it to me underlined it, though I feel that it could hardly have spoken more eloquently if it had been illuminated on vellum by a dozen exceptionally gifted medieval monks) is contained in the first paragraph, which reads in full, under the heading 'Unpaid Leave (other than compassionate)', as follows:

The grant of unpaid leave is not normally approved because it could be held to be unfair to those staff who cannot afford the financial diminution whilst favouring those who can.

If you cannot hear knells while you read that, you must be uncommonly deaf. Note that it is *unpaid* leave that is under discussion; note further that, as the letter goes on to make clear, those who are fortunate enough to slip through the net and obtain permission to take unpaid leave are tied in unyielding knots when it comes to the attendant financial arrangements. For instance:

> ... It should be quite clearly borne in mind that during unpaid leave ... it will be necessary for both the employer's and the employee's shares of the superannuation contribution to be paid by the individual.

And on top of that

> ... incremental credit will be delayed by the length of the unpaid leave.

Very well; having established that those who have unpaid leave gain nothing whatever from public funds, either while they are having it or later, but that on the contrary they have to pay their employers' contribution to their own pension for the period in question, let us go back and contemplate the opening statement again. Before getting down to the substance of it, I must draw attention to the careful use of the subjunctive. The writer does not claim that unpaid leave is unfair to 'those staff who cannot afford the financial diminution'; he does not even suggest that others believe it to be unfair; no, he remains firmly theoretical, and says only that it 'could be held to be unfair'.

I dare say it could. There are very few limits, and those exceptionally flexible, to the capacity for envy, hatred, malice and all uncharitableness that some people, encouraged to feel those sentiments, could manage at a pinch. The point, however, is whether the encouragement should be provided.

The belief that nobody should have anything that anybody else hasn't got has been growing in this country for a long time now — whence, after all, the expression 'politics of envy'. What is more, I have long believed that it is fuelled by a feeling that those whose lack of what others have is caused by their own unwillingness either to save or to work harder should be compensated for their own fecklessness or laziness by a policy of penalizing their more successful rivals.

The largely spurious row over private medicine, for instance, is greatly illuminated by contemplation of the fact that the various forms of medical insurance, which would provide at least the comfort of privacy, are well within the means of some of the most envious and uncharitable opponents of private hospital rooms, most of them no more opposed to having such facilities themselves than Lady Castle was.* Indeed, I believe that much of our taxation policy is designed to ensure that those who save out of their income are no better off by doing so than those who spend everything they earn, though in many cases the spenders earn more than the savers, and it would make no difference to the principle if they didn't.

Some of those who support this kind of policy add hypocrisy to the other unlovely qualities involved by insisting that they are only out to help the 'genuinely unfortunate among us'. It isn't true, and even if it were it remains true also that in the long run (and increasingly in the short) you cannot make the poor richer by making the rich poorer, only by making everybody richer, including the rich. (This, of course, is the lesson that the American and German working classes have learned, and the British have not; the former do not mind if the boss earns more provided that they also do, and the latter, or at any rate their union leaders, mind so much that they would apparently prefer to earn less themselves if by doing so they can ensure that the boss is no better off than he was before.)

Besides, what has even the most horrible cant about equality got to do with what is being done by the North West Thames Regional Health Authority (and, I take it, other health authorities)? I suppose somebody will say that the reason for this odious policy is that the work normally done by staff on unpaid leave has to be done by others while they are away, but such a claim can be ignored; the truth is that there is no purpose in what is

* A fierce and outspoken critic of private medicine, she took care to see that she had a private room when she had the misfortune to need hospital treatment.

laid down other than that stated plainly: to ensure that nobody may have anything that others cannot afford, even though depriving the richer will in no way help the poorer.

What has become of this country when such an attitude can prevail with no public outcry, no political campaign against it, not so much as a protest by a bishop? (Not that that is surprising; it was probably one of today's bishops who thought the wheeze up – I could name at least three who would fill the bill.) Because some employees of the North West Thames Regional Health Authority cannot afford – no, are deemed to be unable to afford, for no evidence is provided – to take a week off without pay in order to stretch their annual paid holiday agreeably, nobody who can afford it is to be permitted to do so. And the only reason given is that this 'could be held to be unfair'.

But what about paid leave? Some employees of the authority, no doubt, can afford, during their regular and official holidays, to go abroad; they must surely be forbidden to do so, since others can go no farther than Bournemouth. Nay, some can manage no better than a caravan parked in a lay-by just off an unpleasant stretch of the M1; let all be reduced to the same level. It follows of course, that a couple who forego many of those luxuries that are now necessities, and with what they save by doing so pay for private education for their children, must be barred from the practice; indeed, those who cannot go so far but buy their children good books and gramophone records, must be outlawed in the interests of those who don't, with a special squad of inspectors, of course, armed with wide powers of entry and search, to enforce the regulations.

And so on and so on and so on. And, I fear, so on. Few among our readers, I expect, will find this tale particularly surprising;* I have no doubt that many could surpass it easily from their own experience. That nothing will happen merely because I have exposed this practice I take for granted. But in after years, when Britain is neither free nor prosperous, I hope somebody will draw

* None did; at any rate this column elicited not a single letter to the Editor, or indeed to me.

the right conclusion; that those who put heavy weights on the backs of the more successful, even when by so doing they do not help the less successful, will end, because they must, by putting heavy weights round the wrists and ankles of those who disagree with what they are doing and have the temerity to say so.

The Times July 7th, 1978

The death march

I DID NOT THINK I would so soon return to the subject of Cambodia, that crucified nation of which the world prefers to know nothing. But I have just read a long excerpt from a forthcoming book on the subject, *Murder of a Gentle Land*, by two American writers, John Barron and Anthony Paul. (The excerpt appeared in *Reader's Digest*, who are also the American publishers of the book, and to whom I am indebted for permission to quote from the work.) And what I have there seen described so far exceeds in evil anything I have included in my own articles on Cambodia, though I had felt sure that I had learned and revealed the worst, that I am compelled to present, today and tomorrow, further and more dreadful details of the pitiless wickedness visited upon a helpless people in the name of communism. And I fear that I have not done with the subject yet: 'the worst is not, so long as we can say, "This is the worst".'

The magazine, in an introduction to the extract, describes the meticulous research and cross-checking that went into the book from which it is taken: several hundred interviews with refugees – in Thailand, the United States and France – in order to build up a complete picture of what has happened since Cambodia fell entirely into the communists' hands. Such verification, and an account of it, is necessary, for the reader, wading breast-high through blood as the story unfolds, must be desperate for a chance to think that it is not true, and even I, who have learned enough of what has happened there to be all too grimly sure that it is true, would dearly love to believe that it is not. For I wrote earlier that the Khmer Rouge have turned a living country into a concentration camp; but this account makes plain that it would be more exact to say that they have transformed it into a charnel-house.

There have been several descriptions already of the emptying of Phnom Penh of its entire population, including all those, however ill, in hospital; it is worth first reminding ourselves, from this new account, of that particular Witches' Sabbath, before we go on to episodes beside which it becomes almost innocent:

Troops stormed into the Prech Ket Melea Hospital ... and shouted to patients, physicians and nurses alike ... 'Out! Everybody get out!' They made no distinction between bedridden and ambulatory patients, between the convalescing and the dying.

Hundreds of men, women and children in pyjamas limped, hobbled, struggled out into the streets, where the midday sun had raised the temperature to more than 100 degrees ... One man carried his son, whose legs had just been amputated. The bandages on both stumps were red with blood, and the son ... was screaming 'You can't take me like this! Kill me! Please kill me!' ... Jon Swain, a young British journalist ... ... wrote that the communists were 'tipping out patients like garbage into the streets ... The Khmer Rouge must know that few of the city's 20,000 wounded will survive ... '

The same afternoon the communists began to purge the capital of all printed matter. Rare and ancient manuscripts from temples and museums; the records of government and business; the contents of libraries; dictionaries, medical textbooks; even personal identity-cards – all were targets. Tens of thousands, perhaps hundreds of thousands, of books were thrown into the Mekong River or burned on its banks. Untold others were burned at a dump, and the libraries of Phnom Penh and Buddhist universities went up in flames.

But nobody knows, and nobody ever will know, how many of the healthy as well as the hospital patients died in what may have been the greatest death march in the whole of human history;

within a week, all the cities of Cambodia had been emptied of
their inhabitants, and a total of some 3,500,000 people forced into
the jungles to fend for themselves. Here are some of the scenes
that Barron and Paul describe:

> From noon onwards, the masses in the streets multiplied as
> communist troops uprooted more and more families. In the
> ever-thickening congestion ... families advanced no more than
> 200 yards an hour ... there was a huge crowd of every age and
> condition, young, old and sick. Some could barely walk. Some
> dragged others ... that evening several thousand people slept
> by the streets or roads ... virtually everybody saw ... corpses
> rapidly bloating and rotting in the sun ... Then the water sup-
> ply ceased throughout the city ... all the way along the Khmer
> Rouge were shooting into the air ... 'Go on! Move on!' they
> shouted ... No stores of drinkable water, no stocks of food, no
> shelter, had been prepared for the millions of outcasts ... The
> very young and the very old were first to die. Adults and chil-
> dren alike slaked their thirst in roadside ditches ... Conse-
> quently, acute dysentery racked and sapped life from bodies
> already weakened by hunger and fatigue ... 'We must have
> passed the body of a child every 200 yards ... troops usually
> demanded that the people walk throughout the day at as brisk
> a pace as the congestion allowed ... soldiers cut down ... people
> who failed to keep pace ... They would give a first warning,
> then a second warning, then they would shoot. Most of the
> ones I saw being killed were elderly ... There was a lorry
> loaded with armed Khmer Rouge. When their truck also
> couldn't move, they just shot at the people to clear the way ... '
> In all of Cambodia, a minimum of 300,000 human beings
> perished during the exodus. And for the survivors, the worst
> was yet to come.

For some it came with almost merciful quickness; these were the
thousands, perhaps tens of thousands, who were exterminated by
the communists, either because they may have worked (as civil
servants or soldiers) for the overthrown regime, or because they

belonged to any group of people – local leaders, intellectuals and the like – who might have served to keep alive the spirit of individuality and humanity that the communists were determined to destroy utterly. So:

The vehicles halted and the officers were ordered to disembark … A minute later, the soldiers along the road began shooting into the officers … For three hours the Khmer Rouge fired into the piles of dead and dying officers … This was only one of many organised massacres perpetrated throughout Cambodia during the first days of surrender … the communists immediately set out to exterminate the entire government officer corps and management echelon of the civil service … By refusing to bury the slain, the communists advertised their deeds … The communists frequently boasted that they had eliminated all prostitution in Cambodia, and they may have been right. Less than a mile outside Sisophon … a lorry driver stumbled upon one example. He saw the crumpled bodies of about 20 young women. Each had been bludgeoned to death … The lorry driver knew some of the women as prostitutes … The communists also killed some students, teachers and other 'intellectuals' for no apparent reason other than the fact that they were educated … On or about April 20 troops marched the whole village [of Phum Kauk Lon] out of their huts … as the people walked among the trees, machine-gun squads lying in ambush cut them all down, approximately 360 men, women and children … a tractor drove past, towing a trailer carrying a group of women aged 18 to 25. As dawn came … along a cart track east of Khal Kabei, where all could see, were the remains of the young women. 'They had been buried up to the necks', said a villager. 'You could only see their heads.' Each had been stabbed in the throat … For more than a week, as the heads became swollen with putrefaction and the smell of death permeated the village, the Khmer Rouge refused to let Khal Kabei arrange a proper burial … From the young women's appearance, especially their carefully groomed long hair, the villagers guessed they were the wives and daughters of officers and senior civil servants ... On April 27, at Mongkol Borev ... a squad of communist soldiers rounded up ten civil servants along with their families, about 60 people in all. They bound the hands of each behind their backs ... One at a time, each official was thrust forward ... The soldiers then stabbed the victim simultaneously, one through the chest and the other through the back ... As each man lay dying, his wife and children were dragged up to his body. The women, forced to kneel, also received the simultaneous bayonet thrusts, then the children and babies ...

And yet I meant it when, before those excerpts, I said that those who died soon and quickly were the lucky ones. Those in the New Villages – that is, the survivors of the forced marches into the jungle – may have been tempted to envy the dead their fate, as the nature of life under communism began to be clear to them.

Each arriving family was allotted a space about five yards square, on which to build a hut. Normally, neither materials nor tools were provided ... The hut completed, everybody joined the common labour force ... They laboured from 6 to 11 a.m. and from 1 to 5 p.m. seven days a week – and in some settlements, three hours at night if the moon was out. Men, women and children were segregated into separate work parties and kept apart in the fields. Except during the midday break ... guards allowed neither rest nor conversation ... About mid-June, while working in the field, Ngy stepped on a sharp piece of bamboo which penetrated almost all the way through his foot. His whole leg swelled, he developed a high fever, and pains shot up to his waist ... That night ... village committee members took turns berating him: 'You must learn to live with pain. You must not be soft. You must not be lazy, trying to get out of work'. There followed a litany: Ngy was free; Ngy was equal; Ngy admitted he had been a lazy malingerer ... by midsummer many villagers were receiving only half a milk tin of rice daily, insufficient to sustain life. Malaria, cholera and typhoid spread. Approximately 1,000 people inhabited the New Village of Ta Orng: about 200 died in June. Sambok Ork contained 540 people when organised in late April; in July and August, two to five died daily ... Out of roughly 800 inhabitants in Phum Svay Sar, about 150 died in the summer ...

The Times March 29th, 1977

And the end of the road

YESTERDAY I GAVE some account of the slaughter visited upon the people of Cambodia by their new communist rulers. I also drew attention to the condition of those who were not killed, but were herded into what can only be described as centres of slavery, the 'New Villages'. But the cruelty and hardship of life there do not exhaust the hazards of survival in communist Cambodia.

> Children were singled out for the most intensive brain-washing. In the village of Khna Sar, university student Ung Sok Choeu observed: 'The only subjects being taught were revolutionary thinking and the aims of the Khmer Rouge struggle, and how to detect the enemies of both. As a result, the children turned into little spies, reporting everything that was said at home.' ... Some children derived a heady sense of power from the knowledge that they could place the life of any elder in jeopardy ... Child spies overheard two police inspectors discussing their former work. Both men were clubbed to death ...

And the madness, as well as the cruelty, of the communist programme for Cambodia can be seen in this account:

> By September ... the people of Ampil Pram Daeum had stripped the jungles of crabs, snails, bamboo shoots, bindweed and all else edible. People looked like skeletons draped with a thin, sickly cover of skin. Of the original 215 ... about 15 per cent had died and only 10 were strong enough to do their jobs. Ten men had been executed ... Through the deathly summer of

1975, the serfs of the New Villages looked to the coming harvest for some relief from their misery. But in the autumn [the authorities] once more convulsed the population by instituting another great migration. More than half a million people suddenly were lifted out of settlements they had built in the south, and scattered anew to start all over again in the north and north-west.

Many, of course, tried to escape, and some succeeded – whence the accounts and descriptions in the book from which I have been quoting. But some failed:

Villages and settlements were evacuated to create a no-man's-land about three miles wide all along the border. The crossings, their approaches and jungle trails were seeded with mines and booby-traps ... Abdul Hadji Mohammad, who was one of the few to escape the persecution of Muslims, remembers: 'We walked for ten nights, moving only when it was dark. All along the way, the jungle smelled of rotting corpses; we could not get away from that smell.' Ouk Phon, who escaped from Phum To Tea ... reports: 'In one spot I saw about 50 corpses tied together with rope, and elsewhere, under a tree, the skeleton of a child, its hands still tied ... Some paths were so thick with skeletons the bones could cut my feet.'

And still the worst was to come, still the mountain of corpses was not high enough to satisfy the leaders of communist Cambodia that the last strength had been crushed from the country's prostrate body.

By 1976 [the communists'] domination of Cambodia was beyond challenge. The population, socially atomised and physically enfeebled, was utterly at the mercy of its new masters. And the New Villages, hewn from the wilderness, were, in their fashion, functioning ... Now [the authorities] could afford to stabilise the country and ameliorate the deathly rigours. But that was not to be. In October 1975, monitors abroad listened as the communist commander in Sisophon received radio orders to prepare for the extermination, after the harvest, of all former government soldiers and civil servants regardless of rank, and their families. Soon word spread among the communist soldiers that teachers, village chiefs and students were to be included in the toll. The killing began during ... 1975. Before the organised slaughter had largely been confined to officers and senior civil servants. Now the lowliest private, the most humble civil servant, the most innocent teacher, even foresters and public health officials, became prey.

The authors of *Murder of a Gentle Land*, after careful checking of their hundreds of interviews with refugees, estimated that at least 1,200,000 men, women and children died in Cambodia between April 1975 and December 1976, as a consequence of the communists' actions. And one of the leaders of the new Cambodia, Ieng Sary,

> ... flew to a special session of the United Nations General Assembly. He left behind a country without universities, commerce, art, music, literature, science or hope ... Upon landing in New York, Ieng Sary boasted, 'The towns have been cleaned'. And when he appeared at the United Nations, delegates from around the world warmly applauded.

The rest is silence. And even worse than silence. Last time I wrote about Cambodia, I quoted Mrs Peggy Duff as saying that the rulers of communist Vietnam were 'working to guarantee human rights': she not only admitted that she had made that grotesque claim – indeed, she virtually boasted of doing so – but added, of Cambodia itself, this explanation of what I had described: 'Phnom Penh was being fed solely by American rice deliveries. When this ceased, the only way to feed the people was to take them to the food and away from death by starvation and disease.' And she went on to say, in a masterpiece of meiosis, 'I regret that the new rulers of Cambodia have been less humane than those of Vietnam.' Perhaps this time someone else will 'explain' the exterminations as part of a programme of preventive medicine, designed to ensure that the victims did not catch cold, and the New Villages as an imaginative form of low-cost public housing.

It was recently reported that the British Bowls Federation is proposing to hold matches against a team of bowls players from South Africa, and that the protests against those who would contaminate English greensward with the wooden spheres of apartheid have already begun. Should the South African bowlsters appear, the protests will doubtless swell in volume and intensity. Yet I somehow doubt whether those even now planning to fill the streets of London in appropriate demonstrations will be equally active and vociferous against a regime which by deliberate action has brought about the deaths of roughly one-sixth of a country's entire population. Nor do I hear any sound from those who insist that the full weight of international pressure be mobilized against Pinochet's Chile. Nor is the House of Commons Order Paper filled with motions of protest in the names of the Labour left. If he is asked to comment (though not if he isn't) we may get a cliché or two from our handsome new Foreign Secretary,* and that will be about all.

As in Britain, of course, so elsewhere. No Cambodia Marchers crowd the avenues of Washington, no Brothers Berrigan† grow hoarse in denouncing the Cambodian leaders, or even in saying penitential novenas for the merry way they dismissed the 'domino theory' while helping to bring about the defeat of South Vietnam (where the new communist rulers are, of course, 'working to guarantee human rights'). Nor are the streets of Stockholm filled with indignant demonstrators, or the boulevards of Paris with the *jeunesse enragée*. As for the United Nations ...

And yet I believe that the free world which ignores, makes light of, or condones what has happened and is still happening in Cambodia does so at its peril. Not just because, not even mainly because, this is further evidence of the true essence and nature of

* Dr David Owen. He said nothing.

† Two American Catholic priests, active in support of the North Vietnamese cause and subsequently in defence of the rulers of the newly unified Vietnam.

communism triumphant, and such evidence grows more urgently necessary as more and more voices are raised to declare that an altogether new species of communism has been discovered in Western Europe. The mortal danger in turning our eyes away from Cambodia is to be found in an entirely different category. John Donne was right; he really was. Evil diminishes us all, and helps to destroy not just our own freedoms, or even lives, but our very souls. Perhaps there is nothing we can do about Cambodia; but unless we continue to feel the evil of it, we have taken a step nearer spiritual death, and brought closer living damnation. The blood of a million dead crieth unto us from the ground. The least we can do, for ourselves as well as them, is to listen.

The Times March 30th, 1977

Damn braces

Pornography: The Longford Report*

THE MOUNTAINS HAVE laboured, and brought forth – well, not a mouse, though it amounts to very little, nor an elephant, though it is extremely large and shortsighted, nor a donkey, though it makes more noise than sense, nor a flatworm, though it does not seem to be sure in which direction it is going, nor a cat, though it will not take advice, nor a tortoise, though it is slow, nor a parrot, though it repeats what it does not understand, nor a hippopotamus, though it excites mirth.

What the mountains have brought forth is a Tigger, which was much given, as I recall, to pulling the tablecloth to the ground, wrapping itself up in it amid the broken crockery, rolling about the room going 'worra-worra-worra', and finally sticking its head out and asking, 'Have I won?'

Far from it. This vast brantub, the contents of which are a thousand parts chaff to one part wheat, is not only useless; it has effectively ruined the market for a serious study, by some such means as an academic team or a Royal Commission, of the problem (if there is one) of pornography. It is also dangerous, in that whatever the good intentions of those responsible for it, it will be used by the unthinking, the demagogic, the freedom-hating and the malevolent, to bolster their demands for further restrictions on publication, exhibition and performance.

The book has many faults, but two are crucial; one is methodological, the other conceptual. The first is the almost total absence of intellectual rigour in the way Lord Longford and his colleagues

* Coronet, 1972.

went about their work. Bits and pieces of statements, opinions, facts, misunderstandings and haphazard research, all of it desperately unscientific and hopelessly undigested, and most of it indiscriminately shovelled together by people clearly quite unskilled in such work, make up a document which at one moment can solemnly review a lot of unsolicited letters about a film ('Growing Up') from people who had clearly not seen it; at another moment can, no less solemnly, offer childishly elementary amateur psychology ('By nature man seeks to form a highly individualised bond. As a baby he cries for attention, and though Freud ... '); and at another moment – indeed, at several other moments – can, faced with evidence against its authors' preformed and immovable opinions, blandly dismiss it. (The *locus classicus* is the report's treatment of the American Commission, mainly composed of experts, which studied the subject and concluded that there was little if anything to fear from pornography, supporting their conclusions with a large quantity of research evidence. Lord Longford and company simply rely on the Minority Report.)

In almost every possible way, the book is a mess. Pseudo-academic reports from sub-committees on such divisions of the group's study as the law, sex education, broadcasting and books rub shoulders with, for instance, one of Peregrine Worsthorne's meandering Sunday essays, elegant paradoxes and all. A penetrating comment on the erotic in literature, by Kingsley and Jane Amis (it is pathetic to see how in other parts of the book this is several times proudly paraded, it being almost the only thing of any genuine distinction in the whole collection), is ruined by an addendum of ramshackle foolishness, calling for a vast apparatus of control over literature, in order to prevent unsuitable varieties ('Not unsuitable *because* of anything, just unsuitable') from falling into the hands of children. Pornography and obscenity are confused, distinguished, confused again, distinguished again, until the reader's head swims with the effort to look both ways at once. Though a number of factual errors are carefully catalogued in a rejoinder to the chapter on broadcasting, Lord Longford has not bothered to correct them. Ken Russell is lumped in with Andy

Warhol, as if they were in any way connected, or even similar. An abusive reference to *Last Exit to Brooklyn* makes it clear beyond argument that the author of the passage has not read it. No sub-group of contributors seem to have looked at any contribution but their own, so that overlapping and repetition therefore abound. The same weight is apparently given to everything put forward as 'evidence', the views of the South End Green Women's Liberation Workshop and Susan Sontag, say, being presented as equal value with, for instance, those of the British Board of Film Censors and the National Council for Civil Liberties. Statistics for venereal disease, illegitimacy, etc., are trotted out with the unproven, and indeed scarcely argued, assumption that they are caused by pornography. And the whole ragamadoglio ends, in a fine flourish of crazy illogic, with a draft Obscene Publications Bill that would abolish the defence of 'public good', thus at last making clear in so many words what has been visible between the lines throughout, that Lord Longford and his group are simply concerned to ban what they find disgusting, even if what they find disgusting does more good than evil.

Worse, however, than the muddled thinking, the slovenly organization, the rambling, confused and repeatedly untenable argument, is the basic assumption on which the entire book rests, which is that sexual pleasure is only obtainable, and certainly only permissible, when accompanied by love. 'Sex only works properly', says one of those who wrote to the group, and whose views are quoted with evident approval and agreement in the report, 'if the person you are having it with is someone you care so deeply about that you will stay around to raise the children who may come'. This claim rattles through the book in a dozen different guises, and (along with the authors' belief that what they find offensive must be harmful) is the chief weapon which they use to attack pornography. The fact that the claim is not only untrue, but manifestly ridiculous, does not seem to have occurred to Lord Longford and his colleagues. It is in fact largely the attitude represented by Lord Longford and the rest of his army of banners that has made so many people unable to enjoy sexual relationships outside society's 'permissible' categories, or frequently inside them either. Blake was wiser: 'Damn braces, bless relaxes.'

It is unlikely that those not professionally obliged to read the whole book will be able to get to the end of it, but if they do (or if, wisely, they start reading at page 460) they will find an enchanting Trojan Horse stabled there. Some of the committee's members, evidently, were troubled by the paucity of evidence one way or the other on the effects of pornography, and an expert psychologist, Mr Maurice Yaffe, from the Institute of Psychiatry, was commissioned to survey the available material. This he has done in a dispassionate, scholarly and meticulously documented forty pages, which come, after the heated amateurism of most of what has gone before, like rain upon the desert's dusty face.

His study effectively demolishes the whole of the preceding report, showing that there is very little evidence at all as to the effects of pornography, that the majority of what there is tentatively suggests that it does no harm, and that, in the final analysis, the Longford report on pornography is no more than an essay in dogmatism.

'One of the most insidious tendencies of recent years', says Mr Jeremy Murray-Brown in a signed addendum to the report's section on sex education, 'is society's increasing reliance on so-called "expert" opinion in preference to natural common sense.' One might ask Mr Murray-Brown how he would like to have his appendix removed by a surgeon acting according to the precepts of natural common sense rather than expert knowledge, but leaving that aside, the call, implicit in his words, for more ignorance and prejudice and less knowledge and objectivity, is unmistakable. I can only say that Lord Longford and his group have responded to that call in full and generous measure.

Observer September 24th, 1972

The victory of Us over Them

FOR THE VICTORY won yesterday in the Court of Appeal – a victory for Us over Them that was overwhelming in its completeness, notable in the severity of the judges' language in condemnation of the Home Office, and (as we shall shortly see) a landmark in English legal history – there is only one possible poet, only one who combines the right trumpet notes with the dash of vulgarity necessary to season what is, above all, a people's triumph. Macaulay, with suitable emendations, is your only man:

> Oh! how our hearts were beating, when at the dawn of day,
> We saw the army of the League drawn out in long array;
> With all its priest-led citizens, and all its rebel-peers,
> And Jenkins's stout infantry, and Lyon's Flemish spears,
> There rode the brood of false Whitehall, the curses of our land;
> And dark Dromgoole was in the midst, a truncheon in his
>   hand ...*

A brief recapitulation, before we continue with merrier music, is necessary here for any newcomer to the story. Last February, the Home Office announced that the colour television licence fee was to be raised from £12 to £18 from April 1st. It then became apparent that a holder of a licence due to expire either at the end of March or within a couple of months afterwards, could, by buying a new one before April 1st, save some money: he would lose the value of the unexpired portion of his existing licence, but the £6 difference between the pre-April and new prices would more than offset this.

* Jenkins was the Home Secretary; Lyon a junior Home Office Minister; Dromgoole the civil servant in charge of the affair.

The Home Office (in a display of incompetence rarely equalled even by that noisome institution they had not realized that the 50 per cent increase would lead many people to take such action) issued unlawful instructions (which, we have only just learned, is always surreptitiously done when the licence fee is increased) to Post Office clerks that no licences should be issued to holders of existing ones before April 1st; these instructions were followed in some instances but not in others, so that some 25,000 prudent citizens managed to buy a licence at the correct and only rate applicable before April 1st, to wit £12; these constituted the volunteer army who fought for law and right, and as whose honorary commander-in-chief I have in this column been privileged to serve, by reporting on and directing the battle, and exhorting the troops to stand firm for justice against illegality.

After April 1st, the Home Office began its campaign to force people who had bought a valid licence at £12 before that date to pay an extra £6 which there was no lawful authority to demand, by threatening, and ultimately purporting, to revoke their licences if they did not pay. Under the Home Office's inexorable and illegal pressure, many of the troops, understandably, gave in; in the end some 5,000 were left holding out.

The weight, it could not be denied, was from the start on the enemy's side. The Executive is powerful, and is constantly seeking ways to extend its power still further; and the Home Office, never squeamish when it comes to misleading, bullying and intimidating the public in its own interests, behaved from start to finish in a manner well calculated to bring all but the stoutest resisters to submission:

Oh! wherefore come ye forth, in triumph from the north,
With your hands, and your feet, and your raiment all red?
And wherefore doth your rout send forth a joyous shout?
And whence be the grapes of the wine-press which ye tread?

But among the brave garrison of 5,000 one determined on a sortie; Mr Andrew Congreve, who has this day ensured himself a place in history beside John Hampden, applied to the High Court for a declaration that the threatened revocation of his licence would be unlawful and invalid.

Mr Congreve is in the best tradition of English heroes; he looks not like a dashing bravo but like a respectable solicitor, which is not really surprising, because that is exactly what he is. And he went to court not for £6 but for the crucial principle that stands at the heart of our law and our liberty, and has since 1689 been enshrined and encapsulated in the Bill of Rights: the principle that no money shall be extracted by the state from the citizen, nor shall anything be done by the state to his disadvantage, save under lawful authority given by Parliament. To establish that doctrine, this country cut off the head of one king and drove another from his throne, and Mr Congreve was not going to permit the doctrine thus established to be overturned merely because the Home Office felt like overturning it. (His valour in the field clearly entitles Mr Congreve to the first and highest honour of this campaign; I therefore hereby award him the Diamond Star of the Order of They Shall Not Get Away With It, with Oak-Leaves, Crossed Swords and Gold Knobs On, and he and his descendants, to the remotest posterity, shall be entitled to a salute from all ranks.)

Appearing for Mr Congreve was Mr Gerald Levy, and I have to say that in the course of a long and varied experience of listening to advocacy I have heard very few expositions so lucid, forceful and persuasive as his. He was helped, of course, by the fact that he was plainly in the right, but even so, it was a masterly performance: he smashed the Home Office case to splinters, showing up the grossness of their errors, the shiftiness of their statements and the illegality of their actions. (Mr Levy being, strictly speaking, a soldier-of-fortune, he cannot be decorated; so notable a contribution to the struggle did he make, however, that it must be recognized. I have therefore created an entirely new Order of Chivalry, and have pleasure in designating him the first Honourable Mercenary Extraordinary; more practically, I give notice that if he does not become a Q.C. very soon, I shall invent, and circulate, a number of most unsavoury rumours about the Lord Chancellor.)*

To the astonishment of everybody (including, I suspect, the enemy), Mr Justice Phillips refused Mr Congreve's application, on grounds as bizarre as can have been heard in the courts for some time. He held that, although a demand for an extra £6 by the Home Office would indeed be unlawful, Mr Congreve must fail because the Home Office had not made a demand, but offered him a set of alternatives to paying, such as giving up his television set. This judgment put me strongly in mind of Mencken's words: 'It is all very lovely, but my duty to my art compels me to add that it strikes me as hard to distinguish from damned foolishness'. But there was no doubt that it was a blow, and great fortitude was required in the face of it:

> They are here! They rush on! We are broken! We are gone!
> Our left is borne before them like stubble on the blast,
> O Lord, put forth thy might! O Lord, defend the right!
> Stand back to back, in God's name, and fight it to the last!

Mr Congreve, with Mr Levy still in the van, went to the Court of Appeal. (It is noteworthy, and fully in character with the Home Office's conduct of this entire business, that although notice of appeal was given at once, purported revocation notices were immediately sent out as soon as the High Court proceedings were finished.)

The appeal judges found unanimously in Mr Congreve's favour yesterday morning. It was a memorable scene, not least for the splendour of Lord Denning's oration. There is no judge living, and there have been few in our history, so ready to protect the citizen against the Executive, and he rose to the occasion magnificently:

> ... nothing unlawful whatever in their trying to save money in this way ... discretion must be exercised in accordance with the

* At present – March 1979 – he remains silkless; I have begun work on the rumours, all of them defamatory and some very unpleasant indeed.

law ... Her Majesty's subjects are not to be delayed or hindered in the exercise of their right except under the authority of Parliament ... a very cynical approach to the law ... a misuse of power conferred ... by Parliament ... these courts have the authority – and, I would add the duty – to correct a misuse of power by a minister or his department ... it was not the policy of Parliament that he was seeking to enforce, it was his own policy. And he did it in a way that was unfair and unjust ... The conduct of the minister, or the conduct of his department, has been found by the Parliamentary Commissioner to be maladministration. I go further, I say it was unlawful ... He had no right whatever to refuse to issue an overlapping licence – or, if issued, to revoke it ... It was perfectly lawful; and the department's dislike of it cannot afford a good reason for revoking ... There is yet another reason for holding the demands for £6 to be unlawful. They were made contrary to the Bill of Rights. They were an attempt to levy money for the use of the Crown without the authority of Parliament: and that is quite enough to damn them ...

And damned they were, not only by Lord Denning, but by his brothers Roskill and Lane, who delivered concurring judgments with almost equal scorn for the knaves who tried to steal our rights for their own convenience.

Their heads all stooping low, their points all in a row,
Like a whirlwind on the trees, like a deluge on the dykes,
The appellate court have burst on the ranks of the Accurst,
And at a shock have scattered the forest of his pikes.

What follows? First, of course, all those who have received purported revocation notices may safely ignore them; their £12, pre-April licences are valid until the date specified on them, and the revocations are what Pope Innocent X called the Treaty of Westphalia in 1648:

Null, void, invalid, iniquitous, unjust, damnable, reprobate, inane and empty of meaning for all time.

H

As for those who paid the extra, believing the Home Office's claim that they were obliged to, they must have the money repaid in full: I think – by God, I hope – that we can at any rate trust Mr Roy Jenkins to see that this is done, and speedily.*

For the rest, it has been a good fight and a valuable one. It should not have been necessary, but then Hampden's action should not have been necessary. It has established something very important indeed, and given us a good deal of pleasure and satisfaction in the course of that establishing:

Oh evil was the root, and bitter was the fruit,
And crimson was the juice of the vintage that we trod;
For we trampled on the throng of the haughty and the strong,
Who sat in the high places, and slew the saints of God.

Well, actually they didn't slay anybody. But what they did was to try to substitute the rule of men for the rule of law, and their own decisions for those of Parliament, in the teeth of the Bill of Rights which says they shall not. When they did that, there were people up and down the country to say that this thing must not, and shall not, be; and lo! it is not to be. The Bill of Rights has been upheld; the rule of law has been upheld; the supremacy of Parliament has been upheld; Mr Congreve has been upheld; all our warriors have been upheld; and we have asserted again the greatest of all the lessons which history teaches, which is that though Goliath is much bigger and stronger than David, and impenetrably armoured, and possessed of fearsome weapons, it remains true, and always will remain true, that a small, smooth pebble, aimed straight, can still topple him. Those whom we have defeated this day will make haste to forget that lesson. Well, we shall remember it.

The Times December 5th, 1975

---

* We could; he did.

At the Cup Final

WHEN I KNEW I was going to the Cup Final, I thought care-fully about the details of my unfamiliar role. I felt I should don a cloth cap and a vivid muffler; bottles of stout would peep from my every pocket; I would compare the game unfavourably to those of 1953, 1949, 1938; I would sing 'Ee-i-addio', shout 'Send him off' and 'Shoot' and 'Put him on the transfer list' and 'Get a white stick, ref'. Carried away, I would rush on to the field and kiss the centre-forward; it would be a perfect day here at Wembley; and the Queen would be looking radiant in pink.

But it wasn't like that at all. I have no cloth cap, no muffler; I don't like the taste of stout; I forgot entirely about the Golden Age. Moreover, it seems that you do not sing 'Ee-i-addio' unless Liverpool are engaged; every time I had one of my shouts ready something else would happen to make it irrelevant; I was not carried away; the sky was overcast; and the Queen was looking radiant in Brussels.

George Jean Nathan once told how he and other New York literati were having a drink in Toots Shor's restaurant before go-ing on to the theatre for the first night of a new production of *Hamlet*, when they conceived the plan of taking the proprietor along. Shor allowed himself to be taken, though he was by no means one for the higher drama, and all went well until about half way through, when the theatre was startled to hear peals of laughter coming from the stout restaurateur. Hasty inquiries were made as to the cause of his merriment, and he replied, 'There are about a thousand guys in this theatre, and I bet I'm the only one who doesn't know how it all comes out in the end.'

And that was the position in which I found myself. About ten minutes after the game began, I realized with a pleasant shock that I had no idea at all whether the play I was watching was good or bad; for this was not only the first time I had been to the Cup Final – it was the first time I had ever been to a football match at all. But before that a number of preconceptions had been destroyed. You can forget all that rubbish about the lonely crowd and Nazi rallies and the submerging of the individual's identity and the feeling of oneness. There was only one moment when I felt part of my 99,999 companions, and they part of me; before the match started, on my way up the hill to the stadium. A great broad river flowed gently, inexorably, towards the turnstiles, with black, important-looking cars nosing through the crowds, as though the whole thing were the funeral of some loved but unofficial hero. All these thousands had exactly the same purpose – to see the Cup Final – and when I finally got in, and stood for a few minutes on the balcony that runs round the outside of the building and looked down on the still-flowing river, I did indeed feel part of a general Leviathan-body larger than anyone or everyone in it.

But once inside, it was very different. The patriots with their banners and blue-and-white hats and huge favours that made them look like so many election canvassers ('I'm calling to ask for your vote on behalf of Sheffield Wednesday') seemed self-conscious, clutching at something that may have once existed, and in other circumstances still might. These were the people who seemed to want to lose their identity, to give all, to show that there are some big brave causes left. But they seemed a small minority, concentrated at either end of the gigantic arena – very friendly and gentle, incidentally, not at all reminiscent of Nuremberg or the Colosseum – where their banners waved, and every now and again their chants would swell up; Wednes*day*, Wednes*day* – Ev-er-ton, Ev-er-ton.

But the rest of us were there to see the Cup Final. Well, we certainly weren't there for the community singing before the game started, and bang went another preconception. A benevo-

lent little man bounced up and down on a rostrum in the middle
of the pitch, and implored us to join in, but only a minority of
us did, and when he called upon us to wave our song-sheets at
the end of the verse, the fluttering was thin and scattered. I have
heard ten times the sound from a twentieth of the numbers singing 'Jerusalem' at the last night of the Proms.

Then the cheering swelled right round the ground, and the two
teams emerged. The twelve-year-old next to me gave it as his
opinion to his friend that Everton were mad to drop Pickering,
whereat his friend agreed, and Princess Margaret appeared, looking radiant in red. The teams lined up; the Royal party halted;
the band struck up the National Anthem; *and stopped after six
bars*. No Godfrey Winn I; but to hear the Royal Marines indulge
in this cheap habit, picked up from shoddy cinemas, was a different kind of surprise.

Then there was the football, and the realization that I didn't
have any idea of its quality, having no standards of comparison
at all. But you don't need them to admire the beauty of the
pitch, rolled smooth as an ice-rink (I've never been to one of
those either) and mown in 116 perfect stripes of equal width. The
turf seems so elastic I half expected the players to bounce yards
high in slow motion every time they took a step, as we are told
will happen on the moon;* but the experts say that on the
Wembley pitch the body seems heavier, not lighter, and the
players tend to feel as if they are at the bottom of the ocean instead. The smoothness is no illusion, though; the ball ran true,
no matter how far or how fast, and it would sometimes get
almost halfway along the pitch, only a few inches inside the
touchline, without trickling over.

To every craft its mystery, but the first surprise never left me.
It was the astonishing accuracy of the passing. Do they have eyes
all round their heads, these men? And if not, how was it that
hundreds of times during the match a running player, his progress blocked, would send the ball far across the ground to a spot

* And later, of course, actually saw happen.

he could hardly have seen, let alone sized up, only to have it come to rest against the boot that had been waiting patiently there for it? This is skill of an order so high that admiration for it enables one almost to understand what the sports writers are talking about when they chatter of ballet, and poetry-in-motion, and much similar camp talk.

The preconceptions were falling fast now. The crowd was sportsmanlike, fair, appreciative. They cheered less than they clapped, and they clapped, for the most part, bold moves from both sides. As even I might have expected, it was the goal-keepers' saves that brought the crowd to its feet most often, and the Wednesday goalkeeper, Springett, in particular, brought off some extraordinary acrobatics, twisting through a seemingly im-passable crowd of blue men to get the ball safely away to a white one.

Like the individualism of the crowd, it is the individualism of the players that stays in the memory. I have seen few pleasanter sights than the unrestrained, unrestrainable joy of the nineteen-year-old McCalliog when he scored the first goal for Wednesday; skipping and leaping, his arms high above his head, he made one realize not so much the awesome, self-imposed responsibility these players carry, with a whole town somewhere watching their every movement, as the very Heaven of being young and scoring a goal in the Cup Final. Is this not every schoolboy's dream? And here was a youth, scarcely out of school himself, who had achieved it waking. Skip, skip; leap, leap; this was his moment, and he will never forget it, nor his happiness.

And at the other end of the scale of human feeling there was the Wednesday player whose momentary mistake, a tiny failure of attention or anticipation, had enabled Everton to bang home the fifth, deciding goal. Triumph and disaster froze together in the same picture; for the want of a horseshoe nail the battle was lost, and the loser lay on the ground and beat the turf with his fists, agonized, hopeless. Springett came out of his goal, knelt, looking suddenly wise and old, beside his colleague, and patted him on the head. There, there; but it was not there, there, and

another man was starting on his long journey with a memory
that would never leave him.

What an extraordinary business it is, when you come to think
of it. In different countries, different cultures, without reference
from one to another, men have formed teams and devised
struggles whose one constant point is to get a ball into a specified
area. Done this way, it is called soccer; if the ball is oval, and they
pick it up, it is called rugby; if the ball is white, and they hit it
with sticks, it is hockey; the same thing in winter is ice-hockey;
on horses, with a round ball again, it is polo; swimming, it is
water polo; if the ball is thrown above the head, it is basketball;
but they all have the same end. I suppose somebody has analysed
its deeper meaning; there are enough intellectual football-
followers to try.

But I cannot say I thought such things until afterwards. At the
time, I was too busy being excited, watching the pendulum-
swing of fortune as the advantage went back and forth, seeing a
promising movement begin only to be stifled before it could
reach the goal, living through the disappointment of Wednesday
as Everton, from two down, became one up. Ten minutes before
the end, the sun came out, and at last it was a perfect day here at
Wembley. *Was* the play good? *Did* it compare with the Finals
of 1953, '49, '38? Who knows? Who cares? Not I. Nor McCalliog; nor the man who lay on the ground, and would not be
consoled.

New Statesman May 20th, 1966

J is for Jew

T ELL IT NOT in Gath, publish it not in the streets of Askelon (actually, as will shortly appear, Gath and Askelon are just the places where people ought to be informed of it), but Mr Shloimovitz is happy. At any rate, he is said to be, and no doubt if he is not he will make haste to let me know; he has never been laggard with his pen, and recks not the cost of postage.

Mr Shloimovitz, I must explain, is the man who for years now has been waging war on the publishers of English dictionaries in this country and in particular on the *O.E.D.* and its tributaries. He has been doing so for the worthiest of motives and with no hope of gain or desire for publicity, and the fact that his entire campaign has been based, from first to last, on a gigantic mis-understanding, of which nobody has ever been able to rid him though many have tried, is neither here nor there. But he is said to be happy because, although he has not succeeded in his princi-pal aim (and if he had succeeded his success would have betokened a colossal scandal in the world of scholarship) a compromise has been reached between him and those with whom he has been battling, which has given him something of what he has asked without their being obliged to give him anything that they could not in honour surrender.

I think it is now time for me to explain what I am talking about.

Mr Shloimovitz is a Jew. (Far be it from me to hold that against him.) Some years ago, on looking into a dictionary under the letter J, he was struck by a realization as overwhelming as that which Keats experienced on first looking into Chapman's Homer, if not more so. For, as any dictionary aiming at comprehensiveness would have to make clear, the word 'Jew' denotes, at any rate in demotic parlance, not only one who is of the Hebrew persuasion, but—as a noun—one who drives hard bargains, one who cheats or is too grasping, and—as a verb—to beat down in haggling, to get the better of a rival by underhand cunning.

On seeing such definitions, Mr Shloimovitz saw red. He in-sisted—in letters to the editors and publishers of dictionaries, in appeals to prominent and influential people, and finally in courts of law—that such unpleasant matter should be excluded from works of reference. It was here that his misunderstanding became apparent; he was altogether unable to grasp just what a dictionary is. It is not a collection of value-judgments on words and their meanings, but a neutral record of words and the meanings people give, or have given, to them. Thus, if (as is undoubtedly the case) the word 'Jew' was used in derogatory senses, the dictionary-makers would be guilty of a shocking betrayal of their calling if they had omitted those senses for fear of giving offence.

This was the principle which our hero simply could not see. He saw instead the perpetuation of ancient, false and cruel allega-tions used against his people throughout the centuries, with hideous results in oppression and persecution. He thought that to leave such offensive matter in dictionaries would help to keep anti-semitism alive; in so thinking he probably overestimated, and substantially at that, the incidence of dictionaries, let alone the incidence of their consultation, among those infected by, or susceptible to, the virus of anti-Jewish prejudice; but he might well have argued that it was better to err on the fearful side than on the confident.

That matter of the kind he objected to was to be found in dictionaries of the utmost respectability cannot be denied. Take the *O.E.D.* itself. Having disposed of the respectable sense ('A person of Hebrew race; an Israelite') it goes on to the colloquial version of the noun:

As a name of opprobrium, of reprobation; applied to a

grasping or extortionate money-lender or usurer, or a trader who drives hard bargains or deals craftily.

Note that this sense is not listed as 'colloq.', though the equivalent verb is:

To cheat or over-reach, in the way attributed to Jewish traders or usurers.

The senses have a long lineage, of course; the noun is first recorded in 1606, the verb (in the *Ingoldsby Legends*, of all harmless sources) in 1845; other authors to use the derogatory senses include Coleridge, Washington Irving and Dante Gabriel Rossetti.

Turning now to the *Shorter*, we find the identical pair of definitions, except that 'money-lender' is omitted from the noun; and, following its parent, the *Shorter* allows the noun to be Standard English but makes the verb colloquial. Before continuing, we should pause to note that neither 'derog.' nor 'low' were used in either the big'un or the *Shorter*, so here was no way out through either of those doors for the compilers; on the other hand, 'vulg.', though the *O.E.D.* does not have it, is introduced in the *Shorter*. But it is not applied to the derogatory definitions of Jew.

Coming next to the *Concise*, we find all editions before the present one, which appeared a few months ago, following the usage of their parent and elder brother, both in definition and labelling. But the first sign of change comes in the new, sixth, edition. The definition has been revised, though not significantly (the 'Israelite' has gone); more important, in the offensive senses, both noun and verb are labelled both 'derog.' and 'colloq.'. Score one for Mr Shloimovitz.

The 1970 revised Brewer (I have no earlier edition) says of the noun, with admirable forthrightness: 'Used opprobriously to denote a mean or hard-fisted person', and a little *Dictionary of English Phrases*, published in 1922, says of 'As rich as a Jew', that it is derived 'from the mistaken belief that all, or most, Jews are wealthy', which seems astonishingly advanced for its era until you notice that the lexicographer's name is Hyamson.

But, of course, we turn for final guidance to *O.E.D. Supplement*, Volume II of which (H–N) has just appeared. The verb comes with the solemn warning: 'These uses are now considered to be offensive', and the noun with: 'As a name of opprobrium'; on the other hand, the editor is careful to say of the definition 'A pedlar' that it is 'In this use not deprecatory'. And to the *O.E.D.*'s list of sources, the Supplement adds Mayhew, Gerard Manley Hopkins, Synge and ('The rat is underneath the piles, The Jew is underneath the lot') Eliot. But Mr Shloimovitz's limited victory, together with the dictionary's integrity, is signalled in the preface, where the following admirable statement of the position appears:

> Offensiveness to a particular group, minority or otherwise, is unacceptable as the sole ground for the exclusion of any word or class of words ... it is therefore desirable to enter new racial and religious terms however opprobrious they may seem to those to whom they are applied and often to those who have to use them, or however controversial the set of beliefs professed by the members of minority sects ... it is also desirable, in order to avoid misunderstanding and consequent hostility, that the somewhat antiquated historical record ... should be brought up to date.

Some stern moralists have rebuked the *O.E.D.*'s editor for conceding even this much, but I think they are being over-strict; the important point is that the principle on which the *O.E.D.* has always operated, which enables the reader to trace the entire history of a word from its earliest appearance, and which has also made it the greatest dictionary in the world, remains intact. And yet, as I say, Mr Shloimovitz, who deserves commendation for his persistence at any rate, is also reported to be content. 'Rest, rest, perturbed spirit'; nobody can any longer be in any doubt that to use the word 'Jew' as a term of abuse is offensive and wrong. Anyone for Nigger?

The Times November 30th, 1976

Unholy passions at Oberammergau

I THINK IT IS incumbent upon me to exacerbate feelings in the row over the Oberammergau Passion Play.* Unlike some of the contestants, I have seen it; I went to the 1960 performance. I have also read the complete text, a course of conduct which also appears to have been thought unnecessary on the part of some of those expressing opinions on the matter.

First of all, let us get Hitler out of the way, together with his heirs and assigns among the neo-Nazis of today. As a lover of Wagner's music, I have often had to face taunts from idiots that I share this particular passion with Hitler. The less implacably idiotic among them can be silenced, I have found, by pointing out that Hitler's musical loves also included Beethoven and *The Merry Widow*, which, if you follow the idiots' logic, suggests either that Beethoven and Lehar were proto-Nazis, or that half the time Hitler was quite a good fellow really; those of us, however, who prefer to use a less exiguous basis of reasoning have long ago concluded that Hitler's musical tastes provide no guidance whatever for an informed discussion of our own.

So let it be with Oberammergau. Hitler praised the play; so did Albert Schweitzer (another Wagnerite, incidentally). That no more makes Schweitzer anti-semitic than it makes Hitler a leprosy doctor; more to the point, it does not make the Oberammergau Passion Play anti-semitic. Nor does the fact that the *Deutsche National-Zeitung* (which is indeed a repulsively Nazified organ) has leaped to the defence of the present text mean that

* The row started over the allegation that the play's text contained matter which was, or which might encourage those who were, anti-semitic.

those who oppose the political and racial views of such people must necessarily take an opposite view on a matter like this. For my part, I can put my position simply: I am damned if I am going to have my moral, political or aesthetic opinions determined or affected by the identity, nature or motives of those who share them.

The only admissible evidence on the question of anti-semitism in the Passion Play will be found in the text and the performance. The performance is a crucial ingredient; no one who has only studied the text on the page (let alone those who have not even done that) can really understand what is involved.

But first, the text. It is important, to start with, to realize that the 1860 version by Alois Daisenberger was not, as is widely supposed, a new play which replaced a text previously in use for many decades or even centuries. The Oberammergau play has been constantly changing over the years, and Daisenberger's version was based firmly upon its predecessors; indeed, his text, which was in any case more an adaptation of the version prepared by Othmar Weis half a century before than a completely new play, can be traced back in some of its elements to the earliest versions of all; as Pastor Franz Bogenrieder, a former parish priest of Oberammergau, has put it, 'the medieval text of St Ulrich and Afra gleams through all the versions, right down to Daisenberger's, just as the underlying colour shines through the old gold of our gothic statues'.

Next, it is important, in considering the question of anti-semitism in the present version, to distinguish between that which *is* anti-semitic and that which may *give rise* to anti-semitism. Daisenberger's text must be acquitted on the first charge. Certainly, the Jews are shown as desiring the downfall of Jesus, but their motive is made clear; they regard the Nazarene's preaching as blasphemous, sacrilegious and subversive of the truth and the moral order. Here is a passage that will make clear what I mean; the Priest Nathanael is speaking:

With our own eyes, and to our shame, we saw the triumphant

entry of this Galilean, how he marched through the gates and streets of holy Jerusalem. You have heard the Hosannas of the infatuated people. You were witnesses how this arrogant man usurped the dignity of the High Priests and had the effrontery to rule as a master in the temple of Jehovah. What is lacking for the entire overthrow of all our national customs and ecclesiastical rites? Another step, and the whole Law given by God to Moses is overthrown by the innovations of this heretic. The statutes of our fathers are despised. The fasts and cleansings abolished, the Sabbath profaned, God's Priests divested of their office, and the holy sacrifice at an end.

That is the spirit in which the Jews are regarded in the present version of the Oberammergau Passion Play, and for the life of me I cannot see anti-semitism in it. (I can, incidentally, see good Biblical warrant for it.) It is said, however, that irrespective of Daisenberger's own feelings, spectators at the Passion Play may come away with anti-semitic feelings instilled or reinforced, because they will gather that the Jews, whatever their reasons, desired Christ's death and helped to bring it about. Of course, the charge of deicide has frequently been put forward as an, or even the, explanation of anti-semitism; it is naïve to suppose that something as deep, old and twisted as that particular plague can be explained in such mechanistic terms, and even more so to suppose that the idea of Jewish complicity in the Crucifixion will come as a revelation to Oberammergau visitors or that they will thereafter look askance at their Jewish neighbours even if it does.

Rational arguments against anti-semitism, after all, are literally meaningless; indeed the statement of the Second Vatican Council exonerating the Jewish people from collective guilt for Christ's death, though a decent and honourable gesture, seemed to me, if put forward as an antidote to anti-semitism, hardly less naïve than the belief in that guilt as a prime cause for Jew-baiting.

I do not, therefore, believe that the present Oberammergau Passion Play is anti-semitic in its intention or nature; and I do not believe that the quantity of anti-semitism in the world will be increased by it. What is more, if I did believe that last proposition from a reading of the text, I would cease to believe it when I remembered my visit to the play.

For in performance, all such questions vanish; indeed any one who *has* seen the play but has *not* read the text must be wondering what the present dispute is about. What the play in performance becomes is an immense, enthralling and wholly persuasive picture of the Passion of Jesus Christ; and that is what it remains, I must stress, whether you believe the Christian interpretation of Christ's life and death or whether you do not. I remember, from my own visit, that as Christ was being nailed to the cross, a jet fighter screamed across the theatre (the stage is open to the sky, and the Bavarian hills can be seen beyond the sets), and made the play's point with considerable succinctness; evil exists, and can be overcome.

Beside the witness of what you actually see and hear, the question of anti-semitism in the play itself becomes as irrelevant as the unspeakable woodcarvings on sale everywhere in Oberammergau, or even the odiously commercialized nature of the entire place. (Or even, for that matter, the grim irony in the fact that Oberammergau in general, and many of the cast in the 1930 Passion Play in particular, had an abominable record of Nazi sympathizing.)

I do not think it matters if the text is or is not changed for the 1980 Passion Play; I hope no one will be put off contemplating a visit by the present dispute; and I promise those who do go a very remarkable experience, untroubled by thoughts of anti-semitism or indeed of any of this world's concerns.

The Times November 28th, 1978

The House of Wagner

WITH THE POSSIBLE exception of the House of Atreus, I cannot think of a line more dreadfully cursed, from generation to generation, than the family Wagner. The genealogy springs into public view, as abruptly as the sunken treasure in the first scene of *Das Rheingold*, with one of the most stupendously original creative geniuses in the entire history of art. Many great artists have been flawed human beings; Richard Wagner was surely unique in the breadth of the gap between his measure as an artist and as a man, in which latter capacity he was about as detestable as it is possible for a man to be. To the hideous warp in his own personality he then proceeded to ally the rancid blood of Franz Liszt, in the person of that mountebank's daughter Cosima, a fitting consort, if we judge by the shadow in her own character, for the monster himself. Then their son, Siegfried, who may well have been the only entirely nice and normal scion the family has so far produced, married a woman who was — is — surely the only human being in existence who could actually give both his mother and his father a start and a beating in the way of character. (A year or so ago — Siegfried's widow has so far outlived her husband by forty-eight years, Cosima having outlived Richard by forty-seven — she proudly announced that her admiration and affection for Hitler were as strong as they had been when he was her regular guest at Bayreuth.)

It has not ended yet, and is unlikely ever to do so. There were dreadful aunts, who quarrelled and denounced and sulked; there were scenes so appalling that from time to time one member of the family would apply for injunctions to prevent another from entering not only the family home but the very town where it stood. Anon, one would cut three minutes from the performance of a work lasting sixteen hours for no better reason than to provoke comment and attract publicity; anon, beside Richard Wagner's grave, Richard Wagner's daughter-in-law was filmed with the rest of Richard Wagner's family, not a single one of them willing to stand near her, let alone speak to her, and she apparently unmoved by the experience. I saw two of them together not long ago. They were all loving smiles for each other; passers-by who knew nothing of their history would never have guessed that there had once existed between them a hatred so intense that one of them had calmly threatened to have the other murdered.

There's no art to find the mind's construction in the face. Go and put the quintet from Act Three of *Die Meistersinger* on the gramophone, and tell me if you can hear the darkness that runs through its creator's story. Better: put on the Siegfried Idyll, and tell me if you can believe that it was written by one of the most selfish men who ever lived, for a woman who was 'astonished at the propensities of the Jews – they can sniff out anything, just like the Jesuits'.

How can this mystery be explained? How can the even greater mystery, of artistic creation itself, be explained? They cannot be, of course; but next best to explaining them is seeing them at close quarters. No closer quarters could well be imagined than those described and recorded in a book which lies before me, dressed in a jacket of tasteful purple; it is 2¾in. thick, and weighs 3lb. 12¾oz., and is roughly half of the complete work, the second half being due to appear sometime next year. It is, of course, the English edition (published by Collins) of *The Diary of Cosima Wagner.*

Long awaited indeed. The diary begins when Cosima, then still the wife of Hans von Bülow (though she had already borne her future husband two children and was expecting his third), went to live with Wagner. Thereafter, she kept it daily, through *Sturm und Drang*, for the fourteen years during which they were together; she made no entry on the day he died, or for any day of the half-century that she lived after that. She died in 1930, and the fate of the diaries in the further half-century that has since elapsed has been pregnant with characteristic Wagner hatred, vilification, paranoia and lawsuits; the diary has not been published until now because it couldn't be.

O Julius Caesar, thou art mighty still! What other artist's spirit, the man dead ninety-five years, can thus walk abroad and turn his sword in our own proper entrails? For the book provides no feeling, in the reader of these thousand pages (and another thousand to come, remember), that it is all battles long ago, of no greater contemporary interest than Beethoven's troubles with his nephew or Mozart's with the Archbishop. On the contrary, the book induces a positively hallucinatory feeling that the man will be on the telephone any minute, demanding money with menaces and writing abusive letters if it is refused.

But that feeling, after all, is parallel to the feeling Wagner's music arouses still. As I have said before, it is possible for a music-lover to dislike or be bored by the works of any other composer without feeling the need to do anything about it except stay away from the hall or the opera house when they are being played; but sane and civilized people, deeply versed in Bach or Beethoven or Berlioz, can and do hate the music of Wagner as though it was a deadly insult directed at their innermost feelings.

Which of course it is; Wagner makes us see those things in ourselves that we would rather – much rather – not see, and many of us find ourselves unable to bear the revelation, while others (I am one of them) are profoundly and forever grateful to him for teaching us so much about ourselves. But what makes the book so remarkable, what makes it, indeed, unique among biographies, is that both sorts of reaction to Wagner are fully satisfied by it. Those who revel in Wagner's music and those who loathe it will alike find the book irresistibly absorbing; so, if there are any such, will those who have no feelings about his music one way or another. For *The Diary of Cosima Wagner* is, as well as being an account of surpassing creative genius at work, a record of two human beings, and their love and life together, unlike any other such story that I have read. And the most amazing thing about it is that although the diarist records, quite unmindful of what she is doing, every odious thought and action either of them had, both of them come out of it as figures not just tragically and irreparably flawed, but also and compatibly of the most immense and wonderful human stature. For from these pages, Cosima emerges as a woman utterly consumed by selfless love, and Richard as a man no less devoured by selfless service of art. I shall try to make good that claim tomorrow.

The Times October 10th, 1978

The other side of the Wagner record

THE RICHARD WAGNERS at home: the very thought seems bizarre, like wondering what sort of nightie Lady Macbeth wore, or whether Oedipus liked mustard on his sausages. And yet there they were, night after night, settling down after dinner to a domestic evening abusing the Jews and reading aloud to one another. What they read, like what they said about the Jews, was faithfully recorded day by day, for fourteen years, in Cosima's diary. The whole record was published in German in 1976; now the first half, running from the beginning of 1869 to the end of 1877 has appeared in English, in a fine translation by Geoffrey Skelton. Yesterday I remarked that this book should throw light on the two greatest mysteries of Wagner's life, which were, first, the contrast between the greatness of his art and the dreadfulness of his character, and second, the springs and nature of his artistic genius. As it happens, the book does indeed provide us with evidence on both those matters, but oddly enough it is more interesting in other areas altogether.

Take the after-dinner reading aloud that I mentioned. Omitting books by authors now quite forgotten, and those read not for pleasure but for some business or duty, we are left with a list which included, in addition to almost every play of Shakespeare's (some of them several times), works by Racine, Renan, Meister Eckhart, Freytag, Luther, Uhland, Scott, Herodotus, Euripides, Aristophanes, T. H. Huxley, Aeschylus, Ranke, Thucydides, Lessing (no, dear, not Doris Lessing), Homer, Cervantes, Plato, Carlyle, Xenophon, Gibbon, Tieck, Schopenhauer, the Brothers Grimm, Sophocles, Goethe, Schiller, Demosthenes, Boccaccio,

Molière, Lucian, Darwin, Beaumarchais, Guizot, the Upanishads, Machiavelli, Balzac, Buckle, Schlegel, Calderon, Voltaire, Gozzi, Hebbel and E. T. A. Hoffmann.

That is the first surprise; the astounding breadth of Wagner's culture; the way he talked about the authors shows that in almost every instance he had a profound understanding of their meaning and their place in his own life and mind. The second surprise follows from that; it lies in the depth and intensity with which he thought and felt about the great questions quite apart from their appearance in his work. Here he is at lunch with Richter, for instance, who says that he would have no objection to being cremated: 'What does it matter to me what is done with me after I am dead?'

> Whereupon R. asks him who this 'I' is of whom he is talking — does he think he never existed before and will never exist again, that his life begins and ends with his own self?

Felix qui potuit rerum cognoscere causas; throughout this immense and detailed record, we see Wagner not only as a reader of almost incredible voracity, but as an eager searcher for knowledge, wisdom and truth. The powerful attraction that bygone cultures had for him was matched by the relentless pursuit of understanding through art, psychology, history, even, occasionally, such 'real' events as the Franco-Prussian War. Almost anything, for Wagner, can set off a train of thought, which once set off, runs along its course giving off sparks of interest and value. 'Where understanding is lacking', he says here (during a discussion of the attacks on *Die Walküre* for its treatment of incest), 'words immediately take its place'; but he belied the aphorism (almost a definition of music, after all) with almost every word he spoke.

This first volume starts with Wagner at work on *Siegfried*; it ends with him no less absorbed in *Parsifal*; in between comes the conception, creation and opening of the Festspielhaus in Bayreuth, and the first complete production of *The Ring*, in 1876. To see the Festspielhaus rise brick by brick from the ground; to suffer with Richard and Cosima, day by day, at setbacks that would have caused Genghis Khan to weep; to hear him talking, almost hour by hour, about his hopes and fears, achievements and plans; this brings us as near as words can reach to the heart of genius. We are no wiser at the end about the eternal mystery of where genius comes from or indeed what exactly it is; but we are much nearer understanding how it operates, how it pours like a flood over any obstacle it can submerge and around those it cannot.

Psychiatrists are going to have a life's work ahead of them studying the dreams of both Richard and Cosima, exhaustively reported here, and no wonder, for the passion, violence and luridness of their sleeping thoughts are the stuff of casebooks rather than diaries. I would hardly expect the creator of Alberich and Fafner, Hagen and Erda, Loge and Hunding, to have an invariably untroubled rest with sweet dreams of buttercups and Mozart, but some of what pours out of his subconscious at night, recounted in the morning, makes one shiver more than a century later, and Cosima's dreams are no calmer. Here is one of his mildest reveries:

> R. cried out loudly in the night; he had dreamed that my father was trying to kill him with an instrument of torture, and I withdrew with cold eyes to the adjoining room, having been instructed by my father to guard the door.

Yet I said yesterday that, appalling though the characters of both Richard and Cosima were, they emerge from these pages enhanced and redeemed. Not quite redeemed, of course; the venom and hatred expressed by both of them against anyone who thwarted Richard's work or wishes in even the smallest particular is not to be excused in this world, any more than the anti-semitism. (Incidentally, though the annotation is in general excellent, the editors are wrong to identify the 'Haman' to whom Wagner is likened by a Jewish writer replying to his pamphlet *Judaism in Music* with an obscure eighteenth-century writer called 'Hamann'. Apart from the double n in the name and the single one in the Diary—though Cosima's orthography, it is true, was no great shakes—the reference must surely be to the Haman who was the chief minister of King Ahasuerus, a proto-Hitler who attempted to exterminate the Jews and whose downfall is celebrated to this day in the Jewish Festival of Purim.) But Cosima's love for her husband is one of the most intense and beautiful in history, and to see it expressed day after day in the Diary to which she entrusted all her thoughts and feelings is to be moved inescapably towards recognizing that this is Isolde herself. Cosima was no slave, no door-mat, for Richard; but a woman with an iron personality of her own (as indeed she was to show in the fifty years of tyranny with which she ruled Bayreuth after his death); but it was entirely at Richard's service.

> As, today, I become so profoundly aware of how much I believe in R., in his mission in life, in his genius, in his kindness, in his love, there gradually arose in me out of my glowing emotions, unshakable though shadowed by unspeakable suffering, a gentle feeling, pale and tender as the new moon rising over a glowing sunset. It spoke, not of fortune or success, nor of rest and joy, either – underlined and silent, it swelled up from my most intense feelings as that fairest of rewards, sweet hope.

The same extraordinary transformation takes place for him. His enemies, though not as numerous as he imagined, were real and implacable; his difficulties, though he made them worse by his behaviour, have rarely been equalled in the history of art. But the murderous fury with which he set about everything that stood in his way can now be seen, with tragic clarity, as the characteristic of a man convinced that he had creations inside him which it was his duty to give to the world, and who truly cared nothing for his own life, repute or happiness, so he could only bring those creations to birth.

Cosima Wagner's Diary is inexhaustibly fascinating; I beg the publishers to proceed to the publication of the second half with all the speed they may.

But one thing I have to add, with a heavy heart; the index is a disgrace – a disgrace to the book and a double disgrace to a great publishing house. There are no subject-entries at all, only entries for names and titles, and those are literally useless, being nothing but strings of undifferentiated page numbers, qualified, in the case of writers or composers, only by sub-entries listing their works (and these also with nothing but numbers). Forty pages have been inexcusably wasted, and a mighty work of enduring human interest defaced and damaged, by this scandalous folly. If Collins wish to regain the respect of their readers, they must have a proper index prepared in time for publication of the second volume, and it must be cumulative for the whole Diary.*

The Times October 12th, 1978

* They promised to do so.

Sandcastles on the road
from Morocco

THERE IS A generally dream-like quality about the dispute over the Spanish Sahara between King Hassan of Morocco (understandably anxious to find something irrelevant but entertaining with which his subjects may occupy their minds to the exclusion of dangerous thoughts about hanging him from a lamp-post) and the men of power in Spain (no less reasonably distracted by the problem of arranging the transition from Franco's rule in a manner that will give them the greatest chance of avoiding a similar fate) which prompts the reflection that King Hassan's impassioned concern for his suffering brothers across the Moroccan border would be less implausible if he had shown rather more for those already enjoying his rule. It also brings vividly to mind both Bismarck's despairing contention that only three men had ever understood the Schleswig-Holstein Question, of whom one was dead, one had gone mad, and he – the third – had forgotten, and Dr Johnson's point, made when asked to pronounce a preference between two bad poets, about the difficulty of establishing a point of precedency between a louse and a flea.

King Hassan has organized a mass march of Moroccans, with himself at its head, into the territory, which has a population of roughly one person for every $1\frac{1}{2}$ square miles (many of whom, it may be confidently asserted, have never heard of either Spain or Morocco); it must be what Shakespeare was thinking of in the scene between Hamlet and the Norwegian captain ('To pay five ducats, five, I would not farm it'), which provoked Hamlet to his memorable outburst:

> Witness this army of such mass and charge
> Led by a delicate and tender prince,
> Whose spirit with divine ambition puff'd
> Makes mouths at the invisible event,
> Exposing what is mortal and unsure,
> To all that fortune, death and danger dare,
> Even for an egg-shell ...

All the same, this has not prevented King Hassan from organizing his mass demo, which is due to set off any minute now, its generally surrealist nature being perhaps best appreciated from yesterday's report that 5,000 Moroccan soldiers, who had spontaneously arrived on the border in answer to the King's call for volunteers, in spontaneously organized lorries each of which had a spontaneously painted picture of King Hassan on the right-hand door, had been 'shouting epitaphs at Spain', information which you will not be surprised to learn has led me to speculate what form these might have taken, and even to try my hand at composing a representative sample, for instance, in the demotic mode:

> Here lies Ali, a loving Dad,
> Who thought Spanish rule was very bad;
> Franco's behaviour gave him a pain;
> Mum and the kids say 'till we meet again'.

Or, for those who prefer a more classical style:

Beneath this stone rests Fatima, an unmarried lady of exemplary piety, who devoted herself singlemindedly to the boycott of Spanish sherry, and departed this life, full of years and virtue, in the knowledge that by so doing she had materially contributed to the downfall of a hated tyrant. *Ubi saeva indignatio ulterius cor lacerare nequit.*

But absurd though everything and everybody concerned in this nonsense undoubtedly is, and unlikely though it is that even a single inhabitant of either the Spanish Sahara or Morocco will be, whatever the outcome of the epic struggle, better off in any particular or to the smallest extent, it does matter. For however savage was Hamlet's scorn, and however justified ('While to my shame I see The imminent death of twenty thousand men, That for a fantasy and trick of fame, Go to their graves like beds'), it must be remembered that he was wrong when he concluded, in his enlightened way, that if the territory was as unimportant and unprofitable as the Norwegian officer said, 'Why then, the Polack never will defend it', receiving when he said as much the melancholy and unanswerable reply, 'Yes, it is already garrisoned'.

So, I am sure, unless the gathering situation in Madrid altogether precludes it, is the Spanish Sahara, and if it comes to fighting I have no doubt that the defenders will acquit themselves stoutly, and that among them will be many of the very Saharans whom the march is supposed to be liberating. And although I take it that he would be a bold Moroccan who refused to join the march and gave as his reason this inability to believe that it would do him or anybody else any good, I am also sure that there will be thousands on it fully persuaded that they are consumed with zeal for the ending of a burning disgrace and the freeing of their soul brothers from the colonialist yoke. It is at times like this that my thoughts always return to the false Etruscan:

> Shame on the false Etruscan,
> Who lingers in his home,
> When Porsena of Clusium
> Is on the march for Rome.

You see, the trouble with the false Etruscan is that he felt every bit as ashamed of himself as Macaulay thought he should be. No matter that the attempt at the restoration of the Tarquins in general and Sextus in particular was disgraceful and indefensible, and that the Etruscans could have occupied themselves far more profitably by getting rid of Lars Porsena and using for the purpose of building a few village schools and some irrigation canals whatever part of his ill-gotten fortune had not already been transferred to a numbered bank account in Switzerland; the fact remains that the call of nationalism, however spurious, indeed however obviously spurious, echoes louder than the call of reason. Some who would not die for liberty will die for Liberia, others who care nothing for truth would lay down their lives for Tristan da Cunha, and I daresay there are those who care nothing for monarchy but everything for Monaco.

Throughout history, rulers have known this, and known how to use it. The pages of Gibbon are littered with emperors whose first action on gaining the precarious throne was to set off on an expedition of conquest, and from that day to this their successors have realized no less that the easiest road to power and security is the one that lies across a neighbouring frontier. Today it is even easier, for the order to march can be accompanied by an assurance that it is designed to unite brother with brother, mingle blood with like blood, free shackled compatriots from alien rule. Whether it is Hitler with the Sudetenland, Ho Chi Minh with South Vietnam, Mao with Tibet or King Hassan with the Spanish Sahara, conquest can now be called liberation, greed rescue, self-preservation self-determination. Many of those Moroccan soldiers who so improbably 'shouted epitaphs at Spain' may shortly need epitaphs for themselves, with few to shout them, but it is by no means certain that they will ask themselves whether it was really worth it as they die. Some will, certainly; and it is these few in every civilization who carry the faint and flickering torch of humanity and reason down the centuries, simply by always measuring pretext against reality and bravely announcing the results of their calculations. But it has generally escaped notice that even Hamlet, in the very scene I have quoted, managed to miss the point, and concluded that greatness lies in the ability to find quarrel in a straw, when honour's at the stake.

So King Hassan will get his volunteers and set off across the frontier as a popular hero, just as Idi Amin increased his popularity at home, rather than decreasing it, by killing or driving out the Asians, and for that matter as Napoleon, by getting most of the *Grande Armée* unnecessarily killed, ensured the devotion of the survivors; depend upon it, if he had succeeded in escaping from St Helena, he would have lasted twice a hundred days, and if he had won the battle of Waterloo he would have lasted for ever. There are always, it is true, the consolations of history, and King Ozymandias of Morocco will leave no more lasting imprint on the sands of time than on those of the Spanish Sahara. But the consolations of history come slowly, and the King of Morocco sets off next week; did I mention that those soldiers of his who shouted epitaphs at Spain also shouted, even more improbably: 'We will not betray the Moroccan Sahara'?

The Times October 28th, 1975

The politics of iniquity

IT HAS NOW been officially stated that Myra Hindley and Ian Brady* will be considered for parole in the course of 1978; considered for parole, not necessarily given it. This, of course, means that the Parole Board, and possibly the Home Office, have now caught up with Lord Longford, who has been pressing the case for such consideration for some time now, notably on a television programme which, a few months ago, caused a considerable uproar. The uproar partly concerned the nature and format of the programme; I did not see it, and since it was impossible to disentangle the row over the programme from the question of substance — to wit, whether either or both of them should or should not eventually be released — I decided to say nothing, though in this matter I am of Lord Longford's opinion. The fuss over the programme having died down, however, it should now be possible to discuss without distraction the case for and against the release of these prisoners, and I propose to do so today. (Strictly speaking, incidentally, a prisoner serving a life sentence cannot be released on parole, only 'on licence', but the principle is the same, and I shall use the more familiar expression.)

The case illustrates to grim perfection the confusion that surrounds — indeed, that constitutes — our society's attitude to imprisonment and the reasons for it. In theory, punishment is meant to reform those who undergo it and to deter any who might be tempted to emulate the action of the punished; in addition, it is sometimes (though not so often as in earlier times) said to be in-

* The 'Moors Murderers' of children.

tended as retribution, so that it ought to be meted out to wrong-doers irrespective of any practical effect it might have. Officially though, the last argument has no place in our penology, and the state's duty is supposed to be limited to ensuring that criminals are punished in a manner which gives the greatest hope that they will not do it again (this includes the element in the theory which is simply concerned with protecting society against those who are too dangerous to be loosed upon it) and the greatest chance of inhibiting others from doing as they did.

The deterrent effect of the life sentence imposed on Miss Hindley and Mr Brady for the appalling crimes of which they were both justly convicted is, and always was, obviously nil. The origins of the impulses that drove them to such evil are buried deep in the human psyche; whatever they may be, they are not to be reached by any probe of reason. Those capable not only of conceiving but of carrying out sadistic practices of the kind involved in their case are incapable of weighing the consequences for their victims, or indeed of understanding them.

Next, reform. Here we come to territory on which there are recognizable landmarks. Lord Longford, who has visited Miss Hindley frequently, and a recently released prisoner who had seen much of her in prison, are both convinced that she has genuinely repented of her crimes, and would be no danger to society or anyone in it if she were now released.

Such testimony is obviously not conclusive. It is however, presumably supplemented by various reports on her behaviour and attitude prepared by the prison authorities and other individuals and bodies whose duties include the making of such observations and the preparation of such studies. Certainly, if the Home Secretary were to contemplate releasing Miss Hindley he would have a formidable body of evidence on which to come to a conclusion. And if he is of the opinion that she has not repented, and that she would be a continuing danger if released, he should say so.

But that brings me to the confusion of which I speak. For it is dreadfully clear that even if it were agreed on all hands that in no circumstances would she ever do anything criminal again, the present Home Secretary* would be reluctant to release her simply because he would be unwilling, for political reasons, to face the inevitable fury. And the inevitable fury is, of course, based on the theory of punishment that is supposed to have no place in our system, to wit the retributive. Myra Hindley did terrible things to innocent children; therefore, runs the instant but unreasoning answer, she must rot in jail for the rest of her life.

But I do not see the force of that 'therefore'. If she is still a potential menace, then she must certainly not be released, at any rate unless such conditions and safeguards are arranged as to ensure that she is unable to do further harm. But if she is not–if, in short, she would be released were she any other prisoner–then her continued incarceration is indefensible.

The abiding hatred of the close families of the victims in this case is understandable (I gather it was expressed with vehemence on the television programme I referred to). Such hatred, like all hatred, is inevitably damaging and corrosive in its effects on those who nurture it; but the horrible wickedness of what was done to their children is such that it would require something not far removed from sainthood to come to terms with the feelings it arouses. But though we surely all feel revulsion at the crimes, and it will be a sorry day for our society when we feel anything less in such circumstances, the rest of us have no right to the desire for revenge that possesses those whose children died.

In particular, the Home Secretary and the Parole Board have no right to such feelings, and above all no right to act on them if they have them. An earlier Home Secretary displayed an unnecessary eagerness to condemn the action of a wise and experienced prison governor who took Miss Hindley out for a walk; that was Mr Robert Carr, and the present holder of the office is unlikely to be less responsive to political pressure than he. It is therefore even more unlikely, whatever advice he may get, not only from Lord Longford and other outsiders who have spent time with Miss Hindley, but from his professional advisers, that

* Mr Merlyn Rees.

the Home Secretary will be willing to authorize the taking of even the first step on the road to her release. Yet I repeat; if all necessary conditions are met, and all fears are satisfied, how can it be right to keep her in jail, when any other prisoner would be released, only because of the ugly clamour that would follow? (And even the Parole Board's chairman, in announcing next year's review, has said that 'likely public reaction' would be taken into account.)

And there is another matter, and that perhaps the most disquieting of all. As far as I know, there has been not a word on the subject from any member of the hierarchies of the Anglican or Roman Catholic churches in this country. Why should there be? Not because it is the duty of Christian archbishops or cardinals to urge mercy for sinners (though the founder of their religion, now I come to think of it, did a good deal in that line), but because, through all the clamour that has arisen over the suggestion that Miss Hindley might be released, there has run the argument that not only has she not purged her sin, but that she never can. The belief that repentance and salvation are beyond a sinner, however terrible the sin, is a heresy of the worst kind; indeed, it makes nonsense of the entire Christian message ('Betwixt the stirrup and the ground ... '). Yet we have heard nothing from the churches (Lord Longford is a Roman Catholic, of course, but I am not talking about lay opinion) in condemnation of such abominable reasoning. I do not, as a matter of fact, expect high church dignitaries, these days, to be less timid than Home Secretaries. But it would be good to hear one of them speak up for Christianity, and it is not at all good to listen in vain for one of them to do so.*

The Times December 21st, 1977

---

* They never did. Nor did the Home Secretary or the Parole Board take any action or make any recommendation.

I

Carry on up the flagpole

You will be so kind as to address me in future as 'Your Excellency' as befits one of my standing, my standing being that of the Honorary Plenipotentiary Extraordinary of the Republic of Burundi, and if you think that I am joking you will speedily discover that you are mistaken, or not, as the case may be.

It all began a few months ago, when I was both delighted and astonished to receive an invitation to propose the toast of 'The Theatre' at the Shakespeare Birthday Celebrations in Stratford-upon-Avon. Delighted because I had never, in all the years I have been going to Stratford, attended the annual whoopee on the Bard's birthday, let alone in such a capacity, and astonished because relations between me and the Bard's home town have for many years been of a distinctly glacial nature, the attainment of Absolute Zero having been announced when the then Mayor, goaded beyond endurance by my latest assault on his fair borough, was asked by an enterprising reporter whether he had any comment on this new outbreak (I cannot remember exactly what I had said, but I seem to recall that even a careful reader would have gained the impression that I had been comparing the place unfavourably with Sodom and Gomorrah), and replied, with a rather closer approximation to the truth than felt entirely comfortable, 'Whenever Bernard Levin can't think of anything to write about, he attacks Stratford-upon-Avon.'

An invitation to be one of the principle guests at the Birthday Banquet, amid the massed ranks of the Diplomatic Corps, the Master of the Rolls and the Bishop of Coventry, seemed to me, therefore, a sign that All was Forgiven, and I hastened to accept, and to prepare my speech; this was to be one of two, the other being made by Lord Denning, proposing the toast of the Immortal Memory.

From time to time, as the day approached, I would receive further information from those in charge of the Stratford celebrations, who seemed to be, and, as it turned out, actually were, extraordinarily efficient. (All is Forgiven on my side, too, you see.) From this I learned that the luncheon was by no means the only item on the agenda; there was also the Procession, and the Unfurling of the Flags of the Nations.

The Procession consists of the chief municipal dignitaries, the Diplomatic Corps, the leading actors from the Royal Shakespeare Company, the clergy, a sprinkling of Peers of the Realm and such, and as many of the townsfolk as wish to join on at the tail of the column. The march, I learnt, was to form up at the Theatre, visit the Birthplace, go on to the tomb in Holy Trinity Church, and return to the Theatre, for lunch in the immense marquee specially erected beside it. But the first stop the Procession makes is for the Ceremony of the Flags, which is where my sudden elevation to diplomatic status comes in. Getting on for 150 flagpoles are erected in the main streets of Stratford for this occasion, and from them fly the flags of every country in the world you can think of, together with a substantial number you cannot. Many countries send their Ambassador or High Commissioner; others are represented by a Minister, Counsellor or the like; but a few are unable to send any official representative, and for these some of the Birthday guests are asked to do the honours. Lord Denning, I gathered, would be unfurling the banner of Mauritius: would I stand in for Burundi?

Now that, you will agree, was an offer I could not refuse, and pausing only to elicit the fact that I would not be expected to sing Burundi's National Anthem, let alone to discuss its exports of copra, bauxite or jute, I accepted that invitation, too, and was only sorry that I did not have time to hire Burundian national costume from Nathan's, such dress being recommended for the various ambassadorial dignitaries. (I settled instead for my famous pink jacket.)

I did have time, though, to start constructing the appropriate fantasies. Those of you who think you know me will guess that my first intention was to park on a double yellow line and claim diplomatic immunity, or to insist on buying several million gallons of duty-free whisky; those who actually do know me will realize that these trivial dreams were secondary, and that what first sprang to my mind was a plan to foment a major diplomatic incident, or better still a world war.

I discovered that my Burundian flagpole was between those of Cyprus and Trinidad, and decided that I would call out to the former, in the hush before the fanfare that was to signal the moment of unfurling: 'I say – our friend from Trinidad tells me that in his country there is a popular saying to the effect that all Cypriots are thieves – jolly amusing, what?' In the event, however, I was too busy disentangling the lanyard: this had obviously been sabotaged by a group of Burundian Irredentists opposed to my home Government, whose action very nearly resulted in the Burundian flag flying at half-mast throughout the ceremony, which would in turn have necessitated an official statement on my part to the effect that our Minister of Agriculture had died during the night, and that I would expect the Diplomatic Corps, in strict order of seniority, to present themselves at my hotel in the course of the afternoon to offer their condolences.

The Procession, preceded by the band of the Royal Engineers, who are Freemen of Stratford, was led by the Chief of Police and the Town Beadle, the latter a magnificent (and perfectly spherical) figure, resplendent in scarlet coat, lace ruffles, cocked hat and staff of office. Marshalling the diplomatic representatives before the column moved off must have been a formidable task for the organizers; I had visions of the scene backstage at the Miss World contest, with harassed officials rushing about crying, 'Peru, Peru, where are you?' or 'Has anybody seen Luxembourg since breakfast?' But that, too, went off without a hitch. I should explain, incidentally, that one of the traditions is that everybody in the procession carries flowers, which are laid on the Poet's tomb when we get to the church; I chose a single elegant, dark red rose (which went rather well, I thought, with the jacket), but some countries had immense wreaths – I thought Denmark would collapse before we arrived.

We marched straight into the Birthplace through the front door, and straight out again through the back; not even the most hurried American tourist, I'll be bound, has ever done the place in a shorter time. As we approached the church, the band fell silent and the bells began to peal; when my rose was added, the tomb was already several feet deep in flowers.

On the front door of my hotel, where the rooms have Shakespearean character or place names (I was in Belmont, the management no doubt remembering that I had once said that if they ever put me in Bottom I'd sue), I found when I returned the memorable rubric 'World Harmony, please use next entrance'. (I had not, of course, forgotten to visit the great Miss Withey of the Chaucer Head Bookshop, who has put together a fine exhibition showing how the few remaining bits of attractive or historic architecture in Stratford are being enthusiastically pulled down.) In the evening, to the theatre, for an enchanting *Much Ado* with Judi Dench and Donald Sinden. Next morning, I made a quick tour of the flags; Switzerland and Rwanda had the largest; Burundi still flew proudly between Trinidad and Cyprus.

I do not believe that if Shakespeare had belonged to any other nation in the world anything like this would happen on April 23rd every year. The French would make it too elegant: the Americans too big; the Germans too accurate; the Scots too sour; the Russians too political; the Italians too untidy. Only this strange, brave, crazy, lovable, ridiculous, indomitable people can do this kind of thing as it should be done, and in the doing keep their eternal tryst with 'Faith, and green fields, and honour, and the sea'. We have lost our faith, the Ministry of the Environment will shortly be arranging the extinction of the last green field, our honour is in pawn a dozen times over; of the four pillars only the sea remains, that same sea of which Heine remarked that it would have swallowed England long ago, if it had not been afraid of getting indigestion. But for a day, in the sunshine at Stratford, the world stood still and saluted Stratford's son. The whole thing was absurd, moving, splendid, and uniquely English, and I would not have missed it for any consideration. Burundi papers please copy.

The Times April 27th, 1976

The blood on the flag

HE JESTS AT scars that never felt a wound. In the account I gave here a few weeks ago of my participation in the Shakespeare Birthday celebrations, I rather made mock of my role as unfurler of the flag of Burundi, and by implication of Burundi itself. For this lightheartedness I have been triply rebuked; offensively by the usual fool who accused me of caring only about white sins in Africa and condoning black ones, civilly by a number of informed readers who wrote more in sorrow than in anger, and usefully by Mr Ben Whitaker, director of that admirably hard-headed organization the Minority Rights Group, who has sent me a report—exemplary in its objectivity, thoroughness and force—written for the M.R.G. by Professor René Lemarchand and Mr David Martin. It is called *Selective Genocide in Burundi*, and from it I have learned in detail what I had previously known only as a vague and half-forgotten impression: that Burundi is no joke, and that the flag I unfurled at Stratford had blood on it.

The modern history of Burundi, which had been part of Belgian-mandated territories adjacent to the Congo, is complex in the extreme (though not nearly so complex as the story of the tribal and political rivalries and hatreds which issued in the appalling story that the M.R.G. report tells). Its details need not concern us now, except to the extent of knowing that it has been an independent state since 1962, that a brief-lived union with Rwanda was dissolved in 1964, and that the tribal conflict that dogs Burundi has also affected Zaire (formerly the Belgian Congo) and Rwanda.

The present situation in Burundi is described by Professor Lemarchand in these terms:

It has become the only state in independent black Africa to claim the appurtenances of a genuine caste society; a country in which power is the monopoly of a dominant ethnic minority (Tutsi) representing less than 15 per cent of the total population ... The pattern of dominance extends to virtually all sectors of life, restricting access to material wealth, education, status and power to representatives of the dominant society.

The Tutsi minority has gained this dominance over the Hutu majority, though it must not be supposed either that the Hutus are a gentle and peace-loving people (in the Hutu rising, in 1972, which gave President Micombero the excuse for the terror and slaughter used to suppress the rival ethnic group, appalling atrocities were committed against members of the Tutsi), or that the conflict is simply one between two ethnic blocs, for there are other groups and interests whose rivalries, ambitions and actions have contributed both to the difficulty of disentangling the rights and wrongs of what has happened as well as to the intensity of the hatreds involved and to the dreadful nature of what has flowed from those hatreds.

But whatever the rights and wrongs, many of the facts seem to be beyond dispute; and these facts are more horrible than anything that has happened in the realms of political or sectarian violence between the slaughter that followed the attainment of independence by India and Pakistan in 1947 and the slaughter going on in Cambodia today. The actions of the rebels in the Hutu rising was similar to that of the *simbas* in the Congo — characteristic, that is, of a reversion to primitive savagery, with the killers resorting to drugs, believing themselves invulnerable through magic, and indiscriminately killing and mutilating men, women and children; Professor Lemarchand estimates the number of victims as approximately 2,000.

But this was as nothing compared with what followed, when President Micombero seized the chance to settle accounts with the Hutu. It began with the imposition of martial law and the systematic extermination, by the army and the revolutionary youth brigades, of anyone believed (no form of trial took place, of course) to have been associated with the rebellion. It continued with the random slaughter of Hutu, in many cases as acts of personal revenge or for the gain of their property. It turned eventually into genocide:

In Bururi the army attacked all Hutu more or less indiscriminately. In Bujumbura, Gitega and Ngozi all 'cadres' of Hutu origins – including not only local administrators but chauffeurs, clerks and skilled workers – were systematically rounded up, taken to jail and either shot or beaten to death with rifle butts or clubs. In Bujumbura alone an estimated 4,000 Hutu were loaded up on trucks and taken to their graves. According to one Tutsi witness 'they picked up almost all the Hutu intellectuals above the secondary school level', and many more, one might add, below the level.
  Some of the most gruesome scenes took place on the premises of the Université Officielle ... and in secondary and technical schools. Scores of Hutu students were physically assaulted by their Tutsi confrères; many were beaten to death... groups of soldiers and jeunesses would suddenly appear in classrooms, call the Hutu students by name and take them away. Few ever returned. At the Université Officielle about one third (120) disappeared in these circumstances. The Ecole Normale of Ngagara ... lost more than 100 students out of a total of 314 ... Not only the Hutu elites were thus physically liquidated ...
  Twelve Hutu priests are said to have been killed, and thousands of protestant pastors, school directors and teachers. In the Bujumbura hospital six doctors and eight nurses were arrested and are believed to be dead ... The repression took on the qualities of a 'selective genocide' directed at all the educated or semi-educated strata of Hutu society ...
  Throughout May and half June, 1972, the excavators were busy every night in Gitega and Bujumbura burying the dead in mass graves ... Those arrested were usually dead the same night, stripped and practically clubbed to death in covered

lorries on the way to prison, then finished off there with clubs at nightfall. Using bullets would have been wasteful ...

From the ... repression a new society has in fact emerged, in which only Tutsi elements are qualified to gain access to power, influence and wealth; what is left of Hutu society is now systematically excluded from the army, the civil service, the university and secondary schools. (The reimposition of school fees in September 1973 has had the effect of further reducing the number of fatherless and other Hutu children in primary and secondary schools; as one missionary put it 'having dealt with the "elite" fathers, the potentially "elite" children are excluded from education'.) Hutu status has become synonymous with an inferior category of beings ...

Of course there has been no rebuke for the slaughterers from the United Nations; nor (also of course) has the Organization of African Unity said a word on the subject. Zaire and Tanzania both sent military supplies to the Micombero Government, though both were probably deceived as to the use to which these were to be put; no such excuse can be made by France:

As one knowledgeable observer put it: 'French military assistants ... were holding the helicopters steady while Burundi soldiers were machine-gunning Hutu rebels out of the side windows ...

Few political conclusions can be drawn from what has happened, and is happening, in Burundi. There is no way of ensuring that these mad dogs who infest our world – the Micomberos and Khieu Samphans, Amins and Castros, Bokassas and Kim Il Sungs, Stroessners and Gadaffis – can be prevented from gaining power, or from using it, once gained, to further their political and personal aims (though in most of these cases there is no distinction in their minds), with bloody and indiscriminate repressions. We are reminded yet again of the fragility of civilization, of the dangers of power, of the dehumanizing effects of ideology; but none of these reflections is of much help to the dead, or for that matter to the survivors. What we can do is to ensure that at any rate people know; and since I inadvertently made it clear that I, for one, did not know of the horrors perpetrated in Burundi, I felt that the least I could do in the way of amends was to contribute my mite today towards the spreading of that knowledge.

The Times May 21st, 1976

Marriage à la mode

Portrait of a Marriage by Nigel Nicolson*

THE MARRIAGE PORTRAYED is that of the author's parents, Harold Nicolson and Vita Sackville-West. Both were homosexuals, which is strange enough; stranger still, the marriage endured, and in almost unbroken felicity, for fifty years. But strangest of all, in the circumstances, it was a love-match from start to finish, as we already know beyond doubt from Harold Nicolson's diaries. (How different, how very, very different, from the home life of our own dear queens.)

Three-quarters of the book is by Nigel Nicolson; it serves as a frame for the other quarter, which is a kind of diary kept by his mother, running for nine months but extending all the way back to her childhood, and giving in particular a detailed account of a tempestuous love affair she had with another woman, Violet Trefusis, which began some five years after the Nicolsons' marriage and continued, on and off, for some three years.

Mr Nicolson found the diary after his mother's death, but before his father's. Now that both his parents, and Violet Trefusis and her husband, are dead, he has published it, and the frame he has built round it serves to fill out the picture. He asks us to share ('Let not the reader condemn in 10 minutes the decision which I have pondered for 10 years') his conviction 'that in the 1970s an experience of this kind need no longer be regarded as shameful or unmentionable', and he is entitled to an unqualified acceptance of his plea.

*Weidenfeld and Nicolson, 1973.

But what Mr Nicolson cannot see is that his mother appears not shameful but ridiculous, not a monster but a poseuse, not perverted but egotistical, and her own part of the book not the tormented confession of a soul in purgatory but a short story rejected by the editor of *True Confessions* combined with the moonings of a schoolgirl who has a crush on the hockey mistress.

'I believe', says Mr Nicolson, 'that she wrote it with eventual publication in mind.' *Believe* is a fine word in the circumstances, I must say; there is hardly a line of Vita Sackville-West's contribution that does not bawl in posterity's face, and if it comes to that hardly a line that is not grotesquely artificial. How's this from the first two paragraphs, for instance?

> I would not give it to *her*—perilous touchstone!, who even in these first score of lines should teach me where truth lies ... I start writing, having spent no consideration upon this task. Shall I ever complete it? and under what circumstances?, begun as it is, in the margin between a wood and a ripe cornfield, with the faint shadows of grasses and ears of corn falling across my page. Unkernelled nuts hang behind me ... I lie on green bracken, amongst little yellow and magenta wild-flowers whose names I don't know ... All day I have been in a black temper, but that is soothed away. There is no place, out here, for temper or personality. There is only one personality present: Demeter.

Two, actually; Demeter appears to have been joined by Judith Starkadder, and subsequently by Christopher Robin:

> She got her mother to ask mine to send me to tea. I went. We sat in a darkened room, and talked—about our ancestors, of all strange topics—and in the hall as I left she kissed me. I made up a little song that evening, 'I've got a friend!' I remember so well. I sang it in my bath.

But then it begins. After an early awakening of her true sexual nature, before her marriage, it lies dormant until Violet seduces her, and then it's a 'mad and irresponsible summer of moonlight nights, and infinite escapades, and passionate letters, and music, and poetry' (and too many commas), and then Violet's intended turns up with 'hair like gold wire, blue eyes starting out of his head, and winged nostrils', and is promptly compared 'to a Crusader, to a greyhound, to an ascetic in search of the Holy Grail' (it must have been those winged nostrils – you never saw a greyhound with hair like gold wire or blue eyes starting out of its head). Anyway, Denys gets in the way only during the day-time, and 'the evenings were ours', whereupon

> I have never told a soul of what I did. I hesitate to write it here, but I must; shirking the truth here would be like cheating oneself playing patience. I dressed as a boy.

There's reckless you are! But when Violet and Denys finally get married, after Vita decides just before the wedding not to go through with the plan for the two women to elope (she had heard from Harold, and 'something snapped in my mind'), the honeymooners and Vita all find themselves in Paris together, and Vita takes Violet away from Denys ('I wanted to say "Don't you know, you stupid fool, that she is mine in every sense of the word?"'), then Denys takes her back from Vita ('That night I dined at the Ritz, and from the open window of her room Violet watched me, and Denys sobbed in the room behind her', and the general conclusion is that 'That day seems to have made a great impression upon him' – well, I suppose it would) after which 'they went away to St Jean de Luz, and I went to Switzerland with Harold', and then they all go back to England, but soon the girls are off again, to Paris ('I used to sit in cafés drinking coffee, and watching people go by' – fancy!) and Monte Carlo ('divine'), where 'a complication arose over Denys announcing his arrival at Cannes' (by now his blue eyes must have been damned near *falling* out of his head, never mind starting), and they all form twos again and go back to London, but then Violet goes off to Amiens, where Vita is to join her, for ever this time, only when Vita follows she takes Denys along, which complicates the situation until Denys says he will leave them and never come back ('Denys cried the whole way'), but he *does* come back, this time travelling with Harold and only a couple of lengths behind Violet's father, and then Harold actually suggests that Violet may have slept with her own husband ('I thought I should have gone mad when he said that') so Vita makes a scene and goes off with Harold from Amiens to Paris, and Violet's father catches the same train, but no sooner do they get to Paris than Violet turns up (maybe she was at the other end of the train), and the two girls go up to Harold's and Vita's room, whereupon Harold bursts in with Denys (how many people were *on* that train, for God's sake?), and Denys swears that he has never done anything unbecoming with his own wife ('I promise you there has never been anything of that kind between Violet and me'), which mollifies Vita a little, 'but still it was bad enough that she should have deceived me even to a certain extent', and then it all gets rather confused, except that at one point Vita goes to Paris, Violet goes to Bordighera and Denys goes to Cornwall (no mention of Harold – perhaps he's just gone to bed), and among other places visited by the various parties are Avignon, San Remo and Venice – oh, now I remember where Harold was – he says he has been 'spending his time with rather low people, the demi-monde', and he sums up by saying 'my heart feels like a pêche melba', and then Violet fades away and Harold and Vita live happily ever after, apart from Vita's having an affair with Virginia Woolf, and another one, just to vary things, with Geoffrey Scott, while Harold ...

The long and the short of the matter is that practically everybody in this ludicrous story has a nice comfortable income, apart from the charwoman whom Vita steps across when visiting Violet early one morning, and of whom she says 'There was a dreary slut scrubbing the doorstep'. When you have plenty of money you can not only afford to rush about between London and Amiens and Paris (where you stay at the Ritz, of course – well, I mean, doesn't everybody?) and San Remo and Bordighera and Monte Carlo and Avignon and Venice; you can also afford (if you are silly enough to want to) to spend your time striking grotesque poses, keening over your own emotions, and saying things like 'I had been vouchsafed insight, as one sometimes is'. The 'dreary slut' scrubbing the doorstep could no more afford the poses than she could afford the travel, and I would dearly like to read *her* diary, particularly if it contained a passage about some stupid, snobbish, affected woman who stepped right on to her nice clean doorstep the minute after she had just whitewashed the bleedin' thing.

Mr Nigel Nicolson had half a century of his parents' happy marriage to write about; half a century in which they loved one another, wrote many interesting books and created one of the great gardens of England. Instead, he has chosen to use a trivial and preposterous exercise in self-indulgence by his mother as the centrepiece of a very different work. He tells us that when he found the diary he 'read it through to the end without stirring from her table'. He should then have put it in the fire.

Observer October 28th, 1973

Valour knows no barriers

I AM SORRY ABOUT the row in Wolverhampton that marred the town's Remembrance Day ceremonies, and not only because anything which mars such an occasion is matter for sadness. But the occasion for the unpleasantness is matter for greater concern than the unpleasantness itself.

The mayor of Wolverhampton, into whose province such matters apparently fall, acceded to a request from the Wolverhampton chapter of the Campaign for Homosexual Equality that they should be represented at the town's commemoration of the dead of the two world wars, and that they should be allowed to lay a wreath in memory of homosexuals who died alongside their heterosexual fellow-servicemen. At this, some of those who had intended being at the ceremony in a representative capacity, including those directing the official ex-servicemen's associations, declared that they would not attend, giving as their reason that they did not want to be associated with homosexuals in any way. And it seems that they did indeed refuse to turn up.

Which is a pity. To start with, it may be asked why the homosexual organization wished to be represented at the ceremony in its collective capacity; could not homosexuals simply go to the commemoration as individuals, and lay wreaths likewise? I suppose they could, and perhaps should; but such ceremonies are normally attended by individuals on behalf of groups, and I am not sure that individual wreaths are permitted except as enshrining such collectively organized gestures; I don't think the public in general, for instance, is allowed to lay wreaths at the Cenotaph, at any rate before the Remembrance Day service.

More to the point, perhaps, is another question; why should homosexuals who died in war be commemorated as homosexuals at all? They were not, after all, fighting in that capacity, nor did they enlist or serve to further the aims of homosexuals (if, indeed, it is not nonsense to talk about 'aims' in that context, which for my part I believe it is); they fought and died, I take it, for much the same reasons as those which inspired the heterosexuals alongside them. What separate standing, therefore, can they have in the matter?

To this, it seems, the Campaign for Homosexual Equality replies that homosexuals in the armed forces were often treated in a humiliating or cruel manner, not for any military failings, but merely for their sexual nature; that, ironically, the Nazis against whom they were fighting were particularly vicious towards homosexuals, many of whom were sent to concentration camps merely because they were homosexuals, and that homosexuals in Nazi Germany had to wear a degrading badge equivalent to the yellow star forced upon Jews; and that a collective action on Remembrance Day by homosexuals is now justified as marking a further step towards recognition of homosexuals as indistinguishable from all other citizens except for this one matter of sexual orientation.

Anyway, whatever their reasons (and I have seen nothing to suggest that those who opposed their attendance in Wolverhampton questioned their motives), a group of homosexuals was invited to take part in the ceremony, and did so; with the result I have described.

A pity. And a greater pity, it seems to me, for what the incident reveals about some of Wolverhampton's heterosexuals. I presume that the town's heterosexual ex-servicemen did not, during the war, refuse to fight alongside homosexuals; I presume they would not claim that homosexuals fought less bravely; I take it they do not insist that heterosexuals who fell in battle should be segregated in death by being put in a different part of the cemeteries in which the war-dead lie. I presume, in short, that they would not say that homosexuals who died in the two world wars should not be remembered, and saluted, on Remembrance Day. Then why do they object to such commemoration being undertaken by the homosexuals of Wolverhampton? After all, the Second World War ended thirty-three years ago; many of the municipal representatives at the ceremony, and many of those attending on behalf of other organizations, would certainly be too young to have fought in it, so there can be no suggestion that the ceremony commemorating the fallen should be confined to the survivors.

The sad truth is, is it not, that the protests, and the boycotting, had nothing to do with the dead of the wars or the most fitting way of commemorating them. It was based on an ancient and lamentable revulsion against homosexuals on the part of people who would, in many instances, be horrified to find within themselves feelings of such revulsion against other groups (racial or religious, say), and might even, if they did experience such feelings, stop to search their hearts to discover why such unjustifiable feelings were rooted there.

For it really is inexcusable to give way to feelings of generalized hostility against homosexuals, just as much as it is in the case of Jew or Negroes, or for that matter blind people or disabled or ugly people. And it is inexcusable not because no homosexual can help being a homosexual any more than any man can help having a darker skin than his fellows (though that is indeed true); it is inexcusable because there is nothing more 'wrong' in being a homosexual than being a Jew or for that matter being one-legged.

No doubt some homosexuals behave badly in their sexual lives; if that is matter for criticism, it must be criticism on the same basis as that applicable to heterosexuals who similarly invite it by their conduct. No doubt some homosexuals flaunt their sexual nature in a manner offensive to others; that is no less true, *mutatis mutandis*, of certain heterosexuals. Certainly, some homosexuals fail to understand the springs of society's failure to accept them fully and to ignore that particular part of their nature as the irrelevance, to every other part of their nature, that it is. But on the other hand, heterosexuals in general are far more guilty of a failure to understand the nature or position of homosexuals, or even to behave with common decency towards them.

And now, it seems, this attitude is to be maintained even in death, and homosexuals who died in war—and for whom the bullets and bombs were, presumably, no less painful to stop than for heterosexuals—are, at least by some in Wolverhampton, deemed unworthy of commemoration.

We have it on the authority of St Matthew that in the resurrection they neither marry, nor are given in marriage, but are as the angels of God in Heaven; similarly, we have it from St Paul that there is neither Greek nor Jew, circumcision nor uncircumcision, Barbarian, Scythian, bond nor free, but Christ is all, and in all. Without wishing to claim the confidence of either of those distinguished sources, I would like to suggest that in the resurrection there will also be neither homosexual nor heterosexual. Even if I am wrong in that belief, I am sure that the dust in the graves of the fallen could not be separated even by the most vigilant Wulfrunian into the constituent parts of heterosexual and homosexual respectively, and that Last Post sounds much the same to the dead of both categories. I do not think that the people of Wolverhampton have anything to be proud of in this business, except for the Mayor and those who supported her in her just and honourable decision.

The Times November 14th, 1978

Benign intentions

WHAT ON EARTH is happening to me? I, who do not normally enter a cinema from one year to the next, have already been twice in 1978. This time it was *Close Encounters of the Third Kind*, a far better film than *Star Wars*, which I saw a few weeks ago. Better in every sense, starting with the 'special effects', which in *Star Wars* consisted largely of interminable repetitions of the same shot—the bobbin-like space fighters whizzing about—but which in *Close Encounters* culminated (after a good deal of similar whizzing) in one of the most magnificent spectacles I have seen on a cinema screen, as the giant space-ship comes in to land. It is much better edited too; though the film deliberately leaves much, including the essential point of it, unexplained until the end, there is no irritating feeling of confusion. But much more important, *Close Encounters* is interesting and exciting at far deeper levels; its enormous success, like that of *Star Wars* (and *Close Encounters* seems to be as popular here as in America, while the other film, curiously, does not), is a portent well worth examining, but it is also saying something on its own account, much more directly and much more effectively.

Of all the arguments against the hypothesis that beings from other worlds may visit our earth, only one has ever seemed to me convincing. It is the proposition that any civilization capable of the technology required to send a vehicle through space would be so unimaginably far in advance of our own that it would not need to send its messengers or observers physically across the light-years; it would be able far more easily to devise means by which we could be inspected in the greatest detail, and if necessary communicated with, from afar. One of the most striking things about *Close Encounters* is that it solves this particular philosophical problem with one single, obvious assumption. I suppose I ought not to give away the most significant surprises in the plot, and I suppose that this particular one comes under that heading, so I shall say no more, except that the moment you see the point you see also the rightness of it. The same is true of an even more startling scene; you will see, towards the end of the film, a group of figures in red combat-suits, arriving at the base at which the space-craft is awaited. The assumption is that they are troops, ready to engage in battle with the unearthly strangers, but when we see them again – taking part in a religious service, which at first reinforces the belief that they are fighting men, now seeking a blessing on their arms – we notice that some of them are elderly and bespectacled, and indeed some of them women, which seems to rule out the hypothesis.

And ruled out it emphatically is, in the very last seconds of the film, when we realize at last who they are and what they are there for – and why the hero, in the last glimpse we get of him, is also dressed in the same uniform, and is being asked by the scientist in charge of the project whether there is any history of mental illness in his family.

At that point, there is an almost audible click in the mind, and that metaphor is particularly apt; the illumination that dawns as the meaning of the whole film becomes clear is as bright, abrupt and dazzling as that of a light turned on by a switch in a dark room. For it is not only understanding that dawns; or rather it is not only understanding in the sense of understanding the facts, of seeing how all the clues come together to provide an explanation. If that were all, *Close Encounters* would be nothing but high-class entertainment, and although it *is* high-class entertainment, and could, indeed have gone much further than it does in the explicitness of its philosophical point without risking its popular appeal, it is also something very much more – which is, after all, why I have chosen to discuss it today.

Why is almost nobody involved frightened, except at the first effects of the space visitors, when homes and motor cars begin to behave as though they are in the epicentre of a massive earthquake? (That, I may say, provides one of the loveliest and most significant items in the whole film, when all the mechanical toys in the infant's bedroom 'come alive', while he watches the resultant *Boutique Fantasque* with saucer-eyed wonder untinged by any fear.) I say almost nobody is frightened, because there is one exception, when the little boy's mother loses a tug-o-war for him (conducted, with a beautiful touch of imagination, through the cat flap) with whatever it is that is pulling him from her. She is terrified on his behalf, but he is eager to go and join his new friends, and before long his confidence is seen to be abundantly justified.

For the point about *Close Encounters* – and this much I can surely say without disclosing anything – is that everything that happens is firmly rooted in an entirely benign intention. Whose intention it is we are left to speculate, but we are given a number of clues to that, too, not least in the words the priest is speaking in the shot of the service, but above all in what creatures we see emerging briefly from the space-craft and in what manner they return to its interior, now not alone.

Within the framework of benignity, there are further clues. If we are ever to communicate with beings from other worlds, we must find a common language, which is unlikely to be an earthly one, particularly Esperanto. In *Close Encounters*, it is suggested that a means of mutual understanding might be sought in musical tones and in hand movements based on the alphabet for the deaf, and we see both methods demonstrated. But the five-note theme that forms the basis of the former attempt is introduced, spectacularly, in a scene in India, in which a group of robed devotees are chanting it in the form of versicle and response. Why India? And why in this particular setting? Whatever you think the answer to those questions may be, you would be wise to assume that there is an answer, and that the choice was not simply a coincidence.

Close Encounters of the Third Kind is a film that lingers on the retina of the mind like the image of a light stared at before the eyes are closed. And the reason is that it offers, in addition to great technical skill and great cinematic excitement, a view, and a view, moreover, of great richness and plausibility. If it is possible that beings from space will one day visit our planet – and you would have to be bone-headed well beyond the point of scientific duty to declare that it is *not* possible – then it is worth wondering what such a visit might mean. Not just consist of; mean. This film offers a clear, consistent and powerful choice among possible meanings, and I believe the huge response the film has had reflects a conviction that the makers' guess is the most likely one. And the feeling that I took from the cinema, which I think few who see the film will fail to experience for themselves, is that the thesis is indeed correct. For the final effect of the film is to send us out with an extraordinarily exalted feeling, of the kind that we get before any work of art that expresses – as all true art does and must – the sense of order and harmony, with its irreducible core of mystery, in the universe. In other words, we emerge with the feeling that not only the film, but the universe, has got the answer right.

The Times May 23rd, 1978

The questions machines cannot answer

As ONE WHO until very recently believed that a semi-conductor is a man who asks you to pass halfway down the bus, I may be in a less than ideal position for commenting on the technological revolution that the microprocessor is about to cause. And indeed, in the matter of understanding how the thing works I am like the man who, challenged to substantiate his claim to know how electricity produced illumination in the form of a light bulb, replied tetchily, 'Nothing to it – you just press the switch and the light comes on'.

However, an equivalent degree of technical knowledge in the case of the microprocessor and all its works is all most of us need for a discussion of the non-technical implications. And, of course, it is these that interest me, and on which I am no less qualified to pass an opinion than the next man, and considerably better qualified than the next but one, who is called Blenkinsop and believes that thunder turns the milk sour.

First, let me put the case for ignoring the effects of micro-electronic technology altogether, not on the ground that it might then go away, but from a rather more practical point of view, to wit, that we have heard this before, and in very recent times, too.

In my own lifetime, which has not lasted nearly as long as many people seem to think, I have seen three technological revolutions – three fundamentally new systems, that is, not just such earth-shaking developments as electric carving knives for taking the fatigue out of cutting the bread for toast, Cling-Wrap film for helping to keep cheese smelling like cheese in a refrigerator otherwise full of unfilleted mackerel or (our beloved Post Office's

K

latest wheeze for averting the danger of making a profit two years running) the Mickey Mouse telephone ('Bring a friend into your life and a smile to your telephone conversation as you lift the handset from Mickey's right arm').

These three revolutions are: the computer, automation (the second only made possible by the first, of course) and peaceful nuclear energy. The first two have certainly changed a great deal in the physical world around us and in the more superficial aspects of the way we live; the third has been an almost complete failure. All three together have made no discernible change in the fundamental structure or operation of society, let alone in our psychology.

Exactly the same prophecies, promises and threats were made about those earlier revolutions as are now being made about the microelectronic one. For instance, in the feature on the subject in yesterday's *Times*, a professor at Bradford University was quoted as saying that 'The next generation may find it needs no more than 10 per cent of its labour force to provide it with all the material goods needed'. Almost exactly these words were used about computerized automation technology in its early days, and even greater claims were made for nuclear energy, which was always said, for some reason, to be about to enable the *Queen Mary* to sail right round the world, without stopping, on a piece of fuel the size of a walnut.

Yet I cannot help noticing that the *Queen Mary* is at present lying off Long Beach, California, and Long Beach is getting positively hysterical at the money she is losing as a stationary tourist attraction. For that matter, the industry which was always held up as the one which was going to be typical of the transformation of Britain's industrial society that would take place as soon as automation had replaced more traditional methods was our motor car industry. Ha. Ha.

The prospect—inviting or alarming, according to taste or position—held out by the microelectronic revolution is that it will make most industrial work unnecessary, and sack almost everybody in industry at once. That again, is exactly what was

said about automation, which hasn't so far even succeeded in reducing the real length of the working week.

And I have not even considered resistance, by industry (both
sides) and government (both parties), to the introduction of the
new technology. At present, many millions of pounds a year are
being paid to help firms of all kinds remain inefficient – not just
welfare agencies like British Leyland but firms which want to
install new machinery that would increase productivity but which
are paid to employ labour for which the new machinery has
eliminated, or would eliminate, the need. By the time microelectronic technology is fully developed here, that attitude – to
say nothing of the Luddism in industry – will be sufficiently widespread and sufficiently tenacious to make it virtually ineradicable.

Perhaps, then, history has yet some surprises in store for those
who insist that the microprocessor is about to transform our
society into something unrecognizably different from its present
form. (Even if it does, incidentally, my own withers are likely to
remain unwrung; it would be a bold silicon chip which would
undertake to write my column. Can the man who puts the
stripes in multicoloured toothpaste say as much about *his* future?)

But let us suppose that the predictions come true; let us suppose
that they come true in full, and that they even do so far more
quickly than any experience of such developments would suggest
is likely. What then?

Well, whatever then, I can tell you what not then. It is possible
that the way we get and spend and lay waste our power will be
utterly transformed by the technological revolution that is coming. It may be, as the experts say, that there will be a huge increase in employment in the service trades, concomitant with the
decrease in employment in the manufacturing trades, though if
so I must make it clear that I am damned if I am going to have
my hair cut by an unemployed Leyland toolmaker. Huge new
'leisure industries' (great God, what a phrase, and what a revelation about what we have become!) may arise; new devices and
processes, hitherto undreamt of, may be introduced, which will
make the electric carving knife as obsolete as sticky tape made

string on parcels; the Ministry of Technology may proliferate so stupendously that it may itself be able to employ all the tens of millions forced out of work by its activities; industrial pollution may vanish, the balance of payments problem may be permanently solved and the silicon chip may replace the potato chip on a million restaurant menus up and down the land. And yet I doubt if human beings will be any different, or the fears, miseries and bewilderments from which they inexplicably suffer notably relieved.

To believe otherwise is to believe in the most Pathetic Fallacy of all, which is the conviction that the essence of a man depends on the cut of his coat. There are at this moment, in countries such as ours, many tens of thousands of individuals who already have everything, in the way of leisure, possessions, facilities and opportunities, that even the most revolutionary technology could provide for the mass of their fellows. Are they any nearer — even by the breadth of a solid-state circuit embossed, together with 29,999 identical brethren, on a piece of silicon one-quarter of an inch across — knowing themselves or understanding their relation to the universe, or the meaning of their journey through life? Do they wake less often in the night, their hearts beating with an inexplicable terror, than he

> Who with a body fill'd and vacant mind
> Gets him to rest, cramm'd with distressful bread?

From the day that *Pithecanthropus erectus* chipped one bit of flint by hitting it with another and discovered that he had invented a cutting edge, the march of technology has gone on unabated. Sometimes more slowly, sometimes (as in our own day) more rapidly; but it has never stopped, and nobody has ever supposed that it would, though one or two have argued that it ought to.

And has that, in itself, got us a day's march nearer home? Can technology create a Rembrandt, or even explain the ones we already have? More: technology can cut wood within a tolerance of a millionth of an inch, and fit the cut bits together with an equivalent precision, and measure the thickness of a film of varnish no less exactly. And with all that, can it make a Stradivarius violin? If it comes to that, who fished the murex up? What porridge had John Keats? Technology provides no answers to any of these questions, or to any of the millions of similar questions that mankind has always asked itself. Yet they are the only questions that matter, which is why mankind has gone on asking them. Whatever life is, it is inside us, not in the machines that produce the goods we use. Whatever our duty may be, it will be done by us, not by microprocessors. Whatever will make us happy, it will make us happy though we are naked and empty handed.

This is not a plea for the simple life, a return to nature, or a general rising against the machines. It is nothing but a warning to anyone who will listen, and it says: put not thy trust in princes. We have long since ceased to put our trust in the princes who wear coronets, but we now rely instead, and no less blindly, on those which wear winking lights and give off a low hum when their buttons are pressed. That trust is as misplaced as the other kind, and although the microelectronic technological revolution may usher in a paradise upon earth, it will usher it in with the serpent already in residence. The silicon chip will transform everything, except everything that matters, and the rest will still be up to us.

The Times October 3rd, 1978

Free speech has to be paid for

THE PICTURE ON the front page of this week's *Sunday Telegraph*, by Paul Armiger, was positively surrealist (as well as a masterpiece of news photography). It showed Mr Martin Webster, one of the leaders of the National Front, marching alone, carrying a Union Jack and a placard reading 'Defend British Free Speech from Red Terrorism', through the streets of Hyde. When I say he marched 'alone', I mean that he was not accompanied by any of his party colleagues; but he could hardly have been lonely, for what made the picture as well as the situation so extraordinary was the fact that Mr Webster was surrounded by a sea, a positive ocean, of policemen. I daresay most readers of the paper might have been content to gasp at the scene and read on; my incurable inquisitiveness, however, compelled me to take a powerful magnifying glass and, at the cost of an even more powerful headache, count the number of police visible. I made it 362.

That, of course, by no means exhausted the number of police on duty in the Manchester area; a very much greater force, not far away, was engaged in seeing that the National Front rally (the point of Mr Webster's symbolic solo procession was that the originally proposed route for his party's general march had been disallowed) did not lead to violence in the form of clashes between National Front members and those who have proclaimed their intention of preventing the Front from making its presence felt or its views known.

A couple of things have to be said at once. First is that Mr Webster displayed considerable courage in announcing and carrying out, his own walk. After all, when he announced it (which was just after his party's march had been prohibited), he could hardly have expected so gigantic an escort, and even with it his action was by no means free from danger; a concerted rush at the police phalanx might not have got to him, but it might well have led to his being accidentally knocked down and trampled upon, and that is to say nothing of the possibility of missiles being lobbed over the police cordon at him or thrown from windows. I once got a cartload of abuse for pointing out that Goering was a brave man, but he was, for all the abuse, and so is Mr Webster. Courage, like sincerity, exists independently of the aim pursued by those who have it, and we can condemn both the aim and the aimers without having to insist that they are all cowards.

The second point to be made is that Mr Webster's protest, again irrespective of the nature, beliefs and intentions of the National Front, was absolutely justified. The National Front is a lawful organization, as is its political mirror-image, the Socialist Workers' Party, and I think it would be just as wrong to suppress the legal activities of the one as of the other. It may be (I shall come to that aspect of the business in a moment) that the National Front, or some of its activities, will be made illegal; but unless and until that happens it has as much right as any group to propagate its doctrine and show itself on the streets.

There are, of course, laws making the incitement to racial hatred a crime, and there have been many prosecutions under these laws. I hope that the greatest vigilance will be exercised by the authorities in respect of what the National Front says and does in racial matters, and that any of its members transgressing the law will be dealt with appropriately; but provided the National Front keeps within the law, it has the right to say what it likes, and that right must be protected.

It was protected in the case of Mr Webster; but the reason for his accompanied walk must be considered. There are powers by the exercise of which political processions may be banned, and the original route for the National Front's proposed march was banned under these powers, on the ground that the probability of serious violence resulting was very high. So indeed it clearly was, but we have to ask why it was, and see what conclusions follow from the answer. The fear of violence comes directly from the threats to use it made by the National Front's equally totalitarian rivals in the Socialist Workers' Party and similar groups. I wrote about those threats (which, incidentally, have as far as I know not resulted in any prosecutions, though incitement to violence is certainly a criminal offence) a few weeks ago, but what happened at the weekend makes it necessary for me to return to the subject. For the re-routing of the National Front march (and, in the circumstances, I believe the Chief Constable's decision to seek the powers to ban the original one was justified, as there certainly would have been violence if it had proceeded, and that is the only consideration the police have to take into account, the political decisions being taken elsewhere) mark a decidedly new stage in the development of the politics of intimidation.

It cannot be right for lawful activities to be forbidden at the behest of a tiny group of the lawless. Yet that is by no means an absurd description of the state of affairs we face. Because the totalitarians of the left have announced that they, and not the law, will decide who is permitted to use the streets for political purposes, and because they have decided and proclaimed that only totalitarians of their persuasion, and not of the equal and opposite persuasion, are to be permitted to do so, their demands are obeyed by the authorities, because they have threatened to use violence if they do not get their way.

That cannot be right, and the police cannot be put into the impossible situation of having to take, on non-political grounds, decisions which are inevitably political ones. But when we look for a political solution to this problem, we come upon the most disquieting signs. The Home Secretary* has been talking about strengthening or amending the law for the purpose of bringing within its scope National Front activities which at present are either outside it, or are so difficult to define in terms of the law

---

* Then Mr Merlyn Rees.

as to make it unlikely or impossible for a prosecution launched against its members to succeed. Now I do not want to see either the S.W.P. or the N.F. banned or restricted; but if the latter is to have its hands tied legally as well as in practice, because of the activities of the former, we have reached a very alarming staging-post on the road to serfdom.

Obviously Mr Rees is not talking in this fashion out of admiration for the S.W.P., or for that matter out of detestation of the N.F., though he certainly does not admire the S.W.P. and he certainly does detest the N.F. His theme is racialism: because the National Front actively propagates racialist doctrines, the argument runs, a special obloquy attaches to it, and special methods of dealing with it must therefore be devised.

I don't see it. The doctrines of the N.F. are certainly repulsive, its leaders vile, its appeal base, and its activities menacing. Every one of those statements is equally true of the S.W.P., and in addition the S.W.P. has declared that it will use, and actually has used, criminal violence in the furtherance of its political ends. Laws must be general, not particular, and if there is a case for further legal sanctions against the N.F. I do not see how they can be drawn up so as to catch only the N.F., and I do not believe that they ought to be even if they can. The cost of the weekend police action has been put at £250,000, which is a high price for the protection of freedom of speech, particularly since it included an unquantifiable sum for the partial suppression of free speech in the prohibition of the N.F. march. A high price, yes; but not too high. And if, as I believe, there must be no partial suppressions of free speech, and certainly not because those who wish to suppress it have announced their intention of doing so by force, then the price must go even higher. And still be paid.

The Times October 12th, 197

Farewell to a friendly Pied Piper

IT IS ALMOST impossible to find a comparison with which to convey the extent of the loss to this country's musical life represented by the appallingly sudden death of David Munrow, the founder and leader of the Early Music Consort. Perhaps if Sir William Glock had been cut off before he had embarked on the work he did for the B.B.C.; perhaps if Sir Robert Mayer had never been born; certainly, apart from those two, no other individual in my lifetime has so enormously enriched (or, for that matter, enlivened) Britain's music-making and music-going.

I was at the last concert he gave, at the Queen Elizabeth Hall a fortnight ago (I think I had not missed any of his group's London concerts for several years), and he was in sparkling form, profoundly and lovingly enwrapt in his music yet jesting with the audience; that, now I come to think of it, is a comprehensive definition of him and of the delight his work conveyed, for I always felt, at one of his concerts, as though I was listening to the music-making of a group of friends—indeed, though I never met him I felt, as I am sure we all did, that I was privileged to *be* one of his friends.

Munrow was only thirty-three, and looked far younger even than that; to judge by his appearance, indeed, one would have guessed he was about nine years old, and I used to wonder uneasily if he wasn't breaking some G.L.C. regulation by appearing at evening concerts, long past his bedtime. Most of his group were, I suppose, much of an age with him, which further enhanced the feeling that they had come together to make music solely for the love of it, and were in consequence slightly surprised to find rows of people out in front listening. In any case, I have no doubt that the members of the Early Music Consort found their work as uplifting and fulfilling as we in the audience did.

As the group's name suggests, they specialized (I hope I am wrong in using the past tense, for although Munrow is clearly irreplaceable, it would be another tragedy if the Consort were now to disband) in music written before music became what it is today (or more exactly became what it is just, after three centuries, ceasing to be): that is, music written before modern polyphony was developed. They stopped, therefore, just short of Bach, though most of the time they dwelt in earlier centuries still, and seemed to take a special delight in discovering, editing and performing older and older music, until they reached the impenetrable barrier of the absence of intelligible notation.

Nothing old is good just because it is old, and this is probably more true in art than anything else. Moreover, works of art which have disappeared from view have generally done so for ominously good reasons. But what was remarkable about David Munrow was that, in searching the archives, libraries and collections of manuscript music where his treasures presumably lay, he displayed absolutely unerring judgment, never presenting anything that had no claim on our attention other than the non-musical one of its great antiquity. (The only other explanation for the astonishingly high quality of the repertoire of the Early Music Consort is that no composer wrote rubbish before the middle of the seventeenth century, but I find that difficult to believe.)

Munrow's last concert was called 'Music by Monteverdi's Contemporaries', which is emphatically not a title to have me hurrying across Waterloo Bridge. The rediscovery of Monteverdi, pioneered by Glyndebourne* when they did their now historic revival of *L'Incoronazione di Poppea* (and then, when the rest of the world had caught up, forged ahead again with the even more

---

* It was pointed out to me, after this column appeared, that even before the Glyndebourne revivals such pioneering on behalf of Monteverdi had been undertaken at Oxford by Sir Jack Westrup. I am glad to give him due acknowledgment now.

wonderful resurrection of *Il Ritorno d'Ulisse*), has been one of the most important of postwar musical developments. The two operas I have mentioned provided me with incomparable musical evenings, as did, even more perhaps, the hearing of his *Vespers* (I recall a performance given in Westminster Cathedral a few years ago by John Eliot Gardiner and his Monteverdi Choir, at an extramural Prom, that was as profound an experience as music has ever offered), but when Glyndebourne tried to do the same for Cavalli they left me, at any rate, behind: I recall saying with some vigour in the interval at *Ormindo* that it was all very fine, but if only the music had been written by Rossini it would have been enjoyable as well.

So if it had not been for the fact that I had long felt that the names of Munrow and his Consort on a concert bill provided an absolute guarantee of delight, I would have hesitated, which would have been a mistake (and a bad one, in the most important sense, as the Queen Elizabeth Hall was packed, and the foolish virgins were queuing on the stairs for returned tickets half an hour before the performance began).

The assembly of musical instruments they deployed was more remarkable than ever; crumhorns, racketts and *chitarroni* rubbed shoulders, or at any rate crooks, strings and reeds, with *rausch-pfeifen* and sackbuts, and some of the things looked even weirder than their names. (I had accused them of playing umbrella-handles, stuffed snakes and draining boards; on this occasion they appeared to have added beer bottles, pistons and wishbones.) But there was nothing weird, though there was much that was strange, about the sounds they produced with these instruments.

Most of that concert consisted of church music, generally solos and duets, and devotional rather than liturgical; almost all of it had an immediacy of appeal, a spontaneous freshness and clarity, that made me forget my problem with minor keys (though a great deal of this music sounds as though it was written not merely before modern counterpoint had been invented, but G major itself), and I took to it in a way that I find impossible with Bach. Of the dozen composers represented, I had heard of only one, Gabrieli (and the only reason was that he figures in histories of Venice), yet it never occurred to me to wonder if they were worth exhuming, or even to classify them as *petits maîtres*, so direct and personal were their voices, so tasteful and 'clean' their work.

'Clean' is the important word. Those seeking a simile in these circumstances usually speak of the sorbet in the middle of a banquet, the palate-cleansing freshness of which enables the gourmandizer tired of beef to turn his attention to mutton. But to speak of Munrow's music in these terms is to belittle it; even the entirely secular sets of dances included in the programme (by Giorgio Mainerio, a sixteenth-century composer of whom, it seems, nothing at all is known), came o'er mine ear like the sweet sound that breathes upon a bank of violets, stealing and giving odour. The fact of the matter is that the work of the Early Music Consort cleansed not just the palate, but the soul, and I can only convey the effect it had on me by saying that as I emerged from the Queen Elizabeth Hall I was powerfully struck by the realization that after what I had heard Beethoven would have sounded coarse and self-centred, while even Schubert would have appeared clumsy and Verdi simply ridiculous. As for Wagner, if the busker at the corner had been playing the Good Friday music itself on his penny whistle, I would have stuck my fingers in my ears and yelled for the police.

I had simply not realized how deeply the music-making of David Munrow and his friends had affected me; I am reminded of my adolescent discovery of music, when after an evening at the gramophone with my coz (he and I started out on that journey more or less together) we would invariably end with the Third Brandenburg, which cleared our heads, physically and spiritually, in exactly the same way as did Munrow. The Consort's popularity was a sign that I had not misread their effect; I remember the first Prom they did, when they were a very new experience indeed, and the young promenaders cheered long and loud.

And then, last weekend, fate played its foulest yet most familiar trick, and took away, in the flower of his years, a man who in the brief span of his music-making (his début as a performer was in 1968) had conveyed us all so often, yet far too rarely, to the enchanted country of the elves that on the sands with printless foot do chase the ebbing Neptune and do fly him when he comes back, the land which provides what is for David Munrow both the perfect and the only possible epitaph:

Be not afeared: the isle is full of noises,
Sounds and sweet airs, that give delight and hurt not.
Sometimes a thousand twangling instruments
Will hum about mine ears; and sometimes voices
That if I then had wak'd after long sleep,
Will make me sleep again: and then, in dreaming,
The clouds methought would open and show riches
Ready to drop upon me; that when I wak'd
I cried to dream again.

The Times May 18th, 1976

Victims of the intellectual consumer society

THIS COLUMN IS about a murderer. Or rather, it is about a new kind of photographic lens, though the murderer never saw or even heard of the lens, and it played no part in bringing him to book. And yet the murderer and the lens – and Mr John Lennon, too, for that matter – are bound in a symbiotic union the implications of which we would do well to heed.

For the past two weeks, in the *Sunday Times* colour magazine, the distinguished West Indian novelist, Mr V. S. Naipaul, has been giving an account of the life and times of Michael Malik, alias Michael X, who is now under sentence of death* in Trinidad for the murder of an associate of his, Joseph Skerritt; Malik was also charged with the murder of an English girl, Gale Benson, but this charge was not proceeded with after he was found guilty on the other.

I met Malik once; I was doing a series of half-hour television interviews at the time, and somebody had suggested that Malik, who was making a good deal of noise at that time as the head of a 'black power' organization in this country (as it turned out, the organization existed only on paper – he gave me a brochure about it – and in Malik's head), might make a good subject for one of the programmes. We spent an hour or so together, but a few minutes were really all that was needed; he was obviously living in a world of fantasy, one of those figures who devise a personality for themselves and then persuade some of the sillier people in our society to accept it as real.

* He was hanged.

Not long afterwards, his imaginary organization collapsed; he was imprisoned for a year on a charge under the Race Relations Act (it was a lamentable case, incidentally – he had been doing no more than 'talking big' about killing white men); Mr Nigel Samuel, son of the property millionaire, who had financially backed another of Malik's pathetic projects, an urban centre to be called 'Black House', ceased to provide money; on bail on another charge, Malik fled to Trinidad, where the fantasy took him over completely and ended in death.

By an even odder chance, I also met Gale Benson once. She called on me to urge me to write about a man called Hakim Jamal, an American Negro fantasist of the same type as Malik, and even more successful at conning the more gullible in this country, especially in the newspaper world. Gale Benson was then living with Jamal, and helping to promote him; to many people she insisted that he was God, though she did not tell me that, and I do not think I would have believed her if she had. I did not write about him.

Both Malik and Jamal were people whom our own society needs to stimulate its own jaded intellectual appetite; it takes them up, plays with them, then discards them when a new sensation appears. (It is worth remembering that the same sort of fashionable folk, *mutatis mutandis*, helped to destroy Brendan Behan in much the same way.)

Anyway, that, these days, is a familiar enough story. But embedded in Mr Naipaul's account of the end of Michael Malik is a sentence that made me pause for a long time before I read on. Malik in Trinidad had kept up the front of being a big shot from London, but the guise was slipping, and people were beginning to see through him. 'But', says Mr Naipaul in words that rang like a knell, 'the visit in April 1971 of John Lennon as his house-guest stilled all doubts.'

Now this was Trinidad, not King's Road, Chelsea; and there were some hard fellows about, by no means to be compared with the fun-revolutionaries of the *Workers' Press* or those young ladies of good family who think it would be so delightful to run a discothèque. And yet the presence of John Lennon was enough to still all doubts.

Such a world needs gods no less than the ancient world did. It makes them out of a Hakim Jamal, and sometimes gets murdered for its pains; it makes them out of a Che Guevara or a Ho Chi Minh, whereat others get murdered instead; it makes them out of a Ronald Biggs* or an Angela Davis,† a Leila Khaled‡ or a Godfather.

And it makes them, again and again, out of those who appear from the infinite variety of sub-cultures that slop from side to side in the bilges of our society, and mump and gag, and caper and yodel, and strut and fret their hour upon the stage, and then are heard no more.

Just such a one – as innocent of taint as of understanding – was John Lennon. There is nothing wrong with Mr Lennon that could not be cured by standing him upside down and shaking him gently until whatever is inside his head falls out. It is not his fault – he appears to be a gentle and bewildered soul – that the spurious *réclame* he has achieved meant that the doubts about Michael Malik were laid to rest by his mere presence in Malik's house; and it is certainly not his fault that Joseph Skerritt and Gale Benson were laid to rest rather more abruptly shortly afterwards. But there it is; such is our world, and such its values, that even in Trinidad, which is full of the very people our own society takes up to make itself feel good, and drops when it is bored, the name of Lennon worked most potent voodoo.

These were my reflections as I finished the second part of Mr Naipaul's account of the short life of Michael Malik. And then I idly turned the pages, and discovered that an expert photographer had examined the lens of a certain brand of camera, and pronounced it good. The manufacturers, understandably pleased, had

* A train-robber who managed to evade capture and made much money from his serialized memoirs.

† An American pseudo-martyr, who disappointed her left-wing admirers by being acquitted instead of martyred.

‡ An Arab terrorist.

illustrated the advertisement for it with an enlargement of a picture, taken with the magic lens, of a lens-testing chart, to show how clear, even when greatly enlarged, the picture remained. And they headed the advertisement 'The photograph that shook the world'.

And, after all, why should they not? A crazy con man convinces a girl with nothing better to do that he is God; another, hardly less crazy, is puffed up like a balloon with the hot air of our society's search for new tastes to satisfy old appetites, and, when the balloon bursts, takes to murder; amid it all, anxious men seek a sign, and find it in the presence of John Lennon, and murmur that all is well.

No doubt the camera with the new lens that takes photographs of lens-testing charts so fine that these photographs shake the world, will sell widely; perhaps Mr Nigel Samuel, who can presumably afford one (it costs £215.50), and presumably now needs a new toy, Michael Malik's 'Black House' having long since collapsed, will buy one – or a dozen, even.

We take up a Michael Malik, and make him what he already was, yet need never have become. We swear our oaths by John Lennon; we read that a photograph of some white lines on black paper has shaken the world, and we neither laugh nor cry. But when the world goes up in flames, and the camera-lens that shook it is cracking in the heat, and the real false gods like Mao Tse-tung are enthroned above the firmament and it is too late to cry out in warning, why, then let us remember that what was wrong with our society is that it forgot what men live by. And what men live by is not Michael Malik, or Hakim Jamal, or John Lennon, or cameras which can take photographs that shake the world.

The Times May 21st, 1974

For art's sake

SINCE NOBODY WRITES a letter to a newspaper without subsequently reading the paper in question in order to discover whether the letter has been printed, I think we may safely assume that the people who stole the Vermeer from Kenwood House, and have since been communicating their wishes and intentions through the medium of *The Times*, will see this. At any rate I hope so, for it is addressed to them. And just as they, in the part of their letter not published (for security reasons) in Wednesday's *Times*, gave certain details of their enterprise which only they and the authorities could have known, in order to establish the authenticity of their letter, so I, in order to assure them that I have studied the original of their message with care, shall point out that they would be well advised, in order to avoid future frustrations, to get the right-hand margin release on their typewriter repaired, for at present it is clearly defective.

They have announced their intention of burning the picture on Sunday, the feast of the Patron Saint of Ireland, 'with much cavorting about in the true lunatic fashion'; perhaps their resolve comes from an imperfect understanding of the Secreta of the Mass for St Patrick's Day ('God of armies, may this unblemished offering prove acceptable to thee ... through blessed Patrick's work this same offering should be made to thy great name among the nations from east to west ... ') though I doubt it. If not, however, I am at a loss to say what exactly their purpose is. They claim to be irked by the fact that 'a capitalist society values its treasures more than humanity', and they may well be right on the point, but to demonstrate, as the burning of the picture would, that they do not value society's treasures at all would not itself indicate any concern on their part for humanity either. In any case, if their motive in stealing the picture was to effect the return of the Price sisters to Ireland* (as their first letter suggested), they might care to note that in this respect at least their heroines share the attitude of capitalist society, for they have appealed to the thieves not to harm the picture, whereas the crime of which they were convicted (conspiracy to cause explosions) suggests that they, at any rate, do not put a very high value on humanity.

But whatever the motives of those who took the painting, it seems worth appealing to them not to carry out their threat to burn it.†

We live in an ugly world, and many people are busily engaged in making it even uglier, some of them without even being inspired by the hope of material reward. Greed, selfishness and cruelty abound; noise, dirt and spoliation surround us on all sides; the heart of man is not noticeably less free than of yore from pride, vainglory and hypocrisy, from envy, hatred, malice and all uncharitableness. If the people who took the Vermeer had instead taken (supposing such a thing to exist) the Doomsday Machine, and proposed to blow the entire planet to fragments with it on Sunday, or even Saturday, it would be difficult – not impossible, but difficult – to maintain that their plan was entirely without merit.

Against this view we have, as we always have had, only three weapons. One of these – the belief in a God who works in a mysterious way his wonders to perform – I am myself unable to wield. Of the other two, the more important – a belief in the theoretical perfectibility of man – is not relevant to the present argument. The final one is the Shield of Achilles, which is the moral consciousness of art, and it is that one that we must raise before 'The Guitar Player', who now has no other defence.

It is not true, though it has often been said, that all great art is

---

* Convicted of terrorist crimes, they were imprisoned in England.
† They did not, and the picture was later recovered unharmed.

healing in its effects.* We do not leave a performance of *Oedipus Rex* or *Tristan and Isolde* with peace in our souls, nor do we gaze with untroubled equanimity on 'The Temptation of St Antony' or 'The Disasters of War', nor close *The Brothers Karamazov* or *The Magic Mountain* and thereafter dismiss them lightly from our minds. One of the functions of art is to bring us face to face with the unbearable, whether it is the unbearable that lies all around us or that which rises in our own hearts. ('Down, thou climbing sorrow', cries Lear in his agony, 'thy element's below'.)

But of some art the claim is abundantly true; there are mighty masterpieces which seek to do no more than celebrate beauty, or joy, or love, or all three together. And of these the works of Jan Vermeer of Delft stand high on the list. We do not know how many pictures he painted; we do know that not many more than thirty have survived. We know that he cared nothing for being in fashion, that he died when he was forty-three, that his widow was left destitute and had to sell two of his pictures to buy bread; that is about all. But we can deduce something else, and that the most important thing. Standing before 'The Servant Pouring Milk', in the Amsterdam Rijksmuseum, or 'Lady at the Virginals', in our own National Gallery, or 'The Guitar Player', in Kenwood House, we can tell that Vermeer cared only for one thing; conveying the truth of what he saw. In the stolen picture the light falls on the left-hand side of the player's face and on the knuckles of her right hand; its source is clearly high above her and to her right, so that the picture on the wall behind her head casts its shadow to the left. The balance of the painting, though almost half of it is virtually empty, is perfect, so miraculously has he caught the attitude of the sitter and the atmosphere in the room. (Bar the door and unroll it, friends, and look at it, and see whether I am not right.)

The work of Vermeer is incapable of doing anybody any harm. The mysterious and haunting quality of the stolen picture, though very powerful, is not disturbing; in it Vermeer tells us nothing

* I would no longer deny this proposition.

about the dark inward of the heart of man. He tells us only that by the most rigorous search, the most penetrating gaze, we can see the truth in that heart.

And if those who now have the Vermeer carry out their announced intention of destroying it, I tell them now that they will thereby have diminished not only the world's pitifully small supply of beauty, joy and love; they will also have struck a blow at the truth. When they have done their work, the lie that stalks the world will be more powerful, and there will be one witness the fewer to Blake's eternal words:

> This life's five windows of the soul
> Distorts the Heavens from pole to pole
> And lead you to believe a lie
> When you see with, not thro', the eye.

'The painting', say the thieves, 'will be burnt on St Patrick's night with much cavorting about in the true lunatic fashion.' I cannot but remember another occasion when the truth was burned, also with much cavorting about in the true lunatic fashion. It was burned in Berlin in 1933, after the Nazis had come to power, and Goebbels made a triumphant speech as the flames mounted into the air, and the Brownshirts brought more supplies to feed them. '*Brenne*, Moses Mendelssohn! *Brenne*, Sigmund Freud! *Brenne*, Heinrich Heine! *Brenne*, Erich Kästner!' Thus they chanted; I forget now who remarked that those who began by burning books would end by burning people.

Beauty is truth; truth beauty. The man who wrote that, O thieves in the night, had much in common with Vermeer, and his name is writ in water, not fire. Your peer, on the other hand, if it is not Goebbels, is Herostratus, who burned down the Temple of Diana at Ephesus for no better reason than that he thought it would make his name remembered. So indeed it has done; but not all remembrance is worth having, and yours will be only a remembrance of the central figures in a night that will live in infamy. No; not the central figures; the minor ones on the edge, just on the edge of the light cast by the flames. 'The Guitar

Player' will be in the middle, hand in hand with Vermeer, and her destruction will testify that he was right, and you were wrong; that he could create, and you could only destroy; that he spoke the truth, and you, lies.

Before you light the match, think on these things; and desist.

The Times March 15th, 1974

Index